MENE, MENE, TEKEL

Eugene Ehrlich

David H. Scott

 HarperCollins*Publishers*

FIRST EDITION

Designer: Joan Greenfield

Library of Congress Cataloging-in-Publication Data

Ehrlich, Eugene.
    Mene, Mene, Tekel / Eugene Ehrlich, David H. Scott.
        p.   cm.
    ISBN 0-06-016456-5
    1. English language—Terms and phrases.   2. English language—Early modern, 1500–1700—Terms and phrases.   3. Bible. English—Versions—Authorized—Dictionaries.   4. Bible—Language, style—Dictionaries.
5. Bible—Influence—Dictionaries.   I. Scott, David H.   II. Title.
    PE1689.E36   1990
    220.5′2033—dc20   89-46527

90   91   92   93   94   CC/RRD   10   9   8   7   6   5   4   3   2   1

To
Harry Ehrlich Wodehouse

FOREWORD

The King James Version of the Old and New Testaments, also known as the Authorized Version, was first published in 1611, almost 400 years ago. And even though there have been many other English-language editions since then, the King James remains the edition of the Bible most admired for the beauty of its language.

Devoted readers do not seem to mind that a sizable amount of the King James vocabulary is no longer commonly understood, that many of its sentences would not pass muster in a college composition class, that the arcane conventions of punctuation and capitalization and paragraph structure were not those practiced in the King James version. Can't the same things be said of William Shakespeare's plays? Not surprising. After all, Shakespeare and the King James scholars were contemporaries and, fortunately for us, they shared his love of words and his gift of expression.

Why do fans of the King James Version remain so loyal? It is my belief that while recent editions may do more to clarify intended meaning, the King James affects readers and listeners more profoundly. *It makes them feel they are reading and hearing the words of God.* Who could ask for anything more?

In fact, this wonderful edition of the Bible has given us much more. Many of the most colorful English words and phrases we hear and read today found their first or most influential use in the pages of the King James: blind leading the blind, crown of thorns, fall by the wayside, giants in the earth, give up the ghost, milk and honey, nothing new under the sun, race is not to the swift, sackcloth and ashes, shibboleth, walls of Jericho, why hast thou forsaken me? And these few are just the beginning.

It was to present and explain a collection of living King James language that *Mene, Mene, Tekel* was conceived. As the reader goes along in the pages of this book, it will become apparent that modern speakers and writers of English have not always been faithful to the original meanings of some words and phrases. How could they be? If there is one fact about language that is set in concrete, it is that language changes and the change cannot be resisted. Fortunately, changes sometimes reverse themselves. Thus, during a long career of teaching in New York City, I was told by a friendly student one afternoon that it is better to be *bad* than to be *good,* and a short while later—perhaps as little as a year, so rapidly does language change—the same student who taught me to be happy because I was *bad* (that is, good) looked pained when I said of another good person that he was *bad* rather than *good.* I was out of date when I used language one year old.

But I am not out of date when I use King James language, that is, language first recorded in 1611 or before. The metaphors remain fresh: blood upon thy head, book of life, bowels of compassion, camel through the eye of a needle, can the leopard change his spots, cup runneth over, ox to the slaughter, reap the whirlwind, strain at a gnat, still small voice, through a glass darkly.

Mene, Mene, Tekel offers many hundreds of such entries in alphabetical order, identifying the source and explaining the context and meaning of each entry. At the end of the book, an Index to Scriptural Passages will help you to locate specific entries.

I hope this volume gives its readers as much pleasure and as much insight into biblical meanings as it has given its compilers. David H. Scott selected and supplied the initial interpretations for the bulk of the entries. Any imperfections that may be apparent now are the result of my own tinkering throughout the volume.

I take this opportunity to thank Isaac Schwartz for his helpful review of entries from the Old Testament. His wise insights into original intentions, combined with his knowledge of Hebrew, proved invaluable in interpreting many phrases.

Eugene Ehrlich

MENE,
MENE,
TEKEL

A

Abraham's bosom
Luke 16:22
a metaphor for paradise or the repose of the dead

The allusion is to the ancient practice of permitting a close friend to rest his head on one's bosom. In the parable of the rich man and the beggar (Luke 16:19–31), Jesus taught that earthly values would be reversed in the life to come. Thus, when the rich man of the parable died, he went to hell, and when the beggar, named Lazarus, died, he was "carried by the angels into Abraham's bosom." The rich man, from "afar off" seeing Lazarus resting his head on Abraham's bosom, and finding hell too hot to bear, asked for mercy: "Send Lazarus that he may dip the tip of his finger in water, and cool my tongue; for I am tormented in this flame."

Not a chance. Abraham turned him down with these words: "Remember that thou in thy lifetime receivedst thy good things, and likewise Lazarus evil things: but now he is comforted, and thou art tormented."

Fair is fair.

See CRUMBS FROM THE TABLE.

Absalom, my son
II Samuel 18:33
the classic cry of a father grieving over the death of his son

Of all David's sons, Absalom was clearly his favorite, but this handsome young man turned out to be the one who would plot to become king in his father's place. Even so, after Absalom's defeat, when he fled but was trapped in the branches of a tree and then killed by Joab, David's general, the aging king broke into anguished cries, expressing grief over loss of a son combined with recognition of his own failure as a father: "O

1

my son Absalom, my son, my son Absalom! would God I had died for thee, O Absalom, my son, my son!"

In William Faulkner's novel *Absalom, Absalom!* the protagonist, Thomas Sutpen, also had several sons and much trouble in his relations with them.

absent in body, present in spirit
I Corinthians 5:3
not with you in the flesh, but with you nevertheless

This is the stuff that congratulatory telegrams are made of. People invited to a celebration they cannot attend often send a message of greetings suggesting that they will be present in spirit. Would they do so if they knew they were quoting Scripture, especially if they were aware of the context in which the words were used? Paul was writing from Ephesus in reaction to reports from his church in Corinth that a marriage had been scheduled that Paul regarded as immoral. In his reply, Paul wrote, "I verily, as absent in body, but present in spirit, have judged already, as though I were present, concerning him that hath so done this deed."

What was this marriage of which Paul disapproved? Verse 1 described it as a fornication, a marriage between a man and "his father's wife." So Paul, rather than sending greetings, was telling his community to expel the pair lest the church be harmed by scandal. And he said his spirit would be there watching over the shoulders of the church members while they came to their decision on expulsion.

Would you now care to choose another message for your next telegram?

Adam's apple
the thyroid cartilage, named for the fruit of the
    forbidden tree in Genesis 3

Popular accounts of the fall from paradise have it that a piece of the forbidden fruit stuck in Adam's throat. Unfortunately, the apple was not mentioned by name in Genesis, so another engaging story goes down the drain. Some biblical scholars have concluded that Michelangelo's interpretation in painting the ceiling of the Sistine Chapel was correct. He showed the fruit as a fig rather than an apple—and countless painters and sculptors have used fig leaves in their work ever since. Other biblical scholars consider that the fruit may have been a grape, citron, orange, or quince.

So you pays your money and you takes your choice.

See EDEN *and* FIG LEAVES.

Adam's rib
a wife

In Genesis 2:21–22 we read a marvelous account of how God created woman: "And the Lord God caused a deep sleep to fall upon Adam, and he slept: and he took one of his ribs, and closed up the flesh instead thereof. And the rib, which the Lord God had taken from man, made he a woman." If curiosity impels us to wonder what God made man of, we need only look to verse 7: "And the Lord God formed man of the dust of the ground." So when we next listen solemnly to "Earth to earth, ashes to ashes, dust to dust," we will know how "dust" found its way into the Christian burial service.

See DUST THOU ART *and* GIVE HONOR UNTO YOUR WIFE.

a little leaven leaveneth the whole lump
I Corinthians 5:6–8
an alliterative way of saying that one rotten apple spoils the whole barrel

Those of us familiar with how bread is baked know leaven as an agent added to dough to cause it to rise. In writing to the members of his church in Corinth, however, Paul was using the word not in this benign sense, but as a metaphor for a corrupting or debasing influence. Paul wrote that the old doctrines must be eradicated: "Know ye not that a little leaven leaveneth the whole lump? Purge out the old leaven, that ye may be a new lump, as ye are unleavened. For even Christ our passover is sacrificed for us. Therefore let us keep the feast, not with the old leaven, neither with the leaven of malice and wickedness; but with the unleavened bread of sincerity and truth."

So Paul was saying that it's better to start from scratch in striving to live better lives.

a little lower than angels
Psalm 8:5
where the human race stands in the grand scheme of
   things

Having asked of God in verse 4, "What is man, that thou art mindful of him?" the psalmist went on, "Thou hast made him a little lower than the angels." Angels were regarded as spiritual beings, serving God at his command and pleasure, so in placing man next in the pecking order, the psalmist was definitely in an upbeat mood.

Mark Twain saw things in somewhat the same light. He put man between the angels and the French.

all flesh is grass
Isaiah 40:6–8
human life is all too fragile and brief

This verse from Isaiah occurs just after the one in which a message from a heavenly voice instructed Israel to prepare a way for the Lord in the wilderness. Here the prophet is instructed to convey further wisdom to Israel: "All flesh is grass, and all the goodliness thereof is as the flower of the field: The grass withereth, the flower fadeth: because the spirit of the Lord bloweth upon it; surely the people is grass."

A disheartening message indeed, but soon followed by one of triumph: "The word of our God shall stand for ever."

See VOICE CRYING IN THE WILDERNESS.

all men are liars
Psalm 116:10–11
a mistaken generalization spoken without forethought

Lest anyone believe the psalmist was offering this thought as a verity, read it in context: "I was greatly afflicted: I said in my haste, All men are liars." Now the record is straight. The psalmist had spoken too quickly and mistakenly. Even so, it is worthwhile to recall "all men are liars" whenever we hear accusations or self-aggrandizing statements.

all that the Lord hath said will we do, and be obedient
Exodus 24:7
a firm commitment to follow the word of God

The last two words of the Hebrew text of verse 7 mean literally "We will do and we will listen." It was with these words that the Israelites undertook to carry out the law—even before they knew what it contained. The early rabbinical commentators used old legends to explain why.

When God completed his Torah, the law, he visited the nations in turn to ask them to accept it. When the descendants of Esau were asked, they wanted to know what was written in the law, and God told them, "Thou shalt not murder." They replied, "We cannot accept it, because the sword is our way of life"—recall Genesis 27:40, "And by thy sword shalt thou live." When God went to the Ammonites and Moabites to ask whether they would accept his law, they too asked what was written in the law. God replied, "Thou shalt not commit adultery." And they said, "We cannot accept this, as our very existence depends on an incestuous relationship between

Lot's daughters and their father"—recall Genesis 19:30–38. God then went to the descendants of Ishmael to ask whether they would accept his law. The Ishmaelites said they could not accept it, as it prohibited stealing, and stealing was their way of life.

Thus did God go to every nation but one, only to be repeatedly turned down. The nation he had not yet visited was the people of Israel. Fearing another rebuff, God inverted a mountain and held it over the Israelites like a huge tub. He told them that if they accepted the Torah, well and good, but if not, he would drop the mountain and they would be buried. At once the Israelites cried out, "We will do and we will listen."

Nothing clears the mind better than a healthy dose of mortal dread.

all the people arose as one man
Judges 20:2–8
a show of unanimity

When the men and women of Israel, described as numbering 400,000 in all, assembled to hear of an atrocity committed by carousing members of the tribe of Benjamin—rape and murder of a man's concubine—"All the people arose as one man, saying, We will not any of us go to his tent, neither will we any of us turn into his house." The crowd went on to promise much more by way of retribution for the offense, but that is not of immediate concern here. Rather, we wish to call attention to the cliché "rise as one man." This idiom is a close translation of the Hebrew original, but the rest of us have turned it into a cliché by repeatedly and boringly rising as one man.

all things are possible
Mark 9:23
the power of faith is unlimited

On first inspection, "all things are possible" seems to be no more than the eternal optimist's credo couched in a mistaken generalization. But when the verse from Mark is given more fully, "If thou canst believe, all things are possible to him that believeth," we understand the remark as an observation on the power of faith.

Quite a different matter.

See NOTHING IS IMPOSSIBLE.

all things come alike to all
Ecclesiastes 9:2
all of us must die

In this verse, the writer of Ecclesiastes was deeply pessimistic: "All things come alike to all: there is one event to the righteous, and to the wicked; to the good and to the clean, and to the unclean." So all things, including death, are at God's disposal and predetermined. Humanity cannot avert his stern decree.

This comes as no surprise to fans of *Richard II*, in which Shakespeare's feckless king, ruminating on his imminent murder, tells us that kings especially must be ready at all times to die:

Within the hollow crown
That rounds the mortal temples of a king
Keeps Death his court.

See, for example, HOUSE APPOINTED FOR ALL LIVING, THREE-SCORE AND TEN, *and* TO EVERY THING THERE IS A SEASON.

all things to all men
I Corinthians 9:22
completely adaptable

Today when this expression is employed to characterize someone—"he's all things to all men"—it implies that the person is lacking in integrity and overly willing to employ any stratagem in hope of gaining an advantage, for example, by espousing liberal ideas when with liberals, conservative ideas when with conservatives. This was not the case with Paul.

Eager to extend his ministry, he identified with all people who might listen to his preaching: "To the weak became I as weak, that I might gain the weak: I am made all things to all men, that I might by all means save some." People would be expected to listen carefully to someone who made such a statement.

And they did, as the record shows.

all things work together for good
Romans 8:28
for true believers, that is

"All things work together for good" may appear to be something out of the mouth of Voltaire's Dr. Pangloss, the incurable optimist, but it is not. Paul here added a proviso that changed the picture markedly. He was discoursing on the importance of belief and trust in God: "We know that all things work together for good to them who love God, to them who are the called according to his purpose."

Those who merely sit back and expect good things to happen to them will be disappointed, but true believers will find in God an active and effective helper.

And then all things will work together for good.

almost thou persuadest me
Acts 26:27–28
close, but no cigar

A useful way of breaking bad news, for example, to a job applicant who manages to make the short list but loses out in the final round. Paul, speaking skillfully and soundly, had done all he could to convince Agrippa that he was innocent of the charges leveled against him. Then he asked, "King Agrippa, believest thou the prophets? I know that thou believest." Then Agrippa said unto Paul, "Almost thou persuadest me to be a Christian." Scholars still dispute the question of whether Agrippa's reply should be taken literally or whether it was a way of saying "Did you really think you could convert me that easily?"

So bear this scholarly disagreement in mind when next you quote Agrippa.

alpha and omega
Revelation 2:10–11
the beginning and the end

Alpha and omega are the first and last letters of the Greek alphabet, therefore the beginning and the end of everything. In these verses from Revelation 2, John heard "a great voice, as of a trumpet, Saying, I am Alpha and Omega, the first and the last." "Alpha and Omega" here refers to God, but in the final chapter of Revelation and elsewhere in the New Testament, the term refers to Jesus as well. It is of historical interest to note that in Isaiah 44:6 we read, "I am the first, and I am the last; and beside me there is no God."

And Isaiah, of course, was written centuries before Revelation.

am I my brother's keeper?
Genesis 4:9
don't ask me; how should I know?

This famous rhetorical question was Cain's evasive rejoinder to God, who was questioning him as to the whereabouts of his brother, Abel, whom Cain had murdered. Beyond the facts of the incident itself, the biblical account is recalled because it addresses the responsibility all people have for one another. "Am I my brother's keeper?" is asked over and over again to this day during discussions of social justice. It almost never helps resolve differences of opinion.

the ancient and honorable
Isaiah 9:14–15
those who hold power

A warning: This high-sounding epithet is not to be applied without first examining the context in which it appears in Isaiah. What did God think of those so characterized: "The

Lord will cut off from Israel head and tail, branch and rush, in one day. The ancient and honorable, he is the head; and the prophet that teaches lies, he is the tail."

The drift is clear—God was not exactly fond of those who held power over his people.

angels unawares
Hebrews 13:2
angels in disguise
See ENTERTAIN ANGELS UNAWARES.

apocalypse
a symbolic depiction of the ultimate destruction of evil
  and the triumph of God

Apocalypse is a second name for the last book of the New Testament, the book of Revelation granted John of Patmos. By extension, an apocalypse is any revelation or disclosure of the future, most often today taken as widespread disaster.

There were many Jewish and Christian apocalypses that failed to make the scriptural canon, and there are portions of canonical books that are apocalyptic—for example, Isaiah 24–27, Daniel, and Joel. Apocalypses have two common characteristics. They express belief in two opposing cosmic forces, good and evil, God and Satan. They also contrast two distinct ages, the present—evil under Satan—and the future—perfect and eternal under God.

No gray areas permitted.

apple of one's eye
Psalm 17:8
a juicy metaphor for anything or anyone held especially
  precious or dear

Never mind that "apple of one's eye" has become a cliché. When the psalmist entreated God, "Keep me as the apple of the eye, hide me under the shadow of thy wings," he did not have in mind some prize fruit. Rather, he was asking for the kind of protection one gives to something cherished or fragile. In his metaphor "the apple of the eye," the psalmist meant the pupil of the eye—to him its most fragile part. And how did "apple" come to be used in this sense? In biblical times, the pupil of an eye was thought to be a globe-shaped solid resembling an apple. The metaphor occurs also in Lamentations 2:18, "Let not the apple of thine eye cease," and in Zechariah 2:8, "He that toucheth you toucheth the apple of his [the Lord's] eye."

Today, a doting grandfather may know the true form and function of a pupil, but he goes on thinking of a favored granddaughter or grandson as the apple of his eye—whether he grasps the biblical allusion or not. And he welcomes every opportunity to take the child under his wing.

See SHADOW OF THY WINGS.

Armageddon
Revelation 16:14–16
any great battle—particularly a final and conclusive
     battle—or scene of great slaughter

In Scripture, Armageddon had a more specific and more terrible meaning. It was the name of the battlefield at or near the strategic Palestinian city of Megiddo. (Armageddon in Hebrew means "Mount Megiddo.") And there, wrote the author of Revelation, the forces of good and evil would one day meet in a decisive encounter, "the battle of that great day of God Almighty," before the day of judgment.

Watch out.

See DAY OF JUDGMENT.

art thou the first man that was born?
Job 15:5–9
just who do you think you are?

A friend, having listened long to Job's continuing complaint of unfair treatment at the hand of God, could contain himself no longer. He accused Job of speaking with the "tongue of the crafty" and then let fly with his best slings and arrows: "Art thou the first man that was born? or wast thou made before the hills? Hast thou heard the secret of God? and dost thou restrain wisdom to thyself? What knowest thou, that we know not? what understandest thou, which is not in us?"

These questions seem to imply that ordinary mortals do not and cannot understand the mysteries of the universe.

A worthwhile thought for all of us.

as a dream when one awaketh
Psalm 73:18–20
a metaphor for impermanence

As Shakespeare wrote in *Hamlet*, "A dream itself is but a shadow." And if it hadn't been for Freud, many of us would not spend countless 50-minute hours striving to recall and find meaning in our dreams. To the psalmist, when the time comes for action by God, those who scoff at him will be destroyed in a moment. Their feet are set in "slippery places." Their prosperity and importance are as transient and unreal "as a dream when one awaketh."

Stock market speculators, are you listening?

See SLIPPERY PLACES.

as for me and my house
Joshua 24:15–16
I don't know about you, but this is the way we see it

During Joshua's farewell to the tribes of Israel, he told the people they had to make a new covenant and choose the God they would serve. It all came down to whether they would go along with the Lord or serve alien gods. It was all or nothing, Joshua said, the Lord was an exclusive God who brooked no rivals, abided no cheating. Joshua put the matter in a nutshell: "If it seem evil unto you to serve the Lord, choose you this day whom ye will serve; whether the gods which your fathers served that were on the other side of the flood, or the gods of the Amorites, in whose land ye dwell: but as for me and my house, we will serve the Lord."

And how did it turn out? "The people answered and said, God forbid that we should forsake the Lord, to serve other gods."

ask, and it shall be given you
Matthew 7:7
as long as you have faith, that is
See SEEK, AND YE SHALL FIND.

a soft answer turneth away wrath
Proverbs 15:1–2
kind words accomplish much

Proverbs offers polished aphorisms on right and wrong ways of living, behaving, speaking, etc., and our own Ben Franklin, brought up on the Bible, carried on this tradition in *Poor Richard's Almanack*. Verses 1 and 2 of Proverbs 15 say, "A soft answer turneth away wrath: but a grievous word stirreth up anger. The tongue of the wise useth knowledge aright: but the mouth of fools poureth out foolishness." So we are advised that our words had best be kindly and courteous, since thoughtless words can lead to trouble.

The advice Polonius gave to Laertes in *Hamlet* was cut from the same moralistic cloth:

Give every man thine ear, but few thy voice;
Take each man's censure, but reserve thy judgment.

See BE SWIFT TO HEAR, SLOW TO SPEAK, SLOW TO WRATH.

as the hart panteth after the water brooks
Psalm 42:1
a metaphor for human longing after God

The complete verse says, "As the hart panteth after the water brooks, so panteth my soul after thee, O God." During the long, hot summers characteristic of the land of the Bible, wild animals had to travel great distances in search of water. Mindful of this, the psalmist compared his need for God's nearness to the compelling thirst of a deer for fresh, cool water in the dry season.

In Christian art, the gentle and graceful hart symbolizes solitude and purity of life.

at the feet of Gamaliel
Acts 22:3
under the tutelage of an inspired teacher

Who sits at someone's feet? A disciple. And whose feet are they? Those of a learned or revered figure.

Gamaliel, a Pharisee, was a teacher of the law who opposed the Sadducees in their campaign for capital punishment for leaders of the Christian movement in Jerusalem (Acts 5:34). Saul, about to be taken into custody and held for trial, said, "I am verily a man which am a Jew, born in Tarsus, a city in Cilicia, yet brought up in this city at the feet of Gamaliel, and taught according to the perfect manner of the law of the fathers."

An excellent way to set the stage for an impassioned appeal. Unfortunately, it didn't do any good. Read on in Acts.

the axe is laid to the root of the tree
Matthew 3:10
judgment is near

The figure is that of imminent destruction even though we moderns mistakenly use it to mean destruction accomplished. Think of a woodcutter resting an axe momentarily on the spot intended to receive the first, the decisive, blow. Now you have

Matthew's intention. John the Baptist, who preached imminent divine judgment, is quoted here. And "the axe is laid to the root of the tree" is best understood as counsel that someone is watching and poised to act. Judgment is near. Trees that do not produce good fruit—people who do not repent and undergo baptism—will be "hewn down, and cast into the fire."

B

Babel
Genesis 11:4–9
today, a confused mixture of voices or sounds, any
   scene of confusion and noise—think of the floor of
   the Chicago commodities futures exchange

The word came down to us in the Old Testament account of
how diverse languages came to be spoken. Babel, from *babhel*,
the Hebrew name for Babylon, was the ancient city where
people began to build a mighty tower, called by us the tower
of Babel. It was intended to reach heaven. While formerly all
people were presumed to speak only one language, "The
Lord scattered them abroad from thence upon the face of all
the earth. . .Therefore is the name of it called Babel; because
the Lord did there confound the language of all the earth."
In short, the Lord decided to punish the presumptuous people who thought they could build a tower reaching all the way
to heaven, by confusing their speech and scattering them
around the earth. One may assume that the punishment was
intended to deter others from trying comparably nervy
schemes.

   One might guess that Babel is etymologically related to
"babble," but the experts do not go along.

Babylon
Revelation 17–19
place of all play, no work

This ancient city on the Euphrates River in southwest Asia
was famous in biblical times for its opulence and culture.
Babylon's hanging gardens, said to have been commissioned
by King Nebuchadnezzar, were an engineering and landscap-
ing marvel, one of the seven wonders of the world. It was in
Babylon that the Jews were held captive between 597 and 538

B.C., the period now referred to as the Babylonian captivity. Today, a Babylon is any city with a reputation for excessive materialism and pursuit of sensual pleasure. F. Scott Fitzgerald, who wrote of American expatriates in Europe after World War I, entitled one of his best short stories "Babylon Revisited." The Babylon of his story was Paris.

Several cities come to mind as candidates for the title of American Babylon.

See HANG OUR HARPS UPON THE WILLOWS *and* SCARLET WOMAN.

Babylon is fallen, is fallen
Isaiah 21:9
a shout of triumph at the fall of a hated enemy

Not the warning cry of a Chicken Little—the sky is falling, the sky is falling. The first half of Isaiah offers the prophet's visions. In one of them, a messenger called out to Isaiah, who was watching from a tower, "Babylon is fallen, is fallen; and all the graven images of her gods he hath broken unto the ground." Apparently, this was what Isaiah foresaw for Babylon when the Medes and Persians got through with it.

See WATCHMAN, WHAT OF THE NIGHT?

Balaam
Numbers 22–24
a misleading prophet or ally

In everyday life, no one would want to be called a Balaam, for this Old Testament prophet, a non-Israelite, got mixed notices in the Bible. Sometimes Balaam was cast as one who would sell his prophetic skills to earn a dollar, at other times as a virtuous person. Balaam is remembered mostly in the phrase "Balaam's ass," an ass that was suddenly enabled to speak words and save its master. In Numbers 22:21–35, Balaam was on his way to see Balak, king of Moab and an enemy of Israel. Along the way, the ass he was riding stopped because it saw an angel obstructing the road, a vision to which Balaam was not privy at first. Balaam gave the ass a considerable beating for refusing to go on, and the ass berated Balaam for mistreating it. Balaam finally was enabled to see the angel and realize that the road had been closed so that he could receive God's instructions from the angel on what to say to Balak.

When Balaam had his audience with Balak, he acquitted himself well in refusing the king's request that Balaam curse the armies of Israel. In Numbers 24:13, Balaam said, "If Balak would give me his house full of silver and gold, I cannot go beyond the commandment of the Lord. . .but what the Lord saith, that will I speak." So instead of cursing the Israelites, Balaam blessed them and uttered favorable prophecies, giving English the allusive phrase "Balaam's curse," which was not a curse at all, and giving Moshe Leshem the title *Balaam's Curse* for his book on modern Israel, published in the United States in 1989. The book's lengthy subtitle clarifies things for those unfamiliar with the biblical account: *How Israel Lost Its Way, and How It Can Find It Again*.

Nevertheless, returning to Numbers, the fact that Balaam mentioned silver and gold when speaking with Balak makes one worry a little bit about Balaam, doesn't it? After all, it was he who brought up the subject of a quid pro quo.

balm in Gilead
Jeremiah 8:22
a remedy for spiritual backsliders

In modern usage, the word "balm" has various meanings, for example, an aromatic ointment made from plants, and anything that soothes, heals, or reduces pain. The balm Jeremiah probably had in mind was an ointment used to heal wounds. It was made from the resin of the balsam tree, which grew in Gilead (today part of Jordan), and it is reasonable to take Jeremiah's phrase as a metaphor for any substance or act promising relief from mental or physical anguish. Jeremiah was experiencing hopeless grief at the condition of his nation. So, after inveighing against those among his people who rejected God's word, Jeremiah cried out, "Is there no balm in Gilead; is there no physician there?" The prophet was asking whether any remedy could be found, any consolation offered, to ease the pain of a people in deep spiritual trouble, to cure an Israel sick to the heart with a malignant disease. Unfortunately, no remedy was at hand.

Balm in Gilead is the title of a 1965 play Lanford Wilson wrote about the seamy side of life in New York City. Sara Lawrence Lightfoot in 1989 used the same title for her inspiring biography of her mother, who had a successful career as a psychiatrist (its subtitle is *Journey of a Healer*). Hurrah, the Bible is alive and well for writers in search of catchy and allusive titles for their works.

Barabbas
Mark 15:7
a condemned criminal pardoned instead of Jesus in
   order to appease the mob

Would you save this man's life?

At the time of the Passover festival each year, it was the practice of the Roman prefect of Judea to release one Jewish prisoner to the people. Pontius Pilate, who served as prefect from A.D. 26 to 36, asked the crowd to decide whether Jesus or Barabbas should be released. Mark 15:7 identifies Barabbas as an insurrectionist who had committed murder, so Pilate may have expected the people to ask for release of Jesus. They chose Barabbas instead, and Pilate acceded to their wishes. The choice between Jesus and Barabbas was between an idealistic peacemaker and a pragmatic patriot. And the idealist lost.

Isn't this the way things usually go?

barren woman
Psalm 113:9
a woman considered incapable of bearing children

In this psalm of praise for God, we read of various merciful acts God performs. For example, in verse 9: "He maketh the barren woman to keep house, and to be a joyful mother of children."

The expression "keep house" requires some clarification. What the King James translators intended was the equivalent of "live in a house." Indeed, the Bible offers numerous examples of women, albeit not emancipated in the modern sense, who nevertheless played roles other than that of homemaker. Consider just two, the prophets Deborah and Miriam in the Old Testament—the former portrayed as a political and military activist, the latter as a leader of other women.

See LIFT THE NEEDY OUT OF THE DUNGHILL, NOTHING IS IMPOSSIBLE, *and* STARS IN THEIR COURSES.

Bartimaeus
Mark 10:46–52
the personification of hope for the desperately afflicted

Bartimaeus, a blind beggar, cried out from the roadside as Jesus passed, "Son of David, have mercy on me." Rebuked by onlookers, he repeated his cry and soon was cured of his blindness by Jesus: "Go thy way; thy faith hath made thee whole." Bartimaeus, in a leap of hope based on unlimited faith, had taken the first step toward a new life.

Fans of the Chicago Cubs, take heart.

See O YE OF LITTLE FAITH.

beat plowshares into swords
Joel 3:12–16
prepare for war
See VALLEY OF DECISION.

beat swords into plowshares
Isaiah 2:4
abandon warfare, enjoy peace
See SWORDS INTO PLOWSHARES.

be doers, not hearers only
James 1:22
you will be judged by your actions, not by your words

Echoing the apostle Paul in Romans 2:13, James told his brethren they would be judged by how they behaved in response to the words of God: "Be ye doers of the word, and not hearers only, deceiving your own selves. For if any be a hearer of the word, and not a doer, he is like unto a man beholding his natural face in a glass: For he beholdeth himself, and goeth his way, and straightway forgetteth what manner of man he was."

"Manner of," employed to this day in the sense of "sort of," was well established in English long before the King James Version of the Bible appeared, but the frequent employment of "what manner of man. . ." by modern speakers and writers surely owes much to its use in James 1:22.

And the message "be ye doers, not hearers only" has broad applications for all of us.

be fruitful and multiply
Genesis 1:22
bear children

In Genesis 1, God created the entire world. After bringing forth birds and fish, God in verse 22 blessed them, saying, "Be fruitful and multiply." Later, in verse 28, he gave the same blessing to the first people. Whether this blessing should be followed slavishly is a subject of dispute, but world population data suggest we may have overdone "be fruitful and multiply."

beginning of wisdom
Psalm 111:10
if you don't know this, you don't know anything

In an oft-quoted sentence, "The fear of the Lord is the beginning of wisdom," the psalmist tells us to revere God. God, not we, created heaven and earth, and God, not we, sustains our life. Proverbs 1:7 and 9:10 and Job 28:28 also tell us that fear of the Lord is the beginning of wisdom. For "fear," understand reverence mixed with dread. For "wisdom," understand knowledge with a tilt toward smarts.

behold the man!
John 19:5
look at him!

A mocking of Jesus.

Pontius Pilate, the Roman prefect of Judea before whom Jesus was tried, had him brought to the courtroom dressed in the mock-royal raiment and crown of thorns the Roman soldiers had put on him. When Jesus appeared, Pilate called out, "Behold the man!"

The Latin phrase for "behold the man," *ecce homo*, is used in English to denote a painting or statue of Jesus crowned with thorns.

Belial
I Samuel 2:12
the personification of evil
See SONS OF BELIAL.

be not righteous over much
Ecclesiastes 7:16
there is such a thing as too much piety

After telling us in verse 15 that the just have perished despite their justness and the wicked have lived long despite their wickedness, the author of Ecclesiastes said, "Be not righteous over much; neither make thyself over wise: why shouldest thou destroy thyself?" The message is moderation in all things; enjoy whatever pleasures the present may offer and avoid excessive zeal for piety or wisdom.

While this may appear to be contrary to orthodox notions of recommended behavior, you can be sure the writer of Ecclesiastes is not telling us to go all out in pursuit of pleasure. See verse 17 for this sobering thought: "Be not over much wicked, neither be thou foolish: why shouldest thou die before thy time?"

But also remember to live while you live.

be not wise in your own conceits
Romans 12:15–16
don't be arrogant

"Your own conceits" here means "in your private opinions," so Paul was warning against adopting an overbearing manner. Paul devoted a long section of Romans 12 and 13 to love as the regulating principle within the Christian community and discussed how to deal with people outside the community. He said to his followers, "Rejoice with them that do rejoice, and weep with them that weep. Be of the same mind one toward another. Mind not high things, but condescend to men of low estate. Be not wise in your own conceits."

In short, sympathetic interest in the lives of others without regard for their social standing helps preserve civility. And too much concern with self has the opposite effect.

be of good cheer
John 16:33
don't give in to despair

Jesus, foreseeing the testings and sufferings his disciples would have to undergo, counseled, "In the world ye shall have tribulation: but be of good cheer; I have overcome the world."

Modern Christians in a world facing growing shortages of food and shelter: Take heed.

beside himself
Mark 3:21
in danger of going off the deep end

When we speak of people who are beside themselves, we are employing idiom that is at least five hundred years old. What we mean is that they are almost out of their senses, whether from joy, anger, grief, or other strong emotion. In Mark 3, we are told that Jesus' work of healing and teaching in Galilee succeeded so well and the crowds he attracted were so large and pressing that Jesus seemed to be in a state of dangerous exaltation. "And when his friends heard of it, they went out to lay hold on him; for they said, He is beside himself."

A phenomenon seen to this day among those who suddenly achieve fame, wealth—you name it.

be swift to hear, slow to speak, slow to wrath
James 1:19–20
sound advice, especially for married couples

The first chapter of the Epistle of James is full of good counsel: "Let every man be swift to hear, slow to speak, slow to wrath: For the wrath of man worketh not the righteousness of God."

Shades of Ben Franklin: "A man in a Passion rides a mad Horse."

See A SOFT ANSWER TURNETH AWAY WRATH *and* LET THY WORDS BE FEW.

bewail my virginity
Judges 11:37–40
what grieves me is that I am childless

Jephthah's daughter—not given the dignity of a name—appeared to believe that among her people it was the bearing of children that made a woman worthy. When told by her father that he had to carry out his vow to sacrifice her, Jephthah's unmarried, thus childless, daughter did not question his determination. She asked only this: "Let this thing be done for me: let me alone two months, that I may go up and down upon the mountains, and bewail my virginity." And when the two months were up, Jephthah fulfilled his terrible vow. Later on in Judges we read, "And it was a custom in Israel, That the daughters of Israel went yearly to lament the daughter of Jephthah the Gileadite four days in a year."

Small comfort.

For an explanation of why Jephthah felt impelled to sacrifice his daughter, *see* JEPHTHAH'S VOW.

bill of divorcement
Deuteronomy 24:1–4
a divorce

No longer common in English, "bill of divorcement" owes whatever life it still has to its use as the title of a vintage movie starring John Barrymore and Katharine Hepburn. Among the Israelites, a man could divorce his wife by presenting her with a written document, in Aramaic called a *get*. In Jeremiah 3:8 this word is translated as "bill of divorce," and in Deuteronomy as "bill of divorcement." Besides ending the marriage, a *get* gave—and to this day among orthodox Jews still gives—the divorced wife the right to remarry, but without a *get* the woman could not remarry. Permissible grounds for a divorce were not spelled out in the Old Testament—Deuteronomy speaks of the husband's finding "some uncleanness in her"—but as long as a bill of divorcement was signed before witnesses and given to the woman, the marriage was at an end. Deuteronomy 24:1: "Then let him write her a bill of divorce-

ment, and give it in her hand, and send her out of his house."
There is no evidence that a wife could initiate a divorce.

"Bill of divorcement" also appears in Mark 10:4. The Pharisees questioned Jesus as to whether it was "lawful for a man
to put away [that is, divorce] his wife." In his reply, verse 9,
Jesus strongly opposed divorce in words familiar to this day:
"What therefore God hath joined together, let not man put
asunder."

Clear enough.

blessed are the poor in spirit
Matthew 5:3–11
blessed are those with no illusions of self-righteousness

The "poor in spirit," verse 3, were those who had no pride,
no self-satisfaction; those literally poor or oppressed; and
those who, though pious, were despised by the elite because
of their failure to observe all the regulations of Judaism.
Thus, we are not surprised to find that "Blessed are the poor
in spirit" concludes with "for theirs is the kingdom of
heaven." In verse 5, the third Beatitude, we read, "Blessed
are the meek: for they shall inherit the earth." The meek were
the unassertive, the gentle, in contrast with the wicked. In this
Beatitude, Matthew echoed Psalm 37:11, "The meek shall
inherit the earth; and shall delight themselves in the abundance of peace."

blind Bartimaeus
Mark 10:46–52
a beggar cured of blindness by Jesus
See BARTIMAEUS.

blind leading the blind
Matthew 15:14
incompetents acting as mentors for other incompetents

In Matthew 15, Jesus characterized the Pharisees as "blind leaders of the blind"—the morally blind leading the morally blind. What is the fate awaiting such leadership? "And if the blind lead the blind, both shall fall into the ditch."

Enough said.

blood upon thy head
II Samuel 1:16
it's your fault

To be human is to fix blame on anyone but oneself. So we are not surprised as we read the following story in II Samuel. A messenger brought David the news that he had slain Saul, at Saul's own request, in fact. David then had the messenger put to death, and by way of justification said over the dead man, "Thy blood be upon thy head; for thy mouth hath testified against thee, saying, I have slain the Lord's anointed." David's words reflect the ancient Hebrews' belief that their kings were anointed by God. Being holy, kings could not be treated in the same manner as ordinary people, and for this reason David's action was justifiable.

To this day, anyone said to have someone's blood on his head—or on his hands—bears the blame for that person's affliction or death. Personnel managers and outplacement specialists—a world-class euphemism—bearing pink slips, beware.

the **book of life**
Revelation 20:12
a register of the names of those who will inherit eternal life

In Revelation, the "book of life" held records of the good deeds done on earth by the righteous—another book was used for the deeds of the wicked. (Philippians 4:3 speaks only of the book of life.) In Revelation, "The dead were judged out of those things which were written in the books, according to their works." And what judgment was visited on those whose names were not in the book of life? According to Revelation 20:15, "Whosoever was not found written in the book of life was cast in the lake of fire." Make no mistake about it, the lake of fire, according to Revelation 20:10, is the place "where the beast and the false prophet are, and shall be tormented day and night for ever and ever."

Enough to make one think twice.

born again
John 3:3
radically recommitted to religious belief

When we refer to people as born-again Christians, we mean they are deeply recommitted to their religious faith as a result of having undergone spiritual rebirth during an intense religious experience. In John 3:3 Jesus said, "Except a man be born again, he cannot see the kingdom of God." In verse 5 Jesus went on to say, "Except a man be born of water and of the Spirit, he cannot enter the kingdom of God." That is, essential to spiritual rebirth are baptism and profound acceptance of God.

The idea of being born again, which appears nowhere else in the New Testament, receives great attention today in public discussion as well as among conservative Christians.

borne the burden and the heat of the day
Matthew 20:12
performed hard work, especially in the service of God

In biblical times, seasonal laborers were paid at the end of each day's work, and the going daily wage was the Roman silver coin called a denarius, in Matthew 20:2 called a penny. Jesus' parable in Matthew 20:1–16 tells of how laborers who had "borne the burden and the heat of the day," that is, who had worked a full day, complained when they were paid the same as those hired later in the day. In rejecting their complaint, Jesus taught that God rewards workers for the kingdom of God who renounce their personal interests. Whether they come to this state early or late, all receive salvation and eternal life. In the words of verse 16, "So the last shall be first, and the first last: for many be called, but few chosen." That is, many hear the message of Jesus, but few respond with a commitment.

Make no mistake. Jesus was not advocating a wage policy. He was being realistic in his assessment of the popular response to a new leader or a new movement.

bowels of compassion
I John 3:17
feelings of pity

It is a commonplace today that many people literally turn their heads away in order to avoid seeing homeless people on city streets. The First Epistle of John gives us a vivid phrase to use in condemning such uncharitable people: "Whoso hath this world's good, and seeth his brother have need, and shutteth up his bowels of compassion from him, how dwelleth the love of God in him?"

One may question why the King James translators chose to use the phrase "bowels of compassion." For centuries the bowels were considered the seat of sympathetic emotions, so while today we are likely to say, for example, that uncaring people shut their hearts to the poor, it once made just as much sense to speak of shutting the bowels. In fact, people in biblical times were anything but certain about which organ was the seat of the emotions. They variously credited the heart, kidney, and liver, as well as other organs.

Incidentally, Isaiah 28:27, commenting less colorfully on those who do not help the poor, had this to say: "He that giveth unto the poor shall not lack: but he that hideth his eyes shall have many a curse."

bow in the cloud
Genesis 9:13–14
a rainbow

In this happy phrase from the Old Testament, God promised that no flood would ever again destroy the earth: "I do set my bow in the cloud, and it shall be a token of a covenant between me and the earth." It is inviting to think that this "bow in the cloud" was the first rainbow ever observed.

a **brand plucked out of the burning**
Zechariah 3:2
a person rescued from imminent danger
See FIREBRAND PLUCKED OUT OF THE BURNING.

bread of life
John 6:35
a metaphor for Jesus as unfailing provider for humanity

In this verse from the Gospel of John, Jesus said, "I am the bread of life: he that cometh to me shall never hunger; and he that believeth on me shall never thirst." The word "bread" here signifies the essentials of life, not luxuries.

bread upon the waters
Ecclesiastes 11:1
something given in charity
See CAST BREAD UPON THE WATERS.

breasts like twin roes
Song of Solomon 7:3
a beautiful bosom

The metaphor is even better when given in full: "Thy two breasts are like two young roes that are twins." Who can think of anything more appealing than a small deer, and when the Song of Solomon speaks of twin deer, my simile runneth over.

Anyone who would wax rhapsodic but lacks evocative words can find no better inspiration than the Song of Solomon.

bricks without straw
Exodus 5:7
a well-nigh impossible task

"Bricks without straw" gives us a model for unenlightened employers trying to crush the spirit of people they employ. When today we say "make bricks without straw," we mean "try to do something without having the proper materials on hand." The result is failure or an inferior end product. The allusion is to Exodus 5:7, in the account of the lives of the Israelites held captive in Egypt. Moses and Aaron had gone to the Pharaoh to ask permission for their people to hold a feast in the wilderness and make sacrifices to God. Not only did the Pharaoh deny the request, but he instructed his foremen to stop supplying the Israelites with the straw needed in making bricks. From then on, they would have to find their own straw and still turn out the same number of bricks they were required to make each day.

See DARKNESS WHICH MAY BE FELT.

brotherly love
Hebrews 13:1
affection, loyalty, fraternity
See SAME YESTERDAY, AND TO DAY, AND FOR EVER.

brother to dragons
Job 30:27–29
an outcast
See COMPANION TO OWLS.

brought nothing into this world
I Timothy 6:7
born without possessions

One of the most difficult lessons to absorb in our wacky world of stretch limos, million-dollar salaries, and money that must be laundered is that there's more to life than VCRs and weekends in Palm Springs. The writer of I Timothy picked up where Job left off in calling to our attention the fact that all of us come into this world without possessions and leave in the same condition: "We brought nothing into this world, and it is certain we can carry nothing out. And having food and raiment let us be therewith content."

George S. Kaufman and Moss Hart were right on the money when they wrote *You Can't Take It with You*.

See NAKED CAME I OUT OF THE WOMB.

burning bush
Exodus 3:2–6
a manifestation of God's presence

The burning bush is an evocative image, usually thought to come verbatim from Scripture even though it does not, and used many times in titles of books and poems. In Exodus 3:2–6, during an account of Moses' experiences, we read, "And the angel of the Lord appeared unto him in a flame of fire out of the midst of a bush: and he looked, and, behold, the bush burned with fire, and the bush was not consumed." Soon enough God spoke to Moses from the bush, saying, "Here am I." And what did Moses do? "Moses hid his face; for he was afraid to look upon the Lord."

To this day the burning bush symbolizes the appearance of God to humankind, and it may be for this reason that orthodox Jews, sensing the divine presence, avert their gaze to avoid seeing God during the most solemn moments of the Yom Kippur service.

See PUT OFF THY SHOES FROM OFF THY FEET.

bury their dead
Matthew 8:22
an obligation of all people

Jesus, intent on succeeding in his mission, told a disciple he must fulfill obligations that superseded even a son's duty to bury his father: "Follow me: and let the dead bury their dead." And who were the dead who would bury the dead? Presumably, those who did not perform missionary work and so themselves could be said to be spiritually dead.

In this phrase from Matthew, Irwin Shaw found an arresting title for his antiwar play of 1936, *Bury the Dead*, but the playwright's intention was far removed from that of Jesus.

by their fruits shall ye know them
Matthew 7:18–20
a test for those who claim to be prophets

Sound advice, especially when applied to the promises of politicians, and particularly politicians running for president: Pay attention to what people do, not to what they say. Jesus, summarizing his test for the genuineness of self-proclaimed prophets, said, "A good tree cannot bring forth evil fruit, neither can a corrupt tree bring forth good fruit." And then he said, "Wherefore by their fruits shall ye know them." Not by their words.

C

Calvary
Luke 23:33
a time of extreme suffering

Small wonder in light of Luke 23:33, which speaks of "the place which is called Calvary" as the site of the crucifixion of Jesus. Archaeological uncertainty about the location of Jerusalem's northern wall has thus far made the site of Calvary impossible to fix. It was near a highway, according to Matthew 27:39, and outside a gate, according to Hebrews 13:12. There is no textual support for the idea that Calvary was a hill, even though many think of it that way.

Incidentally, the name Calvary derives from the Latin *calvaria*, meaning "skull."

For the significance of "skull," *see* GOLGOTHA.

camel through the eye of a needle
Mark 10:25
a self-evident impossibility

Jesus gave all us poor folk much comfort in Mark 10:17–25. What happened was this: A man asked Jesus, "What shall I do that I may inherit eternal life?" Jesus advised him to follow the commandments. The man replied he had done so since youth. Jesus then told him to sell his possessions and give the proceeds to the poor: "Thou shalt have treasure in heaven." The man, who happened to be wealthy, went away unhappy. It was at that point, in verse 25, that Jesus—a master of hyperbole—said to his disciples listening to this colloquy, "It is easier for a camel to go through the eye of a needle, than for a rich man to enter into the kingdom of God." How the disciples, poor fishermen by trade, must have enjoyed hearing Jesus tell off the rich folk!

And how pleased must Roger Waldinger have been to find a title so allusive and pointed for his study of immigrants and enterprise in the New York garment trade, *Through the Eye of the Needle*.

Cana
John 2:1
the village in Galilee where Jesus performed his wedding
  feast miracle
See GOOD THING OUT OF NAZARETH.

can the leopard change his spots?
Jeremiah 13:23
not a snowball's chance in hell

God, through Jeremiah, addressed those of his people who were thoroughly corrupt and so most in need of changing their manner of living: "Can the Ethiopian change his skin, or the leopard his spots? then may ye also do good, that are accustomed to do evil." We must conclude that the task of getting back on the straight and narrow after years of less than laudable living represents more of a challenge than most of us can manage.
  Better to live virtuously from the start than to discover in

middle age that we are no longer capable of doing so.
See STRAIGHT AND NARROW.

carried about with every wind of doctrine
Ephesians 4:14
a metaphor for people lacking conviction or focus

Paul cautioned the new Christian churches against accepting novel doctrines and erroneous ideas advanced by glib talkers: "Be no more children, tossed to and fro, and carried about with every wind of doctrine, by the sleight of men, and cunning craftiness, whereby they lie in wait to deceive." But did Paul intend that the members of his church never consider new ideas? Not at all. He was advising against willy-nilly acceptance of false doctrines advanced by false leaders.

cast bread upon the waters
Ecclesiastes 11:1
today, act charitably or generously without expecting
     anything in return

The writer of Ecclesiastes intended something quite different in this metaphor. "Cast thy bread upon the waters, for thou shalt find it after many days" employs "bread" in the sense of "grain." Whenever one sends grain across the seas, we are told, some will surely get through and bring a good return even though some surely will be lost. Therefore, the verse is recommending that we hedge our bets by spreading our risks. Some part of a risky venture will pay off even though the rest does not.
     Sound advice.
     See LET NOT YOUR LEFT HAND KNOW WHAT YOUR RIGHT HAND DOES.

casting out devils
Mark 1:34
exorcism, a procedure for ejecting demons from the human mind

Several verses of Mark 1 describe exorcisms performed by Jesus. In verse 34 we read, "And he cast out many devils; and suffered not the devils to speak, because they knew him." Exorcism is still practiced today by some Christian churches.

cast the first stone
John 8:7
take the lead in criticizing

Those quick to condemn others for immoral or illicit acts of which they themselves may be guilty are challenged in these words to examine their own lives. John 8 recounts how hostile scribes and Pharisees brought an adulteress before Jesus. They were seeking to trap him into an incautious answer to the question of whether the woman should be put to death by stoning, the punishment prescribed for those who committed adultery. Jesus responded with these words: "He that is without sin among you, let him first cast a stone at her." Verse 9 relates that everybody present except the woman and Jesus left the area, "convicted by their own conscience."

See GO, AND SIN NO MORE.

charity shall cover the multitude of sins
I Peter 4:7–8
love for your fellow humans will do much for you

The First Epistle of Peter, counseling people on how they should conduct their lives, says, "Be ye therefore sober, and watch unto prayer. And above all things have fervent charity among yourselves: for charity shall cover the multitude of sins." The meaning of this thought is best understood by interpreting "charity" as "love of one's fellow humans," the greatest of the three Christian graces enumerated in I Corinthians 13. The strength of this love can overcome faults in the person offering it.

A double benefit, something for the recipient and the rest for the giver.

See SEE THROUGH A GLASS DARKLY.

chief seats in the synagogue
Mark 12:39
the biblical equivalent of two on the aisle

Mark 12, speaking of those who loved the "chief seats in the synagogue," provided a metaphor useful in characterizing people who scramble after prominence by joining only the toniest of country clubs, buying homes only in exclusive enclaves, driving only Mercedes automobiles, and the like. In verses 38–40, Jesus attacked the ostentation of the scribes, the most fortunate of his countrymen, who were given seats in the synagogue even though the other congregants were expected to stand.

children shall rise up against their parents
Mark 13:12
a precursor to the new order

Jesus told his disciples they would encounter terrible events before the kingdom of God was established on earth. For example, "Children shall rise up against their parents, and shall cause them to be put to death." And Jesus meant this literally.

Makes the problems of today's parents seem like nothing.

a clean heart
Psalm 51:10
a metaphor for moral virtue

The psalmist, seeking moral renewal, wrote, "Create in me a clean heart, O God."

See WHITER THAN SNOW.

clearer than the noonday
Job 11:16–17
a metaphor for how your happier future will surely
    appear to you—sooner or later

A friend of Job's told him not to despair of arriving at an
understanding of God's actions. He advised that if Job would
set his heart straight and stretch out his hand to God, his life
would improve and his bitterness disappear: "Thou shalt forget thy misery, and remember it as waters that pass away; And
thine age shall be clearer than the noonday; thou shalt shine
forth, thou shalt be as the morning."
    Clearheaded and ready to face life again, that is.

coat of many colors
Genesis 37:3
a gift expressing love for one's child

The best-known coat in the Bible was given as a gift by a
doting father, Jacob, to his favorite son, Joseph, whom Jacob
especially loved "because he was the son of his old age." In
the land of the Bible, such a gift was a mark of special favor
and was more generally made to an eldest son.
    Don't think for a moment that Joseph's brothers failed to
notice their father's gift.
    For what happened later on, *see* POTIPHAR'S WIFE.

come to thy grave in a full age
Job 5:26
live a long time

You may startle friends if you use "come to thy grave in a full
age" to express the wish that they may have a long life, but
you would be quoting Scripture appropriately. After telling
Job that life would be difficult for him and advising him to put

his faith in God, Job's friend said to him that if he did so, "Thou shalt come to thy grave in a full age, like as a shock of corn cometh in in his season."

See THREESCORE AND TEN.

comfort me with apples
Song of Solomon 2:5
refresh me with apples (for I am faint with love)
See LITTLE FOXES.

the **common people**
Mark 12:37
you and I and millions of others

When do Ivy Leaguers eat pork rinds, knishes, pizza, hot dogs, and kielbasa? When they're running for elective office. During election years, all politicians are friends of the common people. Mark 12:37 says of Jesus, "And the common people heard him gladly." No surprise there. The common people could understand his words and know he was on their side. Besides, ordinary folk have always loved seeing a challenge to orthodoxy and social position.

companion to owls
Job 30:27–29
an outcast

When we recall that owls are mostly up and about in the dark of night while the creatures they prey on are stirring and the owls are hidden from our less competent eyes, we see in "companion to owls" an excellent metaphor for an outcast. Job, regarding himself as God's derelict, society's outcast, vented his despair in some pretty strong language: "My bowels boiled, and rested not: the days of affliction prevented me....I am a brother to dragons, and a companion to owls."

Can you think of anything worse?

a covenant with death
Isaiah 28:15
unprincipled appeasement, a Munich Pact, a death
    warrant

Isaiah warned the rulers of Judah they had erred in relying on
political and military commitments made by Egypt: "Because
ye have said, We have made a covenant with death, and with
hell are we at agreement; when the overflowing scourge shall
pass through, it shall not come unto us: for we have made lies
our refuge, and under falsehood have we hid ourselves."
Isaiah, in verse 18, went on to warn that God would see to it
that the covenant with death, the alliance with Egypt, would
be broken, and "When the overflowing scourge shall pass
through, then ye shall be trodden down by it."
See THIS BROKEN REED.

crown of life
James 1:12
a distinction bestowed on a person who has led an
    exemplary life

In this metaphor the author of the Epistle of James may have
had in mind something like the wreaths of wild olive awarded
winners in the ancient Olympic games. But he was addressing
a subject far more serious than discus-throwing: "Blessed is

the man that endureth temptation: for when he is tried, he shall receive the crown of life, which the Lord hath promised to them that love him."

Any winners in this contest will be those who successfully meet the tests of faith in God.

crown of thorns
Mark 15:17
a metaphor for suffering

The crown of thorns mentioned in Mark symbolizes Christ the suffering servant. So anyone who carries a burden of prolonged and intense suffering may be said to wear a crown of thorns. As recounted in Mark, Pontius Pilate condemned Jesus to death and turned him over to the Roman guards, who were then free to do with Jesus as they chose. Cruel forms of mockery were the guards' particular delight. Understanding that Jesus claimed kingship, they dressed him in a purple robe and crowned him with a wreath made of thorny branches. By way of mocking him further, the guards alternately bowed down before him and spat on him, and struck him on the head with reeds.

Jesus wearing a crown of thorns has been painted by many artists, perhaps the best known being Albrecht Dürer.
See BEHOLD THE MAN *and* PARTED HIS GARMENTS, CASTING LOTS UPON THEM.

crumbs from the table
Luke 16:21
a handout

This biblical metaphor comes closer to reality than does today's smug expression "safety net for the disadvantaged." Luke 16:19–31 recounts Jesus' parable of the rich man and the beggar, named Lazarus, who was "full of sores and desiring to be fed with the crumbs which fell from the rich man's table."

Incidentally, Lazarus soon died and went to heaven.
For the fate of the rich man, *see* ABRAHAM'S BOSOM.

my **cup runneth over**
Psalm 23:5
everything's coming up roses

In this, probably the most popular of all the psalms, an over-flowing cup is used as a symbol for a life of abundance. In saying "My cup runneth over," the psalmist was praising God for the bounty he had seen fit to bestow.

For quite a different symbolic meaning of "cup," *see* LET THIS CUP PASS FROM ME.

D

darkness which may be felt
Exodus 10:21–22
palpable, truly awesome darkness

When the Pharaoh showed no change of heart toward the Israelites despite the many terrible plagues visited upon Egypt, God took yet another step to break the Pharaoh's spirit. He told Moses, "Stretch out thine hand toward heaven, that there may be darkness over the land of Egypt, even darkness which may be felt." Moses did so, and the darkness lasted three days. Those of us who have witnessed a total eclipse, even one that lasts less than an hour, can surely sympathize with the effect all this had on the ancient Egyptians. But was the Pharaoh convinced that he should let the Israelites go? Not quite. It took some smiting of the firstborn to do the trick—and even then, the Pharaoh welshed.

See LET MY PEOPLE GO.

David and Jonathan
I Samuel 13:41
inseparable friends, the biblical equivalent of Damon and Pythias
See PASSING THE LOVE OF WOMEN.

the day of judgment
I John 4:17
the final day for all humankind

For students and felons, a day of reckoning for past sins; for readers of Scripture, the time of God's final judgment on all of humanity, when history will come to a screeching halt: "Herein is our love made perfect, that we may have boldness in the day of judgment: because as he is, so are we in this world." Other passages of the New Testament also speak of this day, among them Hebrews 9:27 and Jude, verse 6. For a description of the judgment scene, see Revelation 20.

days are as grass
Psalm 103:15–16
life is short

Human lives are distressingly brief, in the biblical simile no more than a single season in duration. Together, verses 15–16 say, "As for man, his days are as grass: as a flower of the field, so he flourisheth. For the wind passeth over it, and it is gone; and the place thereof shall know it no more." The image employed in these verses was picked up by Ernest Dowson, the nineteenth-century English poet, in addressing Cynara, an old flame that had flickered but not gone out:

I have forgot much, Cynara! gone with the wind,
Flung roses, roses, riotously, with the throng,
Dancing, to put thy pale, lost lilies out of mind.

And Margaret Mitchell, recognizing a good thing when she saw it, had a title for the only novel she would ever write.

the days of thy youth
Ecclesiastes 12:1
when everything seems too good to be true—and isn't

As everyone who has lived long enough knows, the period of one's youth is carefree and happy mainly in retrospect. Most of today's young people and those of times gone by are, or at some point have been, miserable. Either the author of Ecclesiastes lived in a better time, when the young were full of beans, or he was a person of some years looking back imperfectly at his early years. Whatever the case, verse 1 advises people to think seriously about life before thoughts of death intrude: "Remember now thy Creator in the days of thy youth, while the evil days come not, nor the years draw nigh, when thou shalt say, I have no pleasure in them." Now the perception of Ecclesiastes becomes clear: Youth surely is better than old age.

Faint praise.

the **day the Lord hath made**
Psalm 118:24
an epithet for the Sabbath

In Exodus 20:8–11, the seventh day is established as a day of rest from the week's work, alluding to the day on which God rested after the acts of creation (Genesis 2:2). It has been suggested, in the context of Psalm 118, that the psalmist was offering a litany of thanksgiving for a particular festival. Thus, since the days of the Pilgrims, many an American parent looking out at family and guests gathered around the Thanksgiving table has spoken the familiar words of verse 24: "This is the day the Lord hath made; we will rejoice and be glad in it." In many Protestant churches, ministers use this sentence as the opening call to Sunday worship.

death in the pot
II Kings 4:40–41
danger lurking
See THERE IS DEATH IN THE POT.

death, where is thy sting?
I Corinthians 15:55
death, you have not conquered

Golfers missing a 1-foot putt may see their tantalizing failure as the end of the world and, as though asking for release from eighteen holes of tribulation, may call out, "Death, where is thy sting?" But Paul's First Epistle to the Corinthians tells a different story. Paul saw the resurrection of Jesus as a triumph over death and climaxed his discourse on the subject with "O death, where is thy sting? O grave, where is thy victory?" So Paul felt exultation rather than grief—death had not hurt Jesus, nor had the tomb conquered him.

See THERE SHALL BE NO MORE DEATH.

deep calleth unto deep
Psalm 42:7
a waterlogged metaphor for the distresses that beset the troubled

Verses 5–8 of Psalm 42 constitute a kind of soliloquy mixing self-pity with self-analysis. The psalmist has been unsuccessful in finding peace of mind. An ocean storm rages within him, and his inner tempests are symbolized by nature's wild waters—cataracts, battering waves, and tidal surges. So, in verse 7, we read, "Deep calleth unto deep at the noise of thy waterspouts: all thy waves and thy billows are gone over me."

To balance things off, the Song of Solomon 8:7 supplies a watertight metaphor: "Many waters cannot quench love, neither can the floods drown it." Love conquers all.

Delilah
Judges 16:4–22
a seductive and treacherous woman

Delilah, who lived in Gaza, was paid by the Philistine authorities to find the secret of Samson's phenomenal strength. Catering to his sexual cravings, she wheedled the secret from him. The strength lay in his long hair—his mother had vowed before Samson was born that he would adhere to the Nazirite requirement never to cut it. While Samson slept, Delilah cut off his hair, and stripped of his strength, Samson was immediately caught, blinded, and taken to Gaza (giving Aldous Huxley the title for his novel *Eyeless in Gaza*). As Samson's hair grew back, his strength began to return, and in one final burst of strength, the blind man pulled down the temple of Dagon on great numbers of Philistines and on himself as well.

Delilah has been portrayed in many paintings, among them

those by Rembrandt and Rubens; in an oratorio by Handel; in an opera by Saint-Saëns; and in Milton's dramatic poem *Samson Agonistes*. Whatever her character, this woman apparently fascinates creative people.

den of lions
Daniel 6:16
maximum exposure to danger

A den of lions is any place or situation—an IRS office comes first to mind—in which one is certain to be clawed and chewed to tiny pieces, especially figuratively.

For the biblical context, *see* LAW OF THE MEDES AND THE PERSIANS.

den of thieves
Matthew 21:13
any place where undesirable types gather or hide

The metaphor appears in the accounts in Matthew and Mark of how Jesus drove the moneychangers from the Temple grounds. In Matthew 21:13, Jesus said, "My house shall be called the house of prayer; but ye have made it a den of thieves."

See MONEYCHANGERS.

depart in peace
Luke 2:29
a euphemism for "die a natural death"

In Luke, pious old Simeon was told he would not die until he had seen the Messiah. When Simeon held the infant Jesus in his arms at the Temple, he recognized him as the long-sought savior. Content to die, Simeon said, "Lord, now lettest thou thy servant depart in peace."
See ABRAHAM'S BOSOM.

the **desert shall rejoice**
Isaiah 35:1
everything will be hunky-dory

The first ten verses of Isaiah 35 constitute a poem of exultation anticipating the joyous return to the promised land of a people released by the hand of God from bondage in Babylon. Wonderful will be the further manifestations of God's power: "The wilderness and the solitary place shall be glad for them; and the desert shall rejoice, and blossom as the rose."

Today, vast stretches of the desert in the promised land have been made green and fertile.

For information on the rose mentioned in verse 1, *see* ROSE OF SHARON.

die before your time
Ecclesiastes 7:17
fail to reach the age of seventy
See BE NOT RIGHTEOUS OVER MUCH *and* THREESCORE AND TEN.

the **dog is turned to his own vomit**
II Peter 2:23
recidivism Bible style

A metaphor for a loathsome or disgusting act repeated by a contemptible person. Proverbs 26:11 says, "As a dog returneth to his vomit, so a fool returneth to his folly," and it is to this old saw that the Second Epistle of Peter refers in characterizing backsliders among those newly converted to Christianity. Verse 22 says that it would be better not to convert at all than to convert and then resume one's old life. Verse 23 adds, "But it is happened unto them according to the true proverb, The dog is turned to his own vomit again; and the sow that was washed to her wallowing in the mire."

Animals were held in low esteem by the Jews and early Christians, so such metaphors were particularly telling and are still apt today if you know anything about the habits of dogs and pigs.

See WITHOUT ARE DOGS.

doorkeeper in the house of God
Psalm 84:10
a humble servant of God

People whose life work is directed toward the public good may think of themselves as doorkeepers in the house of God. Verse 10 tells us that peace of mind cannot be obtained in a life dedicated only to pursuit of wealth: "I had rather be a doorkeeper in the house of my God than to dwell in the tents of wickedness."

A striking use of this expression of faith was heard in 1956. Alben Barkley, who served as vice president of the United States from 1949 to 1953, gave a speech that concluded, "I would rather be a servant in the house of the Lord than sit in the seat of the mighty." Within moments, this good man fell dead.

double-edged sword
Hebrews 4:12
something that will yield advantages as well as
    disadvantages

In modern usage, anything termed a double-edged sword need not be a sword at all, but you can be sure it will cut both ways. Thus, truth often helps even when it hurts. A good thing to remember: Whatever we do or say may wound, so let's be careful in choosing our (s)words.

As used in Hebrews, however, "double-edged sword" is a metaphor for incisiveness: "The word of God is quick, and powerful, and sharper than any twoedged sword, piercing even to the dividing asunder of soul and spirit, and of the joints and marrow, and is a discerner of the thoughts and intents of the heart." The referent of the metaphor is the short double-edged Roman sword, sharp on both sides of the blade and therefore devastating in close combat.

Revelation 1:16, in describing John's vision of the Son of man, uses the same image: "In his right hand seven stars: and out of his mouth went a sharp twoedged sword: and his countenance was as the sun shineth in his strength." Why a double-edged sword? Could John have had in mind that one edge would condemn humanity, and the other save it?

See ALPHA AND OMEGA.

doubting Thomas
John 20:25
a die-hard skeptic

This durable epithet describes someone who accepts nothing without irrefutable evidence of its validity. Thomas was not present at the first appearance of the resurrected Christ. When the other disciples reported the appearance to Thomas, he said, "Except I shall see in his hands the print of the nails, and put my finger into the print of the nails, and thrust my hand into his side, I will not believe." A week later, when all the disciples were together, Jesus reappeared and Thomas was given the evidence he demanded.

Notwithstanding, "doubting Thomas" is alive and well in the English language along with "I'm from Missouri."

dove
Matthew 3:16–17
today's term of choice for a person who would wage
  peace rather than war

This gentle bird of symbolic importance is amply represented in the Bible. In Genesis, for example, Noah sent doves out to determine whether the floodwaters had subsided, thus giving doves a lasting significance as messengers of peace and deliverance from anxiety. At the baptism of Jesus, described in Matthew 3, Jesus had a vision of "the spirit of God descending like a dove," and this constituted his messianic call. The dove also plays a role in other books of the New Testament.

While modern artists may use doves as symbols of peace, innocence, and brotherhood, in Christian art the dove represents the Holy Spirit.

See OLIVE BRANCH; WISE AS SERPENTS, HARMLESS AS DOVES; *and* WINGS OF THE DOVE.

down to the sea in ships
Psalm 107:23–24
braving the dangers of the high seas

The Israelites may not have matched the Phoenicians when it came to sailing, but they gave us in Psalm 107 one of the most enduring of seafaring expressions. Poets and writers must

look far to surpass this epithet for brave seafarers: "They that go down to the sea in ships, that do business in great waters; These see the works of the Lord, and his wonders in the deep." The perils inherent in sea voyages of biblical times are described vividly in this psalm and are recalled each winter when newspapers report tragedies at sea. The psalm is a litany of thanksgiving, particularly by the hungry and thirsty who are given food and drink, prisoners who are liberated, the sick who are healed, and seafarers who feel protected on dangerous voyages.

dreamer of dreams
Deuteronomy 13:3–5
today, an idle dreamer or a visionary

In Deuteronomy, a dreamer of dreams was any duplicitous prophet who sought divine revelation in dreams. By way of stern warning against being led away from devotion to the Lord, Deuteronomy says, "If there arise among you a prophet, or a dreamer of dreams, and giveth thee a sign or a wonder, And the sign or the wonder come to pass, whereof he spake unto thee, saying, Let us go after other gods, which thou hast not known, and let us serve them; Thou shalt not hearken unto the words of that prophet, or that dreamer of dreams." Thus are we warned against accepting one-shot demonstrations as adequate proof of a charlatan's claims.
See UNKNOWN GOD.

drive like Jehu
II Kings 9:20
burn up the road

Today we are more likely to speak of a "speed demon" than a "jehu," but both terms denote a fast driver. A jehu is also a driver of a coach or cab, and the term is used in this sense in O. Henry's classic story "A Municipal Report," in which the jehu was anything but a Mario Andretti. As recounted in II Kings, Jehu was a general in King Jehoram's army who set out with a company of charioteers to depose the king, then residing in Jezreel, where he had a secondary castle. When the charioteers came into view across the wide Plain of Jezreel, the watchman on the tower spotted the lead chariot and reported to Jehoram, "The driving is like the driving of Jehu . . .for he driveth furiously."

By the time the incident ended, Jehu and his cohorts had killed the king and more than two hundred others. But it is Jehu's prowess as a driver, not his fierce act of regicide, that keeps his name alive in English.

See JEZEBEL.

a **drop of a bucket**
Isaiah 40:15
nothing, zilch

Today we are more apt to speak of a "drop in the bucket" rather than a "drop of a bucket," but the meaning is the same. Isaiah recounted a vision in which God's majesty and power were seen as dazzling. But what of us? "Behold, the nations are as a drop of a bucket, and are counted as the small dust of the balance." The word "balance" here means "scale," giving us yet another metaphor for the insignificance of people. To weigh objects accurately on a balance, the instrument must be made as clean as possible, so you can imagine how insignificant is the "small dust of the balance," the dust inevitably left even after a thorough cleaning.

dust thou art
Genesis 3:19
one day you'll surely die

Scripture does not miss many chances to tell us of the fate that awaits us all. In this verse from Genesis, we are reminded not only of our mortality but of how we must toil day after day to earn a living by the sweat of our brows. God pulled no punches in laying it all out for Adam, who by that point had disobeyed God: "In the sweat of thy face shalt thou eat bread, till thou return unto the ground; for out of it wast thou taken: for dust thou art, and unto dust shalt thou return."

So not only do we have to work hard to stay alive, but no matter how hard we work we have come from nothing and will return to nothing. The notion of a life after death did not appear until long after the writing of Genesis.

See ADAM'S RIB *and* ALL THINGS COME ALIKE TO ALL.

dwell together in unity
Psalm 133:1
live in peace with one another

A consummation devoutly to be wished: achievement of universal brotherhood. Psalm 133:1 says, "Behold how good and how pleasant it is for brethren to dwell together in unity." The solidarity of the family was the basis of Israel's social and religious strength. If all people were looked upon as brethren today, we might be able to live together in peace.

The idea may seem commonplace, yet it appears to remain beyond our reach, not to mention our grasp.

E

ears to hear
Matthew 11:15
the ability to listen and heed

In Matthew, Jesus said, "He that hath ears to hear, let him hear." Countless times since, mothers have told their children that ears were made to hear with. And Shakespeare's Mark Antony said, "Friends, Romans, countrymen, lend me your ears." The message is the same: Listen to me and don't let my words go in one ear and out the other.

For ears that hear not, *see* MOUTHS THAT SPEAK NOT.

east of Eden
Genesis 4:16
the area outside paradise to which Cain was sent by
   God, who had condemned him to a lifetime of
   wandering
See EDEN.

eat, drink, and be merry
Luke 12:15–21
lead an empty life

Anyone who thinks these words are intended to encourage easy living ignores their biblical context. This is not classic epicurean advice, Bible style. In the parable of the rich fool in Luke, a wealthy farmer saw that his barns could hold no more and decided to pull them down so he could build larger ones. His idea was that when the new barns were built, he would opt for early retirement, saying, "Soul, thou hast much goods laid up for many years; take thine ease, eat, drink, and be merry." Verse 15 makes the point of the parable: "Beware of covetousness: for a man's life consisteth not in the abundance of the things which he possesseth." And what happened? The rich fool died in verse 20, making it clear that possessions are not what life is all about. Isaiah 22:13, in somewhat the same vein, denigrated those who said, "Let us eat, and drink; for tomorrow we shall die."

Incidentally, Ecclesiastes 2:24 took a different, existentialist tack: "There is nothing better for a man, than that he should eat and drink, and that he should make his soul enjoy good in his labor."

In other words, don't worry, be happy—in your work, that is.

Eden
Genesis 2
paradise

When Shakespeare in *Richard II* called England "this other Eden, demi-paradise," he may have been indulging in a bit of chauvinism suitable for Elizabethan England, but think of how big he would have made it today as a travel writer. The primeval paradise that was Eden provided for all human needs, and in the middle, along with "every tree that is pleasant," grew the tree of life and the tree of knowledge. Without meaning to spoil the pleasure of anyone who doesn't know how things turned out, it must be said that Adam and Eve were misled by a certain serpent and given their walking papers. If they had kept their wits about them and obeyed God's instructions, paradise might never have been lost, and Milton would have had to look elsewhere for a subject worthy of a great epic poem—and write other opening lines matching the genius of the ones he did compose:

Of man's first disobedience, and the fruit
Of that forbidden tree, whose mortal taste
Brought death into the world, and all our woe,
With loss of Eden....

Not to mention new closing lines for another epic poem to match those of *Paradise Lost*:

The world was all before them, where to choose
Their place of rest, and Providence their guide:
They hand in hand with wand'ring steps and slow
Through Eden took their solitary way.

The origin of the name Eden is a matter of interest. Although it has generally been thought to be a Hebrew word meaning "pleasure" or "delight," some spoilsport scholars relate it to a Sumerian word meaning "steppe" or "plain." Surely most of us prefer the Hebrew etymology.

Genesis 4:16 also gave us the phrase "east of Eden," where God sent Cain to live a life of wandering after Cain had slain Abel. John Steinbeck used the phrase as the title of his 1952 novel, later made into a film, and based roughly on the biblical story of Cain and Abel, the offspring of Adam and Eve.
See MARK OF CAIN.

Eli, Eli, lema sabachthani
Psalm 22:1
my God, my God, why hast thou forsaken me?
See WHY HAST THOU FORSAKEN ME?

entertain angels unawares
Hebrews 13:2
strangers may turn out to be angels in disguise

A reminder to treat all people well lest we unwittingly come into the presence of someone saintly, someone God-sent. Abraham in Genesis 18:1–8 and Lot in Genesis 19:1–3 both entertained angels disguised as men—with marvelous results for both. Abraham was told by the three strangers he received hospitably that Sarah, his until then barren ninety-year-old wife, would one day bear a child—and she soon did. Lot, living at the time in Sodom, offered to put two strangers up for the night and was warned by them to leave the doomed town before it was destroyed—and he did. Thus, Hebrews

13:2 tells us: "Be not forgetful to entertain strangers: for thereby some have entertained angels unawares."

Today, "entertain an angel unawares" is more likely to be applied to a situation in which a Broadway producer meets someone who unexpectedly offers to foot the bill for a theatrical venture.

the **everlasting arms**
Deuteronomy 33:27
the protective arms of God

It is these everlasting arms that sustain those of faith through every trial. The verse is often used to console people who have suffered the loss of a dear one. By way of blessing the tribe of Asher, Moses said, "The eternal God is thy refuge, and underneath are the everlasting arms; and he shall thrust out the enemy from before thee; and shall say, Destroy them."

every man did what was right in his own eyes
Judges 21:25
anarchy replacing reliance on God

A never-failing recipe for spiritual or political disaster. Judges, closing on a note of despair, says in its final verse, "In those days there was no king in Israel: every man did that which was right in his own eyes." In other words, civil and religious authority had vanished.

Not to worry: Just ahead in the nation's history was Samuel, the charismatic prophet who would refocus Israel's political and moral life—and Saul, Israel's first king.

everyone that shall be found in the book
Daniel 12:1
a metaphor for those who have withstood oppression

The image in Daniel is that of a great register or book of remembrance for the worthy, whether living or dead. To say that someone's name "will be found written in the book" is to congratulate that person on having remained faithful to a cause, fought the good fight, stood up and been counted. In Daniel, the context is a time of trouble, and "At that time thy people shall be delivered, every one that shall be found written in the book."

See FIGHT THE GOOD FIGHT.

everyone that was discontented
I Samuel 22:2
all those in trouble, real or imagined

Charismatic leaders have long known how easy it is to attract the discontented to their banners. And David was such a leader. Fearful of Saul and then of the king of Gath, David made his getaway to a secure cave close to the Philistine border, where he was joined by about four hundred men: "And every one that was in distress, and every one that was in debt, and every one that was discontented, gathered themselves unto him."

every valley shall be exalted
Isaiah 40:4
a metaphor for the power of God

Martin Luther King, Jr., in his great speech of August 28, 1963, said, "I have a dream that one day every valley shall be exalted, every hill and mountain shall be made low." King was drawing on the first half of Isaiah 40:4 for his eloquence, but the remainder of the verse and the beginning of the next are equally inspiring: "And the crooked shall be made straight, and the rough places plain: And the glory of the Lord shall be revealed."

The people of the Bible surely understood this characterization of the power of God.

evidence of things not seen
Hebrews 11:1
things taken on faith
See THINGS NOT SEEN.

evil communications corrupt good manners
I Corinthians 15:33
don't hang out with the wrong crowd

In chapter 15 Paul stressed that God's future gives meaning
to day-by-day human life and urged the Christians of Corinth
to live moral lives. Corinth was a fast track, a thriving commercial center and crossroads of foreign trade abounding
with all the temptations one might expect to encounter in
such a place. In light of this, in verse 33 Paul counseled
Christians to live righteously, to avoid association with people
of doubtful character: "Be not deceived: evil communications
corrupt good manners."

eye for eye, tooth for tooth
Exodus 21:23–27
tit for tat

In Latin called *lex talionis*, "the law of retaliation." While some
take "eye for eye" literally in characterizing Old Testament
justice, such interpretation appears to be wide of the mark.

In a series of if-clauses—if someone does this, then you do
that—we read that the judges will set the punishment for
crimes. And then we come upon, "Eye for eye, tooth for
tooth, hand for hand, foot for foot, Burning for burning,
wound for wound, stripe for stripe." This established the
principle that the punishment must fit the crime. Then we
read, "And if a man smite the eye of his servant, or the eye
of his maid, that it perish; he shall let him go free for his eye's
sake. And if he smite out his manservant's tooth, or his hand-
maiden's tooth; he shall let him go free for his tooth's sake."
These last two cases, in which the masters are punished by

having to free their servants, may be taken as invalidating the idea of slavish adherence to tit for tat. Rather, they showed that when the time came for punishment, no one was to receive preferential treatment because of membership in a privileged class, and any punishment meted out had to be appropriate. All this was a major step up from the vengeful barbarities of earlier societies.

Incidentally, those who think that the New Testament counsels only mercy and forgiveness rather than deserved retribution are directed, for instance, to Revelation 13:10, "He that killeth with the sword must be killed with the sword."

eyes that see not
Psalm 135:15–17
the eyes of an idol
See MOUTHS THAT SPEAK NOT.

eyes to see and ears to hear
Deuteronomy 29:4
a metaphor for the ability or will to learn from experience

Moses, by way of reinforcing his message to the Hebrews to mend their ways, reminded them of their delivery from Egypt with the help of the Lord, concluding sadly, "Yet the Lord hath not given you an heart to perceive, and eyes to see, and ears to hear, unto this day." Ezekiel 12:2 uses the same metaphor: "Thou dwellest in the midst of a rebellious house, which have eyes to see, and see not; they have ears to hear, and hear not."

When will we ever learn?
See EARS TO HEAR.

eyes to the blind
Job 29:15
an apt motto for people and organizations that help the blind

Job, musing about the kindness he had shown the less fortunate in the many days before everything went wrong for him, gave us this memorable metaphor for acts of generosity: "I was eyes to the blind, and feet was I to the lame."
See SING FOR JOY.

Ezekiel's wheel
Ezekiel 1:15–21
a wonderful sight Ezekiel saw in a dream
See WHEELS WITHIN WHEELS.

F

face to face
Exodus 33:11
seeing the Lord directly
See SEE EYE TO EYE.

fade as a leaf
Isaiah 64:6–9
yet another metaphor for the act of dying, the common
    lot of all living things

Before requesting that God help the sinning people of Israel,
Isaiah summarized their condition this way: "We are all as an
unclean thing, and all our righteousnesses are as filthy rags;
and we all do fade as a leaf; and our iniquities, like the wind,
have taken us away." Then Isaiah threw himself and the rest
of the Israelites on the mercy of the court: "Be not wroth very
sore, O Lord, neither remember iniquity for ever: behold,
see, we beseech thee, we are all thy people."
    That is, you made us all.

faith, hope, and charity
I Corinthians 13:13
the three principal Christian virtues, charity being love
    for fellow human beings
See SEE THROUGH A GLASS DARKLY.

faith that moves mountains
Mark 11:23
limitless, unshakable faith

In this verse Jesus said, "Whoever shall say unto this mountain, Be thou removed, and be thou cast into the sea: and shall

not doubt in his heart, but shall believe that those things which he saith shall come to pass; he shall have whatsoever he saith." These words, combining unlimited confidence in God and belief in the power of prayer—with a dash of hyperbole—gave English an enduring metaphor.

See ALL THINGS ARE POSSIBLE, BARTIMAEUS, *and* NOTHING IS IMPOSSIBLE.

faith without works is dead
James 2:21–26
show your faith by the good deeds you perform

The Epistle of James cites the example of Abraham, who "offered Isaac his son upon the altar," and goes on to ask aphoristically, "Seest thou how faith wrought with his works, and by works was faith made perfect?" So there is more to being a Christian than merely professing belief in God: "For as the body without the spirit is dead, so faith without works is dead also." For "spirit," read "breath." Now the message is clear: What is called for is a collaboration between faith— love for God—and works.

See BE DOERS, NOT HEARERS ONLY.

fall among thieves
Luke 10:30
fall in with people of bad character

The current idiom may be "fall in with" rather than "fall among," but the meaning is the same: become acquainted with, especially by chance. Jesus' parable of the good Samaritan in Luke 10:30–37 begins with a marvelously succinct example of narrative technique: "A certain man went down from Jerusalem to Jericho, and fell among thieves, which stripped him of his raiment, and wounded him, and departed, leaving him half dead." Three men in turn came upon the mugged traveler, but the only one who helped him was the Samaritan, a member of a people living in the hills of Samaria, north of Jerusalem, and regarded by Jews as foreign to themselves

even though both groups shared a common heritage.
See GOOD SAMARITAN.

fall by the wayside
Mark 4:3
yield to temptation

Anyone who succumbs to temptation or commits a sin or fails in some way is said to fall by the wayside, once an engaging metaphor but today, alas, no more than a cliché. In the parable of the sower and the soils, in Mark 4, Jesus related how some seeds that were sown "fell by the wayside" and were eaten by birds. Other seeds failed to thrive because they fell on poor soil. By contrast, the seeds that fell on good ground did marvelously well. The various soils are taken to represent the different responses of those who listened to Jesus' message and those who did not.

fallen from grace
Galatians 5:4
relapsed into sin

In day-to-day use, fallen from favor or relapsed from an attained moral position; more freely, out of favor with one's superiors or dropped from a position of power. In Christianity, relapsed into sin.

Paul discovered that converts in Galatia were living not as Christians, but as Jews, that is, in accordance with Mosaic law. By choosing the way of Mosaic law, he said, these converts had lost touch with Christ, through whom God's grace is mediated: "Christ is become of no effect unto you, whosoever of you are justified by the law; ye are fallen from grace."

false prophets
Matthew 7:15
false messiahs
See SHEEP'S CLOTHING.

the **fashion of this world passeth away**
I Corinthians 7:29–31
the end of the world may be drawing near

Not a flash from a Paris couturier, but an admonition from the apostle Paul to behave yourself. The saying is applied today to transitory notions. In I Corinthians 7 Paul was responding to questions put to him on the subject of marriage. He went through all sorts of do-thises and don't-do-thats and then gave us much to ponder: "The time is short: it remaineth, that both they that have wives be as though they had none; and they that weep, as though they wept not; and they that rejoice, as though they rejoiced not; and they that buy, as though they possessed not; And they that use this world, as not abusing it: for the fashion of this world passeth away." Thus, to Paul, everyday concerns counted for nothing in comparison with the apocalyptic events he foresaw.

Nevertheless, his anticipation of an early end to the world proved incorrect.

the **fat of the land**
Genesis 45:18
the best of everything

Before sending the people of Israel back to the land of Canaan, the Pharaoh was intent on seeing the travelers well supplied for their journey: "I will give you the good of the land of Egypt, and ye shall eat the fat of the land." While the Pharaoh had in mind giving the Israelites the excess food of Egypt, modern people who live off the fat of the land—high off the hog, that is—are considered to be living luxuriously.

the **fatted calf**

Luke 15:23–24

the best of everything, set out in a feast welcoming
    someone long absent

Slaughter of a fatted calf symbolizes celebration of a joyous
event. In Luke the celebration was a father's rejoicing in the
return of an errant son. "Fatted calf" had its origin in the
Israelite practice of separating some calves from their mothers and fattening them on special feed to make them ready for
the table during a religious festival or family celebration. In
the parable of the prodigal son in Luke, Jesus related that a
son left home upon receiving his share of his father's wealth.
After wasting the inheritance in riotous living, the son decided to return home. Instead of berating the son, his father
welcomed him warmly and instructed his servants to prepare
a feast: "Bring hither the fatted calf, and kill it; and let us eat,
and be merry. For this my son was dead, and is alive again;
he was lost, and is found."

Jesus was making the point that God welcomes repentant
sinners as well as those who are sinless.

fear God, and keep his commandments

Ecclesiastes 12:12–13

this says it all

See OF MAKING MANY BOOKS THERE IS NO END.

fear of the Lord

Psalm 111:10

reverence mixed with dread

See BEGINNING OF WISDOM.

feet of clay
Daniel 2:31–45
a weakness or flaw in the character of a respected
  person

Anyone who has been held in high regard or has occupied an important position and then proves to have disappointing weaknesses of character may be said to have feet of clay. In Daniel 2:31–45 King Nebuchadnezzar had a dream that Daniel was called on to interpret. The king had seen "a great image, whose brightness was excellent. . .and the form thereof was terrible. This image's head was of fine gold, his breast and his arms of silver, his belly and his thighs of brass, His legs of iron, his feet part of iron and part of clay." In the dream, a mysterious stone fell on the feet and smashed them to bits. The figure then collapsed and broke into tiny fragments, which the winds carried off. For Daniel's complex interpretation, see verses 37–45, which make it clear that nothing is permanent unless it is built on a firm foundation.

Real-estate developers and purchasers of homes in areas susceptible to earthquakes—take heed.

fight the good fight
I Timothy 6:12
fight to the end for what is right

Many a sturdy politician—Tip O'Neill comes first to mind—has taken the edge off a keenly felt electoral or legislative defeat by saying, "Well, we fought the good fight." This is in the same tradition as Grantland Rice's oft-quoted quatrain:

For when the one Great Scorer comes
To write against your name,
He marks—not that you won or lost—
But how you played the game.

The author of the First Epistle of Timothy 6:12, commented on something much more profound, the requirements of faith. After listing activities and attitudes to be avoided by the righteous person, he enumerated some positive actions to be taken: "Follow after righteousness, godliness, faith, love, patience, meekness." And he went on: "Fight the good fight of faith, lay hold on eternal life, whereunto thou art also called, and hast professed a good profession before many witnesses." So the prize for fighting this good fight is eternal life. This thought is repeated in the Second Epistle of Timothy 4:7: "I have fought a good fight, I have finished my course, I have kept the faith."

fig leaves
Genesis 3:7
the original bikinis

In modern English, "fig leaf" denotes anything intended to conceal, usually inadequately and sometimes in defense of an impropriety. The expression has its modern counterpart in "band-aid," meaning a makeshift scheme that provides temporary assistance but does not solve the problem to which it is applied. Once Adam and Eve had eaten the fruit of the forbidden tree, they lost their innocence: "They knew that they were naked; and they sewed fig leaves together, and made themselves aprons." For many centuries afterward, painters and sculptors took pains to obscure the genitals of their subjects, and fig leaves were one of the principal devices they employed for this purpose.
See ADAM'S APPLE.

filthy lucre
I Timothy 3:3
money, mere money

In the First Epistle of Timothy 6:10 we read: "The love of money is the root of all evil"; and in 3:3 we find the expression "filthy lucre." Undoubtedly, and correctly if modern newspaper accounts are to be trusted, the writer saw preoccupation with getting and spending as something that brings trouble. "Filthy lucre" appears in a discussion of qualifications for the office of bishop. For example, blameless character and good behavior are essential. Again, a bishop must be given to hospitality but not to wine. The list goes on, but of interest right now is the requirement that a candidate be "not greedy of filthy lucre," that is, not obsessively interested in acquiring wealth. Although I Timothy lays down additional requirements, the overall intention is by now clear enough. Surely I Timothy has already ruled out dishonest politicians, rascally members of the military-industrial complex, urban real-estate tycoons, and Wall Street types out for quick returns no matter how achieved.

Whatever the intentions of the translators who gave us the great King James Version of the Bible, their expression "filthy lucre" is understood today as something akin to "mere money." This is suggested by the fact that "lucre" has disappeared from the language except when modified by "filthy" or when used by commentators who presume their readers or listeners will themselves supply "filthy." But we still have the adjective "lucrative," which has been around since the sixteenth century and as yet carries no negative connotation.

See BROUGHT NOTHING INTO THIS WORLD *and* ROOT OF ALL EVIL.

a firebrand plucked out of the burning
Amos 4:11
a person rescued from imminent peril, whether by
   human or divine intervention

Zechariah 3:2 uses the same metaphor in "a brand plucked out of the fire." The passage from Amos prophesies that the children of Israel will be punished for rejecting God despite his interventions on their behalf: "I have overthrown some of you, as God overthrew Sodom and Gomorrah, and ye were as a firebrand plucked out of the burning: yet have ye not returned unto me, saith the Lord."

See SODOM AND GOMORRAH.

fishers of men
Mark 1:17–18
an epithet for those who serve as missionaries

In verse 17 Jesus said to Simon and Andrew, both of whom were fishermen, "Come ye after me, and I will make you to become fishers of men." How did they respond? Verse 18: "And straightway they forsook their nets, and followed him."

five were wise, five foolish
Matthew 25:2
be prepared

Verses 1–13 of Matthew 25 relate Jesus' parable of the wise and foolish virgins. The five wise maidens were prepared for the bridegroom's appearance whatever the hour and so were able to join the party when he arrived. The five foolish maidens neglected to prepare their lamps to light the way and so were left out. The message Jesus gave his followers? Only the prepared will enter the kingdom. So be prepared.

The Boy Scouts and Girl Scouts of America sure knew their business when it came to selecting a motto.

See UNTO WHOM MUCH IS GIVEN.

fleshpots
Exodus 16:3
a metaphor for unrestrained living or for places where anything goes

The biblical source of "fleshpots," Exodus 16:3, had in mind something quite different and more salubrious. The Israelites, suffering deprivation in the wilderness, complained to Moses: "Would to God we had died by the hand of the Lord in the land of Egypt, when we sat by the flesh pots, and when we did eat bread to the full." The Israelites were expressing their longing for the relative luxury of cooking pots containing food they could eat. They saw slavery on a full belly as superior to freedom under austere conditions.

For what happened next, *see* MANNA.

the **fool has said in his heart, there is no God**
Psalm 14:1
those who lack faith are morally corrupt

In the Old Testament, "fool" sometimes denotes a morally corrupt person or someone who scoffs at the claims of the righteous that God takes an interest in human beings. Thus, when the psalmist said, "The fool has said in his heart, There is no God....there is none that doeth good," he was not speaking of silly people but of those who lacked faith.

the **foolish things of the world**
I Corinthians 1:27
pursuit of wealth and power

Paul held that everything depended on accepting in one's heart the reign of God's spirit, not on scrambling after temporal advantage. Thus, in defending Christian faith against the charge that preaching the resurrection of Jesus lacked a logical basis, Paul wrote, "God hath chosen the foolish things of the world to confound the wise; and God hath chosen the weak things of the world to confound the things which are mighty."

Wise men steeped in reason were barking up the wrong tree, Paul said, and seekers after power were on the wrong track.

a **fool uttereth all his mind**
Proverbs 29:11
know when to keep silent

The Book of Proverbs heaps scorn upon the unwise who shoot off their mouths without waiting to hear all that is being said: "A fool uttereth all his mind: but a wise man keepeth it in till afterwards."

See BE SWIFT TO HEAR, SLOW TO SPEAK, SLOW TO WRATH *and* LET THY WORDS BE FEW.

forbidden fruit
Genesis 2 and 3
in the modern sense, forbidden pleasure of any sort,
    especially that of illicit love

No wonder so many authors have used "forbidden fruit" in book titles. Ever since the biblical account of the fall of man, poets and philosophers have recognized how hard it is to avoid anything extremely attractive, especially when it is also forbidden. Indeed, one might say that "forbidden fruit" is one of the best-known biblical expressions even though the phrase does not occur in the Bible. In the fall from paradise recounted in Genesis 2 and 3, Adam and Eve were explicitly instructed not to partake of the fruit of the "tree of knowledge of good and evil." But this forbidden fruit was given a seductive attractiveness by the subtle serpent in the garden. The serpent said the fruit offered a way to make human beings become like God, that is independent and free, "knowing good and evil"—able to become free moral agents. It was the eating of the forbidden fruit, Genesis says, that broke the fellowship between God and man.

See EDEN.

in the **forefront of the hottest battle**
II Samuel 11:15
precisely where you don't want to be when the fighting
    begins

King David wrote in a letter to Joab, his general, "Set ye Uriah
in the forefront of the hottest battle, and retire ye from him,
that he may be smitten, and die." David knew what he was
doing. David was having an affair with Bathsheba, who happened to be Uriah's wife and was pregnant with David's child.
So how did things turn out? During the Israelites' attack on
Rabath-Ammon, Uriah bought the farm—bit the dust, that
is—as David knew he would. David married Bathsheba. And
the child she bore died shortly after birth.
     Next week, *Days of Our Lives*.

forgive others to be yourself forgiven
Mark 11:25
harbor no grudges or ill feelings against others

A clear message is conveyed in the words of this verse: "Forgive, if ye have aught against any: that your Father also which
is in heaven may forgive your trespasses." In this century,
psychotherapists have modified the message: Only those ma-
ture enough to forgive others can forgive themselves. God
appears to have been left out of the equation.

forgive them; for they know not what they do
Luke 23:34
a request for forgiveness of unwitting wrongdoers

As the crucifixion of Jesus became a reality, Jesus asked forgiveness for the Roman soldiers who were carrying out the
terrible act of execution: "Father, forgive them; for they know
not what they do."
     Can the rest of us find it within our hearts to forgive those
who do us wrong?
     See PARTED HIS GARMENTS, CASTING LOTS UPON THEM.

for I know that my redeemer liveth
Job 19:25
an expression of faith

This was Job's agonized admission of the mistake he had made in challenging God. It came after his frantic appeal for pity from his scolding friends (verses 21–22), and his unavailing wish that posterity would vindicate him (verses 23–24). The word "redeemer" can also be translated as "vindicator" or "defender," thus evoking the image of a court of justice with a judge, accuser, and defendant. Job sought redemption of his honor, not expiation of sin or guilt.

for this my son was dead, and is alive again
Luke 15:23–24
an errant son has returned home
See FATTED CALF.

forty days and forty nights
Genesis 7:11–14
guess how long it rained

In these verses we learn that "In the six hundredth year of Noah's life, in the second month, the seventeenth day of the month. . .the windows of heaven were opened. And the rain was upon the earth forty days and forty nights." Noah, having followed the instructions of God, was snug aboard the ark during that entire time, and with him were his wife and his three sons and daughters-in-law as well as two of every kind of beast. But forty days and nights! Most Bible scholars— killjoys—look upon "forty" as symbolic of any large number or long time. Thus, for example, they point out that the Israelites wandered in the wilderness for forty years, and the temptation of Jesus lasted forty days.

At any rate, that sure was some kind of rain.

forty stripes save one
II Corinthians 11:24–25
corporal punishment meted out

People who have been made to suffer terribly for a cause may
say they have received forty stripes but one. In Deuteronomy
25:3 it is said that Jews punishing an offender were forbidden
to inflict more than forty stripes. To keep from exceeding that
number, the person holding the whip would stop one stripe
short, and since a whip had three lashes, thirteen strokes
equaled forty stripes save one. Paul, to counter the claims of
competing leaders at his church in Corinth, detailed—flaunted?—his sufferings as a missionary: "Of the Jews five times
received I forty stripes save one." Jewish authorities in Gentile cities had inflicted this punishment on Paul for creating
hostile arguments and divisions within their synagogues while
he was attempting to recruit Jews to the Christian cause.

But Paul had more to say about his sufferings: "Thrice was
I beaten with rods, once was I stoned, thrice I suffered shipwreck, a night and a day I have been in the deep." The full
list is longer, yet the thought persists that not all the blame
could legitimately be laid on the Jews.

freely receive, freely give
Matthew 10:8
teach others what you have learned

In today's churches, "Freely ye have received, freely give" is
an instruction sometimes offered by ministers before a collection is taken. These words in Matthew 10 were addressed by
Jesus to his disciples before they set out on their missionary
work. What the disciples were to give was their teaching and
witness about God.

A financial contribution to a church is supposed to be made
in the same spirit. Whether all TV evangelists have grasped
this notion is not entirely clear.

See LET NOT YOUR LEFT HAND KNOW WHAT YOUR RIGHT HAND
DOES.

friend of publicans and sinners
Matthew 11:19
an epithet for a person accused of consorting with the
   wrong types

While it is easy to understand why sinners may be considered
the wrong kind of birds to flock with, "publicans" requires
some explanation. The British use "publican" to denote a
person who owns or runs a pub, that is, a bar or inn. In Roman
history, however, a publican was a tax collector. And who
among us likes tax collectors? In Matthew 11 Jesus said that
when he enjoyed sociable eating and drinking, he was called
"gluttonous and a winebibber, a friend of publicans and sinners," suggesting that those making the charge were hypocrites.

from strength to strength
Psalm 84:7
supported by faith

Those who become progressively more certain of themselves
as they move through life may be said to go from strength to
strength. In Psalm 84 the phrase refers to the joy of pilgrims
traveling overland to Jerusalem. "They go from strength to
strength, every one of them in Zion appeareth before God."
That is, as they come nearer to the spiritual home for which
they yearn, they become stronger with each difficult day of
travel.
   Not quite the same as pumping iron in a health club.

fruit of the womb
Psalm 127:3
an epithet for offspring

"Fruit of the womb" gives us a happy way to think of children:
"Lo, children are an heritage of the Lord: and the fruit of the
womb is his reward."

And gives clever businessmen a chance at coining a great brand name.

See QUIVER FULL.

full of vomit and filthiness
Isaiah 28:8
hear this, all heavy drinkers, pay close attention

Isaiah accused the Temple priests and prophets of taking so much strong drink that their judgments were marred: "All tables are full of vomit and filthiness, so that there is no place clean." Can you think of a stronger way to characterize the behavior of heavy drinkers?

See DOG IS TURNED TO HIS OWN VOMIT.

G

Gabriel
Daniel 8, Luke 1
a divine messenger

Anyone familiar with the biblical name Gabriel probably associates it with the blowing of a horn on an unusual occasion. Matthew 24:31 states that the second coming will be announced with "a great sound of a trumpet," and tradition has it that Gabriel is the one who will blow that horn, even though the latter thought is not mentioned in Scripture. Gabriel is an angel, one of the celestial beings that appear in human form to carry out commands given by God. He appears in the Old Testament in Daniel 8:16–26, where he interprets a vision of Daniel's. In the New Testament, in Luke, he is the angel who brings Mary and Elizabeth the welcome news that they will bear sons.
See NOTHING IS IMPOSSIBLE.

gain the world and lose your soul
Matthew 16:26
waste your time chasing after money instead of doing something useful
See WHAT IS A MAN PROFITED?

gall of asps
Job 20:12
poisonous venom or the equivalent
See WICKEDNESS SWEET IN THE MOUTH.

gate of heaven
Genesis 28:17
a site redolent of the presence of God
See JACOB'S LADDER.

Gath
II Samuel 1:20
birthplace of Goliath, the Philistine giant
See TELL IT NOT IN GATH.

he **gat no heat**
I Kings 1:4
he couldn't perform sexually

The four verses that open I Kings tell of the second king of Israel, who was suffering the effects of senility. "Now King David was old and stricken with years; and they covered him with clothes, but he gat no heat." A woman was brought to the king to see whether she could cause him to get heat. To no avail: "The damsel was very fair, and cherished the king, and ministered to him: but the king knew her not." Alas, the requirements that peoples of Bible lands put on their leaders were rather different from those employed in modern democracies. When David failed to know so fair a damsel, the fact of his impotence gave rival claimants to the throne sufficient reason to remove him from office. Soon enough, those who wanted to succeed David made their moves. As things turned out, it was Solomon who gained the throne.

Gehenna
Matthew 5:22
hell or hellfire
See HELL FIRE.

generation of vipers
Matthew 3:7
unworthy or sinful people

This metaphor, used by John the Baptist in addressing the Pharisees and Sadducees, suggests a brood of poisonous snakes slithering away from an approaching grass fire. And what was this grass fire John warned of? A fiery judgment is coming: "O generation of vipers, who hath warned you to flee from the wrath to come?"

It is difficult for authors to beat the Bible when it's time to find a book title. Philip Wylie in 1942 proved this for the umpteenth time when he published *Generation of Vipers*, his attack on American mothers. Wylie's scathing denunciation of what he called "momism" is largely ignored today, but in its time was a cause célèbre and, naturally, a bestseller.

Gethsemane
Mark 14:32
a scene or occasion of great suffering

A gethsemane, like a calvary, represents a profound test of character or spirit. Gethsemane was the site where Jesus prayed just before Judas betrayed him and where Jesus was taken into custody by the Romans: "They came to a place which was named Gethsemane: and he saith to his disciples, Sit ye here, while I shall pray." Although the actual location of Gethsemane is not known for certain, both Mark and Matthew imply that it was near the Mount of Olives, east of Jeru-

salem. Whatever its precise location, the site is forever associated with the agony of Christ.

get thee behind me, Satan
Mark 8:33
get lost, you tempter

This expression, more conventionally paraphrased as "Get
out of my sight," is well established in our everyday language
as a way of shooing off a would-be tempter. In Mark 8 Jesus
used these famous words in rebuking Peter: "Get thee behind
me, Satan: for thou savorest not the things that be of God, but
the things that be of men." Satan, of course, was the arch-
tempter who had done his best to tempt Jesus at the start of
his ministry.

giants in the earth
Genesis 6:4
an epithet for people of great stature and strength

Of such people we are wont to say, "They don't make 'em like
that no more." Genesis 6:4 says, "There were giants in the
earth in those days; and also after that, when the sons of God
came in unto the daughters of men, and they bare children to
them, the same became mighty men which were of old, men
of renown." To shed a little light on biblical euphemism,
these giants were the offspring of unions of young women and
divine beings.

Giants in the Earth, Ole Rölvaag's novel published in English
in 1927, recounted the terrible struggles of Norwegian immi-
grant farm families, latter-day giants in the earth trying their
best to settle the forbidding Dakota Territory.

See GOLIATH.

Gideon's army
Judges 7:2–8
true believers, able to conquer even when outnumbered

God doesn't always make things easy for those who believe, and the story of Gideon's military success against the Midianites is a case in point. While Gideon's great army was preparing for battle with the Midianites, God said, "The people that are with thee are too many for me to give the Midianites into their hands, lest Israel vaunt themselves against me, saying, Mine own hand hath saved me." In accordance with God's instruction, anyone "fearful and afraid" was thereupon encouraged by Gideon to leave. "And there returned of the people twenty and two thousand; and there remained ten thousand." God, still not pleased, told Gideon to lead the rest of his soldiers to water and observe how they drank. Three hundred did not bend their knees to drink, but cupped water in their hands and lapped it up. And God said the three hundred who had not bowed down were enough to lick the Midianites. So it happened that Gideon's tiny but totally dedicated army routed the enemy.

Today, a Gideon's army—whether a military force or not—is one from which all the fearful and relatively unskilled have been weeded out, leaving a team totally dedicated to the task at hand. Anyone who has ever spent the night in a hotel room knows the work of Gideon's International. This small but dedicated Gideon's army does not bow down as it goes about its mission of providing free Bibles for hotel guests.

Gilead
Jeremiah 8:22
a district of ancient Palestine
See BALM IN GILEAD *and* SHIBBOLETH.

gird up your loins
Job 38:3
get ready for action

Finally ready to confront the challenge made by Job, God decided to put it to him straight so Job would understand what kind of God he was: "Gird up now thy loins like a man: for I will demand of thee, and answer thou me." Put up your dukes. You're in for a real fight. In short, God wanted direct answers to direct questions.

A word should be said of the literal meaning of "gird up one's loins." Think of the loose, flowing garments men wore in biblical times. Now consider how difficult it would have been to take anyone on in serious combat when so encumbered. Since the loins are the hips and lower abdomen, girding up one's loins meant tucking one's knee-length, shirtlike tunic under one's belt.

In II Kings 9:1 the prophet Elisha, instructing a messenger to carry an important message to Jehu, told him, "Gird up thy loins and take this box of oil in thine hand." In that case, the idea was to impress the messenger with the need to make haste.

give honor unto your wife
I Peter 3:1–7
excellent advice

But read on. Modern women may not be entirely happy with I Peter 3, which is concerned with telling people how to keep their consciences clear. Consider, for example, verse 1: "Ye wives, be in subjection to your own husbands." Now quickly go on to verse 7: "Likewise, ye husbands, dwell with them according to knowledge, giving honor unto the wife, as unto the weaker vessel, and as being heirs together of the grace of life: that your prayers be not hindered."

That helps balance the scales, although exception can be taken to the metaphor "weaker vessel." How well we all know the strength shown by many women in bearing up under grief and adversity that would pound most men into the ground.

Nevertheless, Peter provided Antonia Fraser with an appropriate title for her 1984 book, *The Weaker Vessel: Woman's Lot in Seventeenth-Century England*.

give up the ghost
Psalm 22:1
die; relinquish all hope
See WHY HAST THOU FORSAKEN ME?

the glory is departed from Israel
I Samuel 4:21
a way of saying that one's country has lost its honor and the respect of other nations

In Samuel's account, "The glory is departed from Israel: because the ark of God was taken" encapsulated one of the tragedies of Israelite history. Soon after learning of Israel's defeat by the Philistines and loss of the holy ark of the covenant, the wife of Phinehas gave birth to a son. Her sense of loss was compounded by additional tragedy. Phinehas and her brother-in-law had been killed in battle, and her father-in-law, upon news of the defeat and the loss of his two sons and the ark, had fallen and died of a broken neck. The ark, regarded as the dwelling place of God and imbued with his presence, was "the glory." The devastated mother, expressing grief over capture of the ark, named her child Ichabod, which means "without honor."
See also QUIT YOURSELVES LIKE MEN, AND FIGHT.

gnashing of teeth
Matthew 8:12
giving vent to rage
See WEEPING AND GNASHING OF TEETH.

go, and sin no more
John 8:11
the words Jesus used in dismissing a woman who had
     been taken in adultery

Explicit in this expression of forgiveness is recognition of past
guilt.
See CAST THE FIRST STONE.

God and mammon
Matthew 6:24
God and pursuit of wealth

"Mammon," a transliteration of an Aramaic word meaning
"wealth," is used in English to mean the deification of riches.
In this verse Jesus warned of the perils of seeking wealth: "No
man can serve two masters: for either he will hate the one, and
love the other; or else he will hold to the one, and despise the
other. Ye cannot serve God and mammon." There is no deny-
ing that Jesus asked his followers to make stark either-or
choices. In this exchange, he wanted them to entrust their
lives to God, eschewing anxiety about food, clothing, and
shelter.
    Despite Jesus' injunction, in the present century God seems
to be running a distant second to mammon.
See FILTHY LUCRE.

God save the king
I Samuel 10:24
let the king live!

In introducing Saul to the Israelites, the prophet Samuel said
of their first king, "See ye him whom the Lord hath chosen,
that there is none like him among all the people?" And what
did the people shout? "God save the king."
    Ever since, this is what the English and many other peoples
have said—in translation, of course—upon the coronation of
a new king.

God's business
Luke 2:41–49
all the things to be attended to on God's behalf or in God's service

These verses from Luke 2, which include the phrase "my Father's business," offer a brief account of an episode in the life of Jesus that is of special interest to parents—especially intelligent parents who are aware that at some point they must begin to relinquish control of their children's lives. Mary and Joseph had journeyed to Jerusalem at the time of the feast of the Passover, taking with them the child Jesus, then twelve years old. When the time came to depart, Mary and Joseph left Jerusalem along with the other Galileeans in their caravan and did not miss Jesus until hours had passed. They had allowed their son some independence in Jerusalem, and Jesus had occupied himself with listening to the rabbis and putting questions to them.

When Mary and Joseph went back to Jerusalem to find Jesus, they came upon him in the Temple area and chided him for giving them a scare. And how did Jesus answer them? "How is it that ye sought me? wist ye not that I must be about my Father's business?"

A marvelous way for a child—a special child in this case—to say, "Don't you know I'm all grown up?"

gold, and frankincense, and myrrh
Matthew 2:11
gifts brought to the infant Jesus by the wise men who had been directed by Herod to go to Jerusalem

Gold, of course, was the precious metal. The other gifts, derived from fragrant resins, chiefly from south Arabia and the east coast of Africa, were much sought after by kings, princes, and other affluent people. Frankincense was the principal ingredient of the incense used in worship. When burned, it obscured the odors characteristic of agricultural villages before running water became commonplace. Myrrh was also used in incense as well as in cosmetics and was important in embalming.

See WISE MEN FROM THE EAST.

the **golden bowl**
Ecclesiastes 12:6
a metaphor for life

Ecclesiastes 12 discusses the inevitability of death, reminding the young especially that the grave is the finish line for every member of the human race. In a series of metaphors in verses 2–6, we read of the waning powers of the aging, with verse 6 characterizing death as the time when "the silver cord be loosed, or the golden bowl be broken at the fountain, or the wheel broken at the cistern."

Proving once again that the Bible is tops for literary titles, not only did Henry James use the title *The Golden Bowl* for one of his novels, but Sidney Howard called one of his plays *The Silver Cord*, in his usage a metaphor for the cord that binds mother and child together.

See DAYS OF THY YOUTH, *and* TO EVERY THING THERE IS A SEASON.

the **golden calf**
Exodus 32:4
today, a seldom-used metaphor for money or material
    goods as objects to be ardently sought after

During the exodus from Egypt, a golden calf was the idol set up by Aaron and worshiped by the Israelites in direct contravention of God's command. Aaron "made it a molten calf: and they said, These be thy gods, O Israel, which brought thee up out of the land of Egypt." This is far from the only biblical mention of this incident, nor is it the only example of the making of idols by errant Israelites.

In these times of computerized chasing after wealth, we can expect "golden calf" to make a linguistic comeback.

Golgotha
Mark 15:22
a time of extreme suffering

Today, both Golgotha and Calvary—whether capitalized or not—denote a time of extreme sacrifice or suffering. In the New Testament both are given as names for the site where Jesus was crucified by the Roman soldiers.

The name Golgotha derives ultimately from the Aramaic word for "skull," and the New Testament refers to the site of the crucifixion as "the skull" and "the place of the skull." These names are thought to reflect the habitual use of Golgotha by the Romans for carrying out crucifixions. Unfortunately, the Roman army in its destruction of Jerusalem in A.D. 68–70 obliterated many landmarks outside the city's northern walls, making it impossible thus far to locate Golgotha, or Calvary, with any accuracy.

See CALVARY *and* GETHSEMANE.

Goliath
I Samuel 17
any giant in size, power, or influence

In the First Book of Samuel, Goliath was the heavily armed Philistine giant whom David brought down with a slingshot and then decapitated, using Goliath's own sword. The encounter is memorable because David had been a real long shot. Too young to enter the army, David worked for his father as a shepherd and had some experience in using a slingshot to prevent wild animals from ravaging his flock. Thus it was that David, taking on Goliath mano a mano, "smote the Philistine in his forehead, that the stone sunk into his forehead; and he fell upon his face to the earth."

But just how big was Goliath? According to verse 4, "six cubits and a span." While no one now knows for sure just what these ancient measurements were, a cubit is estimated to be 18 to 22 inches, and a span about 9 inches. This would place Goliath's height at somewhere between 9 feet 9 inches and 11 feet 3 inches—big enough. Elsewhere, Goliath's

height is given as four cubits and a span, which would mean he was about 6 feet 9 inches tall—still big enough.
See GIANTS IN THE EARTH.

gone with the wind
Psalm 103:15–16
a metaphor for the brief life of a human being
See DAYS ARE AS GRASS.

a **good name**
Ecclesiastes 7:1
good reputation

What is better than a good name? Hardly anything. After all, Ecclesiastes 7:1 says, "A good name is better than precious ointment." But the story is not complete without the rest of the verse: "And the day of death than the day of one's birth." Now the thrust of the verse is less clear. And when a succeeding verse tells us that sadness is better than laughter, we tiptoe out to muse silently and recall familiar lines from Shakespeare's *Othello*:

Good name in man and woman, dear my lord,
Is the immediate jewel of their souls.

good Samaritan
Luke 10:33
a person who goes out of his way to help someone in trouble

Luke 10:30–37 recounts how "a certain Samaritan" gave assistance to a traveler who had been waylaid and assaulted and had not been assisted by well-placed Jews who had passed by. The Samaritans, residents of the district of Samaria, were for many centuries despised by Jews because of differences in religious practices. Even so, this anonymous Samaritan acted as a good neighbor and responded to the need of another human being without regard for class or religion. The irony is that in our litigious times many state legislatures have felt impelled to enact what are called "good Samaritan laws." These statutes are intended to offer legal protection to physicians and others who give aid to strangers in physical distress.

See FALL AMONG THIEVES.

the **good that I would I do not**
Romans 7:18–19
I know what's right, but I don't do it

Jewish and Christian writers did not invent the idea that even good people have a propensity for doing the wrong thing. Five hundred years before Paul wrote his Epistle to the Romans, Euripides wrote in *Medea*, "I know, indeed, the evil that I purpose; but my inclination gets the better of my judgment." Paul in Romans 7 suggested that people have both good and evil in them, and at any time one attribute or the other predominates, with the result that we sometimes act honorably and sometimes sinfully. In verse 18 he said, "For I know that in me (that is, in my flesh) dwelleth no good thing: for to will is present with me; but how to perform that which is good I find not." So people, despite good intentions, are not always able to control their actions. As Paul said in verse 19, "The good that I would I do not: but the evil which I would not, that I do."

Modern children often account for their acts of mischief—or worse—in similar language: "I don't know why I did it. I knew it was wrong, but I just couldn't help myself."

Come to think of it, that's a lot better than saying, "I knew what I did was wrong, but I didn't think it was illegal."

any **good thing out of Nazareth**
John 1:46
a great achievement arising from a humble source

A classic put-down by a big-city type to any suggestion that the boondocks have something to offer. Nathanael, urged by Philip to join him in becoming a disciple of Jesus of Nazareth, showed skepticism—and scorn—in putting the question "Can any good thing come out of Nazareth?" At the time, Nazareth was an insignificant farming village, and Nathanael was a native of Cana, a more important town. How could one expect big things from a tank town? While the remark attributed to Nathanael may have been a local folk saying, it's more entertaining to take it as an original and condescending remark. In any event, Nathanael eventually acceded to Philip's urging and was accepted by Jesus as a disciple.

Nazareth, of course, went on to great biblical importance, while Cana played a lesser role as the site of the wedding feast miracle described in John 2:1–11.

good will toward men
Luke 2:14
kind feelings toward others

The full verse reads, "Glory to God in the highest, and on earth peace, good will toward men," suggesting that a new era was beginning on earth. Who could ask for anything more? Originally sung by an entourage of angels, "a multitude of the heavenly host," this verse is known in hymns and oratorios as the Gloria in Excelsis Deo, Latin for the hymn "Glory be to God on high."

good works
Acts 9:36
acts of kindness or good will

This verse says, "There was at Joppa a certain disciple named Tabitha, which by interpretation is called Dorcas: this woman was full of good works and almsdeeds which she did." Later, in verse 39, we find that Dorcas had made coats and garments for widows while she was in Joppa. It is worth pointing out that Tabitha was an Aramaic name and that Tabitha/Dorcas died and was restored to life by Peter, verse 40. But to this day it is as Dorcas that this charitable woman is remembered for her good works, and many churches since the early nineteenth century have sponsored Dorcas societies, whose function is to provide clothing for the poor.

And what of Tabitha? Nothing.

gospel
Mark 16:15

> in everyday use, something undeniably true; in the biblical sense, the good news preached by Jesus that the Kingdom of God was imminent

"Gospel" is part of the title of each of the first four books of the New Testament: for example, The Gospel According to St. Matthew. Mark's injunction in 16:15 "Go ye into all the world, and preach the gospel to every creature" has been taken literally by Christian missionaries who go to all the continents of the earth in their zeal to spread the word. As evidence of this spirit, consider the so-called missionary hymn, which begins, "From Greenland's icy mountains to India's coral strands...."

"Gospel" can be traced back to an old English word, "god-spell," a translation of the Greek word *euangélion* meaning "good news," which makes "gospel" a distant cousin of "evangel," "evangelical," "evangelism," and "evangelist," among others.

go through fire and water
Psalm 66:12

> do anything required, no matter how dangerous

Moderns may say "come hell or high water," but the meaning is the same—brave any danger, endure any test. Shakespeare, in *Merry Wives of Windsor*, wrote, "A woman would run through fire and water for such a kind heart." Psalm 66, a hymn of praise and thanksgiving, recalls some of God's mighty acts for his people. In verse 12 the psalmist said, "Thou hast caused men to ride over our heads; we went through fire and through water: but thou broughtest us out into a wealthy place."

go to the ant, thou sluggard
Proverbs 6:6
learn the virtue of work

The sayings of the so-called writers of wisdom literature were collected in Proverbs, written long before the days of La Fontaine and about the time of Aesop. In Proverbs 6:6 idlers are told to work hard: "Go to the ant, thou sluggard; consider her ways, and be wise."

To this day, the ant epitomizes industry, and while some Roman philosophers and modern writers have sung the praises of idleness, the evidence in Proverbs is that the people of ancient Israel were cut from different cloth.

grain of mustard seed
Mark 4:31–32
a metaphor for the smallest of beginnings

It was believed that the tiny seed of the Palestinian mustard bush produced the largest of shrubs. Thus, the verses from Mark say of Jesus' message about the coming of the kingdom of God, "It is like a grain of mustard seed, which, when it is sown in the earth, is less than all the seeds that be in the earth: But when it is sown, it groweth up, and becometh greater than all herbs, and shooteth out great branches."

As the American writer David Everett (1769–1813) pointed out, "Tall oaks from little acorns grow." Not unexpectedly, Emerson topped him with "a thousand forests in one acorn." One thing is clear: From tiny beginnings can come great results. And it is this thought that encourages social activists, missionaries, and capitalist entrepreneurs to dream.

graven image
Psalm 135:15–17
an idol
See MOUTHS THAT SPEAK NOT.

greater love hath no man
John 15:13
a popular eulogy for brave people who have given their
lives to protect their fellow human beings

Jesus, as he readied himself for the agonizing road to death,
set the example for all his followers: "Greater love hath no
man than this, that a man lay down his life for his friends."

great is Diana of the Ephesians!
Acts 19:24–29
self-interest blinds the eyes to moral and ethical values

In Ephesus, when the preaching of Paul was beginning to
show results, the silversmiths became upset because sales of
their silver shrines for the temple of the goddess Diana were
dropping. One of the silversmiths, Demetrius, called his fellow craftsmen together and gave them a rousing talk, "And
when they heard these sayings, they were full of wrath, and
cried out, saying, Great is Diana of the Ephesians. And the
whole city was filled with confusion." So intense was this
response that Paul was impelled to leave town.

It would appear that people whose pocketbooks are threat-
ened may choose to ignore right and good words addressed
to them—as though we didn't know.

great men are not always wise
Job 32:2–9
they don't know it all

After Job's three friends finished working him over, a new
voice was heard, that of a younger man angry with Job because he had "justified himself rather than God." At first the
young man buttered Job up by expressing his respect for the

wisdom of older people. Soon enough, however, he began to warm up to his real message: "Great men are not always wise: neither do the aged understand judgment." And from that point on, he really got on Job's case.

So have respect for people of reputation, but don't take everything they say as gospel.

grind the faces of the poor
Isaiah 3:15
a stark metaphor for treating the poor abysmally

In biblical times and for a long time thereafter, grain was ground between hard and heavy millstones, and one can imagine the effect such an implement would produce if poor people's faces were given the same treatment. In this verse from Isaiah it is the affluent, the ruling class, and the royal family that are doing the grinding. God is seen as sitting in a court of justice and charging the powerful, "What mean ye that ye beat my people to pieces and grind the faces of the poor?"

The question is all too pertinent today.

hair shirt
Daniel 9:3
a sign of humility, penitence, and contrition
See SACKCLOTH AND ASHES.

the **hairs of your head are numbered**
Matthew 10:30
God has his eye on you

To encourage the disciples, who would encounter persecution when they began to spread the gospel, Jesus said God was watching over them closely: "The very hairs of your head are all numbered."

the **half was not told me**
I Kings 10:7
seeing is believing

The queen of Sheba had heard accounts of Solomon's wealth and wisdom but wanted to see for herself. So she went to Jerusalem along with a bejeweled retinue that was something to behold. And what was her response on meeting Solomon and seeing the opulence of his court? "Howbeit I believed not the words, until I came, and mine eyes had seen it: and, behold, the half was not told to me: thy wisdom and prosperity exceedeth the fame which I heard."
   In short, she was bowled over.

the **halt and the blind**
Luke 14:15–24
the handicapped

Plainly visible in the everyday life of the land of the Bible were the poor, the maimed, the halt [lame], and the blind. To a great many of us today, such people are all but invisible. Jesus, in the parable of the great banquet, had in mind the rejection he had experienced among the elite of Judaism: "A certain man made a great supper, and bade many." When the event was to begin, excuses poured in from the invited guests in rebuff of the host. So, giving instructions that no previously invited guests were to be allowed in, he sent his servants out to find "the poor, and the maimed, and the halt, and the blind" to fill the banquet hall.

The meaning is clear: If the elite won't accept Jesus' message, give it to the underdogs of the world.

See MAKE LIGHT OF.

handwriting on the wall
Daniel 5:25
the jig is up
See MENE, MENE, TEKEL UPHARSIN.

hanged our harps upon the willows
Psalm 137:2
gave up music for the duration

In "There Is a Tavern in the Town," an old song still sung today, the singer recalls a lost love and vows to hang his harp on a weeping willow tree. This image derives from Psalm 137, which recounts how the Jews exiled in Babylon refused to sing "the Lord's song in a strange land." Having no heart for music, the psalmist said, "We wept when we remembered Zion. We hanged our harps upon the willows." In similar fashion and also celebrated in a popular song, recent years have seen the practice of tying ribbons around the trunks of trees to signify that loved ones held hostage or imprisoned in foreign lands have not been forgotten.

See BABYLON.

hast thou found me, O mine enemy?
I Kings 21:19–21
the response of choice for someone on the lam who
    realizes he has been tracked down

King Ahab's scheming wife, Jezebel, arranged for a man called Naboth, owner of a vineyard Ahab coveted, to be falsely accused of blasphemy by the town elders. The charge was rammed through, and Naboth was put to death by stoning. Ahab, strolling in the vineyard that soon would be his, encountered the prophet Elijah, who had been instructed by God to confront the king, and Elijah said, "Hast thou killed, and also taken possession?" Ahab replied in these guilt-ridden words: "Hast thou found me, O mine enemy? And he [Elijah] answered, I have found thee: because thou hast sold thyself to work evil in the sight of the Lord. Behold, I will bring evil upon thee."

A warning for all those planning a crime against humanity: Somewhere out there is a relentless Simon Wiesenthal who will not let you rest.

See JEZEBEL.

have we not all one father?
Malachi 2:10
a rhetorical question saying it all on behalf of the
    wonderful condition formerly known as brotherhood

God may have been addressing the Jews in this message, sent via the prophet Malachi, but it can surely be taken as applicable to all people: "Have we not all one father? hath not one God created us? why do we deal treacherously every man against his brother, by profaning the covenant of our fathers?"

Why shouldn't we give all people the same respect due

members of our own families? Why shouldn't we treat one another with warmth?

having nothing, yet possessing all things
II Corinthians 6:10
inner contentment does not depend on being wealthy

The apostle Paul, writing to members of his church in Corinth, drew a series of contrasts between what others perceived his life to be and the actual nature of his life as he knew it. Finally, he wrote, "As sorrowful, yet always rejoicing; as poor, yet making many rich; as having nothing, and yet possessing all things." Once we recall that what Paul held dearest was God's love, these paradoxes are resolved. One can look sad but rejoice inwardly. One can lack money but enrich the lives of many by preaching. One can own nothing but possess all important things.

heap coals of fire on his head
Romans 12:20
reduce someone's animosity by treating him kindly

Paul counseled his followers that there was more than one way to skin a cat. "Therefore if thine enemy hunger, feed him; if he thirst, give him drink; for in so doing thou shalt heap coals of fire on his head. Be not overcome with evil, but overcome evil with good." By repaying bad treatment with good, you can awaken your enemy's conscience and force him to see his wrongdoing. Above all, don't try to surpass your enemy's terrible behavior with worse behavior of your own.

If we keep in mind that Paul was not advising us to kill with kindness, the counsel he offered may be worth a try. Are you game?

See VENGEANCE IS MINE; I WILL REPAY.

hear, O Israel
Deuteronomy 6:4–9
listen to me, all my people

Shema, the Hebrew word for "hear you," opens the definitive statement of Jewish faith: "Hear, O Israel: the Lord our God is one Lord; And thou shalt love the Lord thy God with all thine heart, and with all thy soul, and with all thy might."

With these words (or the Hebrew original) begins the prayer known as the Shema, which continues through verse 9. The Shema is recited twice each day in Jewish ritual. It is also recited when confronting martyrdom; for example, that suffered by Jews in the Holocaust. The Shema is an affirmation of faith and love of God.

See LOVE THY NEIGHBOR.

hearts and minds
Philippians 4:7
faith and understanding
See PEACE OF GOD WHICH PASSETH ALL UNDERSTANDING.

the **heavens declare**
Psalm 19:1
a metaphor for the strength and beauty of natural forces

In praise of the self-evident hand of God, the psalmist said, "The heavens declare the glory of God; and the firmament showeth his handiwork." The firmament in biblical times was seen as a solid dome covering the flat earth, and on that dome moved the sun, moon, and stars in their courses. The psalmist is saying, How majestic is the God who created these well-ordered, reliable marvels!

he heapeth up riches
Psalm 39:6
how a person given to meaningless pursuit of wealth
   spends his time

It is difficult for most of us to understand why people already wealthy are preoccupied with acquiring more, why people who win the grand prize in a lottery continue to buy lottery tickets, why corporate raiders fresh from a successful foray can't wait to do their thing again. Psalm 39:6 does nothing to clarify the situation; it merely expresses the enigma more pithily: "He heapeth up riches, and knoweth not who shall gather them."

Life is short. There must be better things to do with one's time.

See EAT, DRINK, AND BE MERRY.

He is risen
Mark 16:6
Christ's resurrection

These words, the foundation of New Testament faith, are recalled in many hymns and much sacred music.

hell and destruction are never full
Proverbs 27:20
you'll get what's coming to you

Proverbs 27:20 says in its entirety, "Hell and destruction are never full; so the eyes of man are never satisfied." Those who long for more than they have may find themselves in deep trouble, for hell always has room for the (un)deserving. And there will always be candidates for admission.

hell fire
Matthew 5:22
the fire burning in hell, punishment in hell, or a place of
   extreme suffering

In Matthew we read, "Whosoever shall say, Thou fool, shall
be in danger of hell fire." "Hell fire" is a translation of
Gehenna, a Greek rendering of a Hebrew place name for a
valley in ancient Palestine where refuse was continually
burned. In the New Testament, Gehenna is the place where
the wicked receive final punishment.

But why, in the line from Matthew 5, did Jesus condemn
those who say, "Thou fool"? In the Jewish religious sense, a
fool was not always a stupid person, but someone godless and
wicked. Thus, anyone addressed as "fool" was considered to
have given way to angry temper, which Jesus said would be
judged as severely as would an act of violence.

helpmeet
Genesis 2:18
a wife

To most of us, a "helpmate" means a wife or a husband. But
"helpmeet" is one of those glorious boners so dear to the
hearts of William Safire and others who take pleasure in
pointing out solecisms and curious if not downright spurious
etymologies. It all began in Genesis 2:18. God, having created
man, observed, "It is not good that the man should be alone;
I will make him an help meet for him," that is, a help suitable
for him. In the seventeenth century, a persnickety hyphen
crept in to do its work, giving us "help-meet," and the inexo-
rable forces of language did the rest, soon enough dropping
the hyphen, and Presto! "helpmeet."

here am I
I Samuel 3:4
I'm ready to do your bidding

The boy Samuel was being trained by the priest Eli to obey the call of God. While sleeping, Samuel thought he heard Eli call to him. So Samuel went to Eli and said, "Here am I." Eli said he had not spoken the words Samuel heard, whereupon Samuel returned to his bed. Twice more in his sleep he heard what was actually the voice of the Lord. Finally, on instruction from Eli, when Samuel heard the voice of the Lord once more, he replied, "Speak, for thy servant heareth." Samuel was ready to do God's bidding.

he taketh the wise in their own craftiness
Job 5:8–13
hoist with their own petards

A way of saying that even the most cunning of schemers eventually get what's coming to them. In an attempt to persuade Job to take his problems to God, Job's friend spoke glowingly of the power that "doeth great things and unsearchable; marvelous things without number." Continuing in this manner, the friend told Job that God also deals with the overly clever and the willfully contrary: "He taketh the wise in their own craftiness: and the counsel of the froward [those disposed to disobedience] is carried headlong."

The implication for Job was clear: If God can do so much for and to humanity, he will do no less for and to Job. Should not the rest of us—particularly those who think they are smarter than anyone else—take this thought to heart?

he that is not with me is against me
Matthew 12:30
you're either for God or against him

Matthew's words find use today in hardball politics, which values partisan advantage over people's welfare. Recall the so-called White House enemies list, which was brought to light in the Watergate hearings. In Matthew, of course, the intent was far different. In the midst of public controversy with the Pharisees, Jesus called on his listeners to make an either-or choice between God and Satan: "He that is not with me is against me; and he that gathereth not with me scattereth abroad." Either you believe in God or you oppose God.

See HOW LONG HALT YE BETWEEN TWO OPINIONS?

hewers of wood and drawers of water
Joshua 9:27
unskilled laborers; drudges

During an assault on Canaan, the Hivite, or Gibeonite, soldiers were intent on joining the fight against Joshua but grew fearful of his vaunted might. Instead of fighting, they tricked the Israelites into agreeing not to harm them. The Israelites lived up to the agreement but not without some cost to the Gibeonites: "And Joshua made them that day hewers of wood and drawers of water for the congregation, and for the altar of the Lord, even unto this day, in the place which he should choose."

Must it be pointed out that even today, when governments faced with labor shortages admit great numbers of foreign workers, the jobs the foreigners are allowed to fill are not exactly the first rung on a career ladder? At least Joshua kept his word and did not turn the Gibeonites out when there was a downturn in the nation's economy.

both his ears shall tingle
II Kings 21:12
the news will make his ears hurt

Manasseh, a king of Judah, was up to something the Lord thoroughly disapproved of—fooling around with ventriloquists and wizards and, especially, worshiping the stars and planets and setting up altars to Baal. As a result, God sent word through his prophets: "Behold, I am bringing such evil upon Jerusalem and Judah, that whosoever heareth of it, both his ears shall tingle."

In other parts of Scripture it is the cheeks that tingle, sometimes the entire human body. But whatever parts are involved in this classic example of psychogenic response, it is unanticipated news, good or bad—not frostbite—that evokes the response.

See ITCHING EARS.

his life is bound up in the lad's life
Genesis 44:30
a way of describing the deep love a father feels for his
  son

These words are particularly affecting when we consider that the father of whom they were said was Jacob, who had twelve sons in all, among them Judah, Joseph, and Benjamin. Judah pleaded with Joseph not to separate their youngest brother, Benjamin, from their father: "His life is bound up in the lad's life." If Joseph persisted, he said, the loss of Benjamin would "bring down the gray hairs of thy servant our father with sorrow to the grave."

Not to worry. It all ended happily.

holier than thou
Isaiah 65:2–5
obnoxiously pious

It wasn't hard to get under Isaiah's skin. For example, he condemned people "which walketh in a way that was not good, after their own thoughts. . .which eat swine's flesh . . .Which say, Stand by thyself, come not near to me; for I am holier than thou. These are a smoke in my nose, a fire that burneth all the day."

Although these were just some of the ways to provoke the prophet, Isaiah did give us the makings of the enduring phrase "holier than thou" to apply to people making a hypocritical show of righteousness or piety, and for this we are eternally grateful.

Could it be that God loves hypocrites, since he makes so many of them?

the **Holy Ghost**
Mark 1:1–8
the divine spirit held to empower Christian individuals
   and communities, and a vehicle of God's revelation

These verses introduce John the Baptist and set the stage for
the appearance of Christ.

hope against hope
Romans 4:18
continue to hope in the face of ample evidence that
   hope is useless

By way of explaining that promises depend on faith, Paul used
the example of the patriarch Abraham, who had no logical
grounds for hope that he and his wife, Sarah, well past the age
of childbearing, would ever have a child. After all, Abraham
himself was "about an hundred years old." Yet Paul described
Abraham as one "Who against hope believed in hope, that he
might become the father of many nations, according to that
which was spoken, So shall thy seed be." As we all know,
Sarah did give birth to Isaac—when Abraham was a hundred
years old and Sarah was ninety—so Abraham's faith in the
promise made by God was fulfilled.

See ENTERTAIN ANGELS UNAWARES.

the **hope of the hypocrite**
Job 27:8
self-deception

Self-deception may work for a while, but reality will eventually
take over. And when it does, watch out! Job, arguing that he
was a true believer, not a pretender, asked a rhetorical question: "What is the hope of the hypocrite, though he hath
gained, when God taketh away his soul?"

hosanna
Mark 11:9
a shout of praise

In biblical use, a hosanna—a Hebrew word meaning "save, we pray"—was an exclamation of adoration or an appeal for deliverance addressed to God.

house appointed for all living
Job 30:23
yet another metaphor for death

The grave is humanity's inevitable fate no matter how hard people try to avoid it. Job, ever the realist, was part way through his final accusations against his divine adversary when he said, "I know that thou wilt bring me to death, and to the house appointed for all living." For Job, the house was death unavoidable, and death was the place of eternal darkness.

See ALL THINGS COME ALIKE TO ALL, THREESCORE AND TEN, *and* TO EVERY THING THERE IS A SEASON.

house divided against itself
Matthew 12:25
a recipe for disaster: inner division is fatal

In Abraham Lincoln's time, orators could take it for granted that their audiences would comprehend biblical allusions. So when Lincoln spoke out in 1858 against the idea of a nation half slave and half free, saying, "A house divided against itself cannot stand," the people listening surely recalled Matthew 12:25: "Every kingdom divided against itself is brought to desolation; and every city or house divided against itself shall not stand.''

This verse is part of a response by Jesus to the charge that in his acts of healing he was possessed by "Beelzebub the prince of the devils,'' that is, by Satan.

how are the mighty fallen
II Samuel 1:19
in biblical times, a sincere lament; today, most often an expression of derision

This shift in meaning is understandable when we consider how few of today's mighty are estimable: A president who chooses to resign when impeachment threatens? A preacher who becomes front-page stuff in the likes of the *National Enquirer*? An Olympic star whose muscles owe too much to the encouragement of steroids? When David learned of the deaths of Saul and Saul's son Jonathan, he said sadly, "The beauty of Israel is slain upon thy high places: how are the mighty fallen!" And he meant just that.
See TELL IT NOT IN GATH.

how art thou fallen from heaven, O Lucifer
Isaiah 14:12
an I-told-you-so of the first water

This taunt of Isaiah's can be applied to anyone whose star has seemed fated to rise forever and then, suddenly and permanently, falls out of sight. But despite what some may think, it has nothing to do with Satan, even though he did indeed fall from heaven and his name was to become associated with Lucifer's. Verse 4 speaks of a "proverb against the king of Babylon," making it clear that Isaiah was addressing the king when we read in verse 12, "How art thou fallen from heaven, O Lucifer, son of the morning! how art thou cut down to the ground, which didst weaken the nations!" Lucifer, in the Latin of the Vulgate, means "light bringer," and the Hebrew word translated in verse 12 as Lucifer is better translated as "day star" or "morning star." (Notice that in the verse from

Isaiah "Lucifer" is followed by "son of the morning.") The epithet "morning star" is well applied to the Babylonian king, because morning stars cannot be seen at night, and the king had boasted that he would rise to heaven and challenge the Lord.

Instead it was the king's fate to be cast down to the very bottom of hell—and eternal night.

See HOW ARE THE MIGHTY FALLEN.

how forcible are right words!
Job 6:25
give it to me straight

In this verse from Job we are admonished, along with Job's well-intentioned friend, to speak plainly and honestly. Experiencing inner turmoil over what he perceived as undeserved afflictions visited upon him by God, Job found himself tired of the platitudes his friend was giving him by way of consolation. Ready for some straight talk, Job declared, "How forcible are right words!"

how long halt ye between two opinions?
I Kings 18:21
make up your mind

Political pollsters, take notice: Here are the words to use when the people you poll persist in sitting on the fence. The prophet Elijah put the matter squarely to the unresponsive Israelites—either you're with God or with those who worship Baal: "How long halt ye between two opinions? if the Lord be God, follow him: but if Baal, then follow him." Alas, "The people answered him not a word." Was Elijah dismayed? Not hardly. Since the Israelites did not respond, Elijah carried off the contest by himself, with considerable help from God. See verses 17–40.

I

I appeal to Caesar
Acts 25:11
I'll fight this all the way to the Supreme Court

As a citizen of Rome, Paul could demand to be tried under Roman law. When the Jewish religious authorities in Jerusalem pressed their complaints against him before Festus, the Roman governor based in Caesarea, Festus kept putting Paul off. Finally, the apostle made one last appeal: "If I be an offender, or have committed any thing worthy of death, I refuse not to die: but if there be none of these things whereof these accuse me, no man may deliver me unto them. I appeal to Caesar." And Festus had to comply with Paul's demand.

Paul made it to Rome, but whether he ever came to trial and how he met his death are not related in the New Testament.
See ALMOST THOU PERSUADEST ME.

if a man die, shall he live again?
Job 14:14
is there a chance that God is on Job's side?

Job was in the midst of a search for some Emersonian compensation for the misery he suffered. Knowing in his heart of hearts that death was forever, but speculating that there might be some slight hope before God for a person who had died, he said, "If a man die, shall he live again? all the days of my appointed time will I wait, till my change come." This haunting question is considered by many to be one of the most significant in the entire text of Job. When it is coupled with his apparent willingness to wait for an answer—had he another choice?—we may take it as an indication that Job was not entirely pessimistic.

And isn't it hope, no matter how fleeting, that keeps the tough going when the going gets tough?

112

if God be for us, who can be against us?
Romans 8:31
God's help will tip the scales

"If God be for us, who can be against us?" initiates the climax to Paul's long discourse on the new life as the basis for the believer's faith. To have divine power on one's side in the struggles of life is to ensure victory over all other forces. More than one aphorist owes a good deal to this line from Romans. Abolitionist Wendell Phillips, for example, gave us "One on God's side is a majority."

if his son ask bread
Matthew 7:9
a child in need of help

In verse 9 Jesus asked a rhetorical—and difficult to parse—question: "What man is there of you, whom if his son ask bread, will he give him a stone?" In verse 11 Jesus went on to ask, again rhetorically, "How much more shall your Father which is in heaven give good things to them that ask him?"

if I forget thee, O Jerusalem
Psalm 137:5–6
a passionate expression of love for one's homeland
See RIVERS OF BABYLON.

I have trodden the winepress alone
Isaiah 63:3
no one helped me

God is not always depicted as a benign father. In the bloodthirsty language the writer of Isaiah employed, the Lord said, "I have trodden the winepress alone; and of the people there was none with me: for I will tread them in mine anger, and trample them in my fury; and their blood shall be sprinkled upon my garments, and I will stain all my raiment." (Revelation 19:15 echoes Isaiah: "He treadeth the winepress of the fierceness and wrath of Almighty God.")

So, after introducing the prophecy with the homely metaphor of a winepress, out of which the juice of grapes is forced, the writer of Isaiah got down to the real business at hand: The enemies of Israel will get theirs, for God is capable of bringing destruction on nations without any help from human beings.

How many of us, on hearing Julia Ward Howe's "Battle Hymn of the Republic," recognize the biblical origins of its first, metaphorical stanza?

> Mine eyes have seen the glory of the coming of the Lord;
> He is trampling out the vintage where the grapes of wrath are stored;
> He hath loosed the fateful lightning of His terrible, swift sword;
> His truth is marching on.

And, from John Steinbeck: Thank you, Julia, for an unforgettable book title.

increased knowledge, increased sorrow
Ecclesiastes 1:16–18
vexation, frustration, and an increasing sense of futility await those who strive for deeper understanding of life's mystery

The author of Ecclesiastes, whose identity is not known for certain but who appears to have had a reputation for wisdom, tried to discover whether knowledge offered guidance to what is good and true. He could find no answers. Indeed, the more he learned, the more mysteries he found: "I gave my heart to know wisdom, and to know madness and folly: I perceived that this also is vexation of spirit. For in much wisdom is much grief, and he that increaseth knowledge increaseth sorrow."

Sounds as if we all should try to learn less.

See OF MAKING MANY BOOKS THERE IS NO END.

inherit the wind
Proverbs 11:29
be repaid with evil
See THEY HAVE SOWN THE WIND.

in much wisdom is much grief
Ecclesiastes 1:16–18
knowledge can never solve all life's mysteries
See INCREASED KNOWLEDGE, INCREASED SORROW.

in the wilderness a lodging place
Jeremiah 9:2
Walden Pond, Camp David—any sylvan hideaway

Unfortunately for the prophet Jeremiah, at the time he longed for such a lodging place he was seeking more than solitude and open spaces. What he really wanted was to get away for a time from his own people, whose actions were causing him considerable anxiety: "Oh that I had in the wilderness a lodging place of wayfaring men; that I might leave my people, and go from them! for they be all adulterers, an assembly of treacherous men."

Can you blame Jeremiah for wanting to get away?

I shall not be moved
Psalm 16:8
a firm avowal of perdurable faith

The psalmist recognized the eminence and strength of the Lord, saying, "I have set the Lord always before me: because he is at my right hand, I shall not be moved." This verse, combined with a metaphor from Psalm 1:3, "And he [the true believer] shall be like a tree planted by the rivers of water," was picked up in the spiritual "We Shall Not Be Moved" and used later as a song by the labor and civil rights movements:

Just like a tree that's standing by the water,
We shall not be moved.

Ishmael
Genesis 16:12
an outcast

An angel prophesied that Ishmael would be "a wild man; his hand will be against every man, and every man's hand against him"—in short, an outcast. To Hagar, Sarah's servant, was born a son fathered by Abraham and called Ishmael. This happy event came about after the apparently barren Sarah had given Hagar to Abraham as a concubine so that he might have an heir. Isaac, Abraham and Sarah's son, was conceived somewhat later, after Sarah had fallen out with Hagar and sent her along with Ishmael into the desert. An angel—the very one who made the prophecy about Ishmael's fate—appeared in time to save the unfortunate pair from starvation. Can anything beat the Bible for storytelling?

Melville gave the name Ishmael to the narrator of *Moby-Dick* and made him the only survivor of Ahab's obsessive hunt for the great whale. Someone had to survive to tell the tale, but why the character named Ishmael? Was it because he was sustained by a belief in love and human solidarity? Or because he was protected by God? After all, Ishmael in Hebrew means "God has heard."

is it lawful to give tribute to Caesar, or not?
Mark 12:14
an unanswerable question

Anyone wishing to stop a debating opponent dead will admire the artfulness of this question, the biblical equivalent of putting someone between Scylla and Charybdis or between a rock and a hard place. A group of Pharisees and nationalists intent on entrapping Jesus asked, "Is it lawful to give tribute to Caesar, or not?" If he answered yes, the nationalists would be angered. If he said no, he would be in danger of arrest by the Roman governor for treason.

For the response made by Jesus, *see* RENDER UNTO CAESAR.

is it nothing to you, all ye who pass by?
Lamentations 1:12
stop and think

Could there be a better inscription for a memorial to the millions who died in the Holocaust or to the uncountable number of soldiers and civilians who died in the Vietnam War? The writer of Lamentations, traditionally thought to be the prophet Jeremiah, was in deep despair over the sinfulness that prevailed among his people. And he said to anyone who would listen, "Is it nothing to you, all ye that pass by? behold, and see if there be any sorrow like unto my sorrow, which is done unto me, wherewith the Lord hath afflicted me in the day of his fierce anger."

Step aside, Job, you've met your match. Whether Jeremiah did or did not write this book of the Old Testament, so characteristic of the prophet were such lamentations that by the eighteenth century the English word "jeremiad" had emerged, with the meaning "a lengthy complaint or prolonged lamentation."

See LET THE DAY PERISH WHEN I WAS BORN.

is not the sound of his master's feet behind him?
II Kings 6:32
the hatchet man is on his way

During the Syrians' siege of Samaria, when there were food shortages and enormously inflated prices, the king of Israel sent for the prophet Elisha to punish him for counsel that had been given to a hungry woman on how to survive the food shortages. (If you have the stomach for it, see verses 26–30 for the barbaric advice she received.) Elisha, before the messenger of the king could reach him, told the elders, "See ye how this son of a murderer [the king] hath sent to take away mine head? look, when the messenger cometh, shut the door, and hold him fast at the door: is not the sound of his master's feet behind him?" This was done, and Elisha suffered no harm.

is not this great Babylon?
Daniel 4:30–31
prideful words and certain to portend the downfall of
    any power-hungry potentate who utters them

With this question began a self-serving announcement by
King Nebuchadnezzar, who had rebuilt the city of Babylon to
serve primarily as a royal residence: "Is not this great Babylon, that I have built for the house of the kingdom by the
might of my power, and for the honor of my majesty?" In the
very next verse, "While the word was in the king's mouth,
there fell a voice from heaven, saying, O king Nebuchadnezzar, to thee it is spoken; The kingdom is departed from thee."

All you modern creators of monuments to self: Are you
listening?

is Saul also among the prophets?
I Samuel 10:11
have you joined the kooks?

Said of those who unexpectedly lend support to a cause they
earlier and vigorously opposed. Consider, for example, a
leader of the National Rifle Association suddenly issuing a call
for abolition of gun ownership by private citizens. In biblical
times, bands of prophets engaged in communal ecstatic practices, in Scripture referred to as "prophesying." Some of the
people revered these prophets, but many others scorned
them. Against this background, Saul's prophesying brought
concern to the people who had known him for some time.
And they said, "What is this that is come unto the son of Kish?
Is Saul also among the prophets?"
  Et tu, Brute?

itching ears
II Timothy 4:3
ears that enjoy gossip

The writer of the Second Epistle of Timothy gave us this
engaging metaphor in a discussion of the weakness of people

who fall prey to teachers who pander to them: "The time will come when they will not endure sound doctrine; but after their own lusts shall they heap to themselves teachers, having itching ears."

To this day we say of those who egg on scandalmongers that they have itching ears.

See BOTH HIS EARS SHALL TINGLE.

it is more blessed to give than to receive
Acts 20:35
help those who need help

This passage in Acts makes no mention of giving money, but it is in this sense that its words are most often taken, especially when a Christian congregation is offered the collection plate. In Paul's farewell speech to the Christians of Ephesus, he said, "I have shewed [shown] you all things, how that so laboring ye ought to support the weak, and to remember the words of the Lord Jesus, how he said, It is more blessed to give than to receive." There are endless ways to provide support for those who need it—visiting the sick, comforting the bereaved, and working at community shelters are but a few. Yet financial support for a church or synagogue is essential and comes best from those who are part of the community.

it is not good that man should be alone
Genesis 2:18
all men should marry

Right on the money. Who among us does not benefit from being in the company of others?

See HELPMEET.

I was blind, now I see
John 9:25
don't split hairs

John 9 relates how Jesus restored the sight of a man who had been blind from birth. The healing occurred on the sabbath, so the Pharisees saw the marvelous act as a breach of the law forbidding labor on that day. Insisting that anyone who broke the sabbath law must be a sinner, they tried to disprove the healing by questioning the man and his parents. The once-blind man replied, "Whether he [Jesus] be a sinner or no, I know not; one thing I know, that, whereas I was blind, now I see."

Pragmatism at its best: If it works, don't knock it.

See JUDGE NOT BY APPEARANCES *and* SABBATH WAS MADE FOR MAN.

I was sick, and ye visited me
Matthew 25:36
you performed your ethical duty

Nursing homes and hospices welcome volunteers who take this statement to heart. Visiting the sick was one of the ethical virtues praised in Jesus' parable of the last judgment. The other virtues he praised were feeding the hungry, giving water to the thirsty, sheltering strangers, clothing the naked, and visiting the imprisoned.

J

Jacob served seven years
Genesis 29:1–30
he paid his dues—and then some

Jacob, who was no slouch when it came to pulling off scams, met his match in dealing with Laban, his future father-in-law. Jacob wanted to marry Rachel, the "beautiful and well favored" younger of Laban's two daughters. Laban agreed to the match if Jacob would first work for him as herdsman for seven years. Jacob agreed. And why not? Verse 20 says, "Jacob served seven years for Rachel; and they seemed unto him but a few days, for the love he had to her." When the seven years were up, Jacob asked for Rachel's hand. But Laban set out a feast at which, it is presumed, Jacob drank too much. When he awoke in the morning, Jacob found that Laban had pulled a switcheroo. With Jacob in his bed was the elder sister, Leah, not Rachel. Soon enough, Jacob struck a new deal, specifying that at the end of the week-long wedding celebration Laban would give him Rachel as well. And all Jacob had to do this time was work another seven years for Laban.

Love may conquer all, but bait-and-switch has also been successful for a long time.

For evidence of Jacob's own conniving, *see* VOICE IS JACOB'S VOICE.

Jacob's ladder
Genesis 28:12–17
a means of climbing into heaven

In a dream, Jacob saw a ladder reaching up to heaven. It was this dream that gave us "Jacob's ladder," a name for a rope or chain ladder used by seamen, and "Jacob's-ladder," a name for a common flower whose leaflets have a ladderlike arrangement. In Jacob's dream, he saw "a ladder set up on the earth, and the top of it reached to heaven: and behold the angels of God ascending and descending upon it." Then Jacob heard the voice of God promising great things: "Thy seed shall be as the dust of the earth, and thou shalt spread abroad to the west and to the east, and to the north, and to the south: and in thee and in thy seed shall all the families of the earth be blessed." On awakening, Jacob exclaimed, "This is none other but the house of God, and this is the gate of heaven."

And "gate of heaven," denoting a place heavy with a sense of the presence of the divine, remains with us as a popular name for cemeteries.

Jael
Judges 5:26
one tough cookie

Anyone who believes women play only passive roles in Scripture should consider Jael. It was she who murdered Sisera, commander of the Canaanites in a great battle with a force of Israelites. Using a hammer, she drove a tent pin through his temple while he slept.

Active enough for you?
See STARS IN THEIR COURSES.

jawbone of an ass
Judges 15:14–17
any weapon that's handy—tire iron, baseball bat,
    Saturday night special

As related in Judges, a gang of Philistines got under Samson's skin, so he picked up the jawbone of an ass and slew a thousand Philistines. Could this have been an exaggeration? Verse 14, by way of explaining Samson's act, adds, "The Spirit of the Lord came mightily upon him." At any rate, when done, the triumphant Samson crowed, "With the jawbone of an ass have I slain a thousand men." He then tossed the jawbone aside, and the place was thereafter known as the Hill of the Jawbone.

a **jealous God**
Exodus 20:5
a God intolerant of defection or unfaithfulness

Jehu
II Kings 9:20
the biblical Barney Oldfield
See DRIVE LIKE JEHU.

Jephthah's vow
Judges 11:30–31
a hastily made commitment yielding tragic results

Jephthah, an Israelite military leader, vowed that if he returned victorious after battle with the Ammonites, "Whatsoever cometh forth of the doors of my house to meet me, when I return in peace from the children of Ammon, shall surely be the Lord's, and I will offer it up for a burnt offering." Return Jephthah did—and victorious—but the first to emerge from his house was his only child, a daughter. Jephthah fulfilled his vow, since at that time nothing, not even humane actions, took precedence over keeping a vow. And the rest of us are warned not to make a vow unless we first think things through completely.

One cannot help but wonder what person or animal Jephthah had in mind for possible sacrifice when he made his terrible vow.

For a sidelight on the tragic story, *see* BEWAIL MY VIRGINITY.

Jerusalem, Jerusalem
Matthew 23:37
a sorrowful farewell to a place held dear

In Matthew 23, Jesus lamented what had happened to Jerusalem, the beautiful and holy city, which was so hard on prophets, notably Jeremiah. The characterization attributed to Jesus, "O Jerusalem, Jerusalem, thou that killest the prophets, and stonest them which are sent unto thee," is set in what appears to be a piece of prophetic preaching. Taken at face value, verse 37 is an expression of Jesus' heartbreak that Jerusalem had not welcomed his message.

a jewel of gold in a swine's snout
Proverbs 11:22
a metaphor for a beautiful woman who behaves
   indiscreetly

The verse reads in full, "As a jewel of gold in a swine's snout, so is a fair woman which is without discretion."

Jezebel
II Kings 9:30–33
an impudent or shameless woman

In the past, the word "jezebel" was also applied to a woman who painted her face, and "painted woman" to this day remains a euphemism for "prostitute." What did Jezebel, wife of King Ahab of Israel, do that her name became an English word—and earned the ultimate linguistic accolade of losing its initial capital letter? First of all, I Kings 21:25 tells us that Ahab worked "wickedness in the sight of the Lord, whom Jezebel his wife stirred up." (Aha, it's always the woman's fault.) She was accompanied by priests of the cult of Baal, who were the objects of Israelite religious animosity.

II Kings 9:30–33, recounting the history of the period after Ahab's death, contributed further to Jezebel's reputation. These verses relate how, "When Jehu was come to Jezreel, Jezebel heard of it; and she painted her face, and tired her

head, and looked out at a window." Jehu, while carrying out
the murder of Jehoram, Ahab's successor and a son of Jezebel, ordered that the queen mother be thrown out of her
second-story window by "two or three eunuchs." This they
did, and "some of her blood was sprinkled on the wall, and
on the horses: and he trod her under foot."

So much for Jezebel. Nice chap, Jehu.

See DRIVE LIKE JEHU; HAST THOU FOUND ME, O MINE ENEMY?;
and STILL SMALL VOICE.

Jonah
Jonah 1–4
any person considered to bring bad luck

Despite this bum rap, Jonah's biblical sea voyage, stay in the
belly of a great fish, and trials at Nineveh constitute a parable
on the breadth of God's mercy and forgiveness. Jonah was a
Hebrew prophet commissioned by God to proclaim his judgment upon sinful Nineveh, capital of Assyria. Fearing that
God would pardon the hated Ninevites if they asked for forgiveness, and seeking to avoid the assignment, Jonah boarded
a Mediterranean ship bound in the wrong direction. When
God caused a great storm to come up, the crew members
offered prayers for their safety to their various gods, but to no
avail. Jonah, found asleep and not in prayer, was brought
before the crew. He confessed his disobedience to God and
urged the crew to toss him overboard as a way of calming the
storm. When all else failed, this was precisely what the sailors
did. And the storm subsided.

But what of sinful Nineveh? The people repented, and God
spared them. So right from the start Jonah had correctly
sensed he would be forced to swallow a bitter pill.

jot or tittle
Matthew 5:18
the least bit

When we promise to do things strictly by the book, we may
say we'll deviate "not a jot or tittle," that is, not in the slight-

est. And in doing so we are close to Jesus' language and intent in Matthew 5:18. Jesus was charged by scribes and Pharisees, the latter group considered to be those scrupulously observant of the letter of Jewish law, with undercutting the law of Moses. Not so, said Jesus: "Think not that I am come to destroy the law, or the prophets; I am not come to destroy but to fulfill. For verily I say unto you, Till heaven and earth pass, one jot or one tittle shall in no wise pass from the law, till all be fulfilled."

"Jot" derives from ι (iota), the smallest letter in the Greek alphabet, which has its English counterpart in the letter "i." A "tittle" is a dot or other small mark used in writing or printing. Thus was Jesus promising that he would not teach even the tiniest change in the law.

jubilee
Leviticus 25:9–10
today, any occasion for rejoicing

We moderns recognize especially silver, gold, and diamond jubilees—twenty-fifth, fiftieth, and sixtieth or seventy-fifth anniversaries. Among the Israelites, the word "jubilee" had a highly specific meaning. Every fiftieth year was a jubilee, or jubilee year, a year of restoration and emancipation. Farmers' fields were to be left uncultivated, slaves were to be set free, and houses that had been sold since the previous jubilee were to revert to their original owners or to the heirs of those owners. The sounding of the ram's horn heralded the start of a jubilee: "Then shalt thou cause the trumpet of the jubile [*sic*] to sound on the tenth day of the seventh month, in the day of atonement shall ye make the trumpet sound throughout all your land."

Judas
Mark 3:19
a traitor

Taking our cue from Mark, we think of a Judas as a traitor or a person treacherous enough to betray a close friend. Mark

3:19, along with many other passages in the New Testament, associates Judas Iscariot (not to be confused with Saint Judas, an honorable man who became one of Christ's apostles) with the betrayal of Jesus: "And Judas Iscariot, which also betrayed him...."

See KISS OF DEATH *and* THIRTY PIECES OF SILVER.

judge not by appearances
John 7:24
good advice

A difficult precept for the great number of people who are quick to condemn on weak evidence. In healing a man on the sabbath, Jesus angered those who felt he had violated the law forbidding all work on that day. Admitting to the healing, Jesus told his critics that the law did not forbid work performed on the sabbath in circumcising a boy, so why should it forbid healing? Jesus went on: "Judge not according to the appearance, but judge righteous judgment."

Righteous judgment, it seems, may now and then include going beyond the letter of the law—but with some care and thoughtfulness.

judge not, that ye be not judged
Matthew 7:1
make sure your own hands are clean before you lay into others
See MOTE IN THE EYE.

the **just and the unjust**
Matthew 5:45
this covers all of us

In the land of the Bible, the average annual rainfall ranged from insufficient for most agricultural purposes to barely enough. Matthew 5:45 says in praise of God, "He maketh his sun to rise on the evil and on the good, and sendeth rain on the just and the unjust." So we all have an equal chance at nature's bounty.

James Gould Cozzens found in Matthew 5 the title for his novel *The Just and the Unjust*, which probed the inevitable conflict in human affairs between what should be and what can be.

K

keep the faith
II Timothy 4:7
don't abandon your faith when things get tough

Nowadays, the phrase advises trust and persistence in whatever enterprise you are part of. In the New Testament, where this thought is expressed over and over again in many different ways, it means keep to the precepts of Christianity even in the face of Roman oppression.
See FIGHT THE GOOD FIGHT.

kick against the pricks
Acts 9:4–5
engage repeatedly in self-defeating behavior

"Kick against the pricks" is a metaphor found also in Acts 26:14 for struggling hopelessly against fate, for hurting oneself by protesting when there is no chance of winning. The allusion is to oxen, which kick reflexively when goaded, although they accomplish nothing thereby and only increase their pain. The great beasts will continue to kick without knowing what is causing their pain each time, but humans can be expected to learn from analogous experiences.

For Saul of Tarsus, the future Christian apostle Paul, the doctrine preached by the disciples of Jesus was so radical it seemed to undermine everything he believed. For this reason, Saul had been making life tough for the Christians, even threatening them with bodily harm. As Saul was on his way from Jerusalem to Damascus, where he intended to play rough with Christian converts, he suddenly experienced a manifestation of the risen Jesus Christ. "And he fell to earth, and heard a voice saying unto him, Saul, Saul, why persecutest thou me? And he said, Who art thou, Lord? And the Lord said, I am Jesus whom thou persecutest: it is hard for thee to kick against the pricks."

So while it is only human to resist change, especially great change, nothing is gained by butting one's head repeatedly against a stone wall.

Unless one enjoys feeling pain, that is.

kingdom divided against itself
Mark 3:23
conflict within a group
See HOUSE DIVIDED AGAINST ITSELF.

kingdom of God
Mark 1:14
domain of God's sovereignty

This is Mark's expression for one of the thoughts central to the message of Jesus, who preached "the gospel of the kingdom of God," that is, God's sovereignty over hearts and minds and wills. To Jesus, the coming of the kingdom was imminent, and repentance and turning to God were essential for salvation.

kingdom of heaven
Matthew 18:3
domain of God's sovereignty

This expression has the same meaning as "kingdom of God." Like any reverent Jew then as now, Matthew avoided use of the name of the divinity. In Matthew 18:3 Jesus was asked by his disciples, "Who is the greatest in the kingdom of heaven?" His response was, "Except ye be converted, and become as little children, ye shall not enter the kingdom of heaven." Jesus saw children as having the required qualities: a sense of dependence and of trust in those who love them, a sense of wonder and expectancy, receptiveness and honest directness, and absence of consciousness of rank or race.

How many of us, children included, can claim to possess all these qualities?

See KINGDOM OF GOD.

king of terrors
Job 18:11–14
death personified

Painting a vivid picture of psychic disintegration, a friend confronted Job with image after image of the dread fate that awaited the unhappy, guilt-ridden man: "Terrors shall make him afraid on every side, and shall drive him to his feet....His confidence shall be rooted out of his tabernacle, and it shall bring him to the king of terrors."

Not a pretty picture.

kiss of death
Mark 14:45
an act leading ultimately to disaster or death

The kiss of Judas, the original finger man, was a kiss of betrayal, a treacherous gesture of affection whose real purpose was to mark someone for execution. In short, the kiss of Judas was a kiss of death. Mark 14 recounts how Judas, acting in concert with the chief priests, agreed to identify Jesus for the Temple guards by kissing him during the feast of the Passover, thus enabling them to arrest the right person. Verse 45 relates that this is what Judas did: "As soon as he was come, he goeth straightway to him, and saith, Master, Master; and kissed him." The crucifixion of Jesus was one step closer.

Today, a kiss of death denotes an act or event that destroys any hope of success in an enterprise.

See THIRTY PIECES OF SILVER.

L

the **laborers are few**
Matthew 9:37
a call for help

Jesus, teaching and healing throughout Galilee, was attracting
great audiences. Seeing the helplessness of those who heard
him—Jesus called them "sheep having no shepherd"—he
perceived himself both as gathering a scattered flock and
harvesting grain. But his task was pressing, he said, and he
could not accomplish it alone: "The harvest truly is plente-
ous, but the laborers are few."

Volunteers for good causes are seldom in great supply.

laborer worthy of his hire
Luke 10:7
one who has earned all the help he is offered

This may sound like a statement made by a union leader, but
it is not. In saying "For the laborer is worthy of his hire," Jesus
was telling his disciples to accept offers of hospitality when
they were out on their missions. The laborer was the disciple,
and his hire was food and lodging. The service rendered was
the carrying of the message of ultimate significance—the
coming of the kingdom of God.

labor of love
I Thessalonians 1:2–3
a true calling

Any work performed without regard for payment but for the
sake of the work itself may be called a labor of love. The
phrase was used by Paul in thanking and complimenting the
members of his church in Thessalonica: "We give thanks to
God always for you all, making mention of you in our prayers;

Remembering without ceasing your work of faith, and labor of love, and patience of hope in our Lord Jesus Christ, in the sight of God and our Father." And a labor of love it must have been for the church members pursuing their missionary work amidst the hostile dominant community of the Macedonian port city.

as a **lamb to the slaughter**
Isaiah 53:7
silently, unprotestingly, meekly, gently, innocently

Verse 7 continues a description of the suffering of Israel (interpreted by some Christians as a prophecy of the coming of Jesus Christ): "He was oppressed, and he was afflicted, yet he opened not his mouth: he is brought as a lamb to the slaughter, and as a sheep before her shearers is dumb, so he openeth not his mouth." Today, the unwary who fall for slick sales pitches or get-rich-quick schemes are described as lambs being led to slaughter. But the modern metaphor collapses when such lambs come to life again after a time and fall for the same schemes all over again.

At least when real lambs die, that's the end of the story.

See LOST SHEEP *and* MAN OF SORROWS.

lamp unto my feet
Psalm 119:105
a metaphor for a source of guidance, of intellectual or
   spiritual light

Psalm 119:105 reads, "Thy word is a lamp unto my feet, and
a light unto my path," meaning that God's commandments
and precepts have given the psalmist guidance throughout his
life. We have a second metaphor in "light unto my path."

land of Canaan
Genesis 12:1–8
ancient Palestine
See PROMISED LAND.

land of darkness
Job 10:20–21
a metaphor for the finality of death

At the time when the Book of Job was written, the concept of
a life after death had not emerged. Even though we have
become accustomed to the despair of poor Job, we are struck
by his forlorn cry: "Are not my days few? cease then, and let
me alone, that I may take comfort a little, Before I go whence
I shall not return, even to the land of darkness and the shadow
of death."
   Give me a break.
See LAND OF THE LIVING.

land of milk and honey
Exodus 3:8
ancient Palestine
See MILK AND HONEY.

land of the living
Job 28:12–13
the finite world

When a person returns to consciousness after a serious accident or a bout with a dangerously high fever, we are apt to say, Welcome back to the land of the living. But the land of the living, to Job at least, was far from a paradise. Job was a man who demanded real answers to pressing questions. And so, in the midst of an extended paean to wisdom in chapter 28, he asked, "Where shall wisdom be found? and where is the place of understanding? Man knoweth not the price thereof; neither is it found in the land of the living." Apparently, wisdom is not to be found in man's finite world, the land of the living. The implication is that God is the only source of wisdom.

See BEGINNING OF WISDOM *and* LAND OF DARKNESS.

the latchet of whose shoes I am not worthy to stoop down and unloose
Mark 1:7
an expression of profound humility

John the Baptist was speaking of Jesus in uttering this thought: "There cometh one mightier than I after me, the latchet of whose shoes I am not worthy to stoop down and unloose." "Latchet" is an archaic term for a strap used to fasten a shoe.

the laughter of a fool
Ecclesiastes 7:5–6
a metaphor for foolish words

The writer of Ecclesiastes here tells us, "It is better to hear the rebuke of the wise, than for a man to hear the song of fools. For as the crackling of thorns under a pot, so is the laughter of the fool." Anyone who has ever tried to cook over a fire fueled only by kindling will readily appreciate this metaphor. A lot of sparkling and crackling but no enduring heat.

law of the Medes and Persians
Daniel 6:8
unalterable law

Like "cast in concrete," this phrase denotes anything that must not be changed. Bureaucrats, envious of Daniel's rise in favor with the Persian King Darius and knowing Daniel's devotion to the God of Israel, urged the king to enact a law prohibiting prayer to any god except the king himself: "Sign the writing, that it be not changed, according to the law of the Medes and Persians, which altereth not." The king signed the law, but Daniel continued to pray to God, whereupon the king had Daniel thrown into a den of lions. Things turned out all right for Daniel, who was rescued by an angel.

And the bureaucrats? They were thrown into the same den—without a protecting angel.

See DEN OF LIONS.

let all things be done decently
I Corinthians 14:40
be fair and thoughtful

Good advice for town meetings and for families gathered together to find solutions for vexing problems. Paul was addressing the members of a church he had founded in Corinth, who were then attempting to solve some problems and settle some issues. Finally, after reviewing all the problems and offering his solutions, Paul wrote: "Let all things be done decently and in order." These gentle words are worth recalling by those working in community with others and especially by those who find themselves appointed to sit in judgment of their fellow human beings. Small wonder these words have been used as a motto by modern Presbyterians.

let my beloved come into his garden
Song of Solomon 4:16
come join me, my darling

Words expressing the yearning of a young bride awaiting the appearance of her husband and the love they will share: "Awake, O north wind; and come, thou south; blow upon my garden, that the spices thereof may flow out. Let my beloved come into his garden, and eat his pleasant fruits."

let my people go
Exodus 5:1
grant us our freedom

The Old Testament supplied this traditional plea of all peoples demanding freedom from bondage. Consider the old spiritual:

Go down, Moses,
Way down in Egypt land,
Tell old Pharaoh,
Let my people go.

Moses and Aaron confronted the Pharaoh with these words: "Thus saith the Lord God of Israel, Let my people go, that they may hold a feast unto me in the wilderness." And did the Pharaoh accede? He did not.

For what happened next, *see* BRICKS WITHOUT STRAW.

let my right hand forget her cunning
Psalm 137:1
may I lose all my skills and knowledge
See RIVERS OF BABYLON.

let my tongue cleave to the roof of my mouth
Psalm 137:6
may I be struck dumb
See RIVERS OF BABYLON.

let not the sun go down upon your wrath
Ephesians 4:26–27
don't go to bed mad

Advice that has endured to this day—consult any marriage manual: Be sure to settle all the day's disagreements before retiring for the night. In Ephesians Paul directed this thought not toward married couples, but toward members of newly established Christian churches that were experiencing internal disagreements and attacks from outside: "Be ye angry, and sin not: let not the sun go down upon your wrath: Neither give place to the devil."

William Blake, who seems always to have put things better, expressed Paul's thought this way in "A Poison Tree":

I was angry with my friend;
I told my wrath, my wrath did end.
I was angry with my foe;
I told it not, my wrath did grow.

let not your left hand know what your right hand does
Matthew 6:3
keep your good works to yourself

The perfect text for government officials who arrange arms shipments to terrorists while professing to have nothing to do with them? Unfortunately not, at least in the sense in which these words were originally intended. Jesus gave this message in a context of almsgiving, a feature of Jewish piety, saying, "When thou doest alms, let not thy left hand know what thy right hand doeth." He was counseling against blowing your own horn. By not telling even your closest associates about your giving, only God and you will know about it.

Isn't that the way charitable contributions should be made?
See FREELY RECEIVE, FREELY GIVE.

the **letter killeth, but the spirit giveth life**
II Corinthians 3:5–6
strict adherence to rules may not always be wise

People err in following rules slavishly when their zeal results
in injustice. Paul argued that Jewish law, the old law, had a
deadening effect because it was so difficult to obey. People
were led, therefore, either to hypocrisy or to despair over
their inability to meet its many demands. By contrast, Paul
pointed to the simplicity of Christianity: "Our sufficiency is of
God; Who also hath made us able ministers of the new testament; not of the letter, but of the spirit: for the letter killeth,
but the spirit giveth life."

Strict constitutional constructionists: Are you listening?

let the day perish when I was born
Job 3:3
I'm in deep trouble

This thought from Job reverberates to this day, when people
in the depths of mental depression are apt to say "I curse the
day I was born" or ask "Why was I born?" In verse 3 Job says,
"Let the day perish wherein I was born, and the night in which
it was said, There is a man child conceived." This lament
continues through many verses, asking many why questions.
Finally, in verses 25–26, the crushed Job says, "The thing
which I greatly feared is come upon me, and that which I was
afraid of is come unto me. I was not in safety, neither had I
rest, neither was I quiet; yet trouble came."

You want to know what despair is? Job will tell you what
despair is.
See LORD GAVE, AND THE LORD HATH TAKEN AWAY.

let the heavens be glad, and let the earth rejoice
I Chronicles 16:31
give thanks for all God's blessings

By way of thanksgiving to the Lord, David in this verse says: "Let the heavens be glad, and let the earth rejoice: and let men say among the nations, The Lord reigneth."

let there be light
Genesis 1:2–3
the words spoken by God before one of his first acts of
    creation

Teachers have long tried to shed light on obscure subjects with which students struggle. When success rewards these pedagogical efforts, we may say their students have seen the light. Genesis 1 reports that God was able to create light instantaneously. Before the act of creation began, the earth "was without form, and void; and darkness was upon the face of the deep....And God said, Let there be light: and there was light." Just like that. And why not? Unlike other gods, the Lord God of Israel did not arise after a struggle with chaos, the sea, or some fire-spouting dragon. God the creator, the sovereign, has no past, no ancestors, no personal life—God just is.

And all the forces of nature obey God without hesitation.

let the wicked fall into their own nets
Psalm 141:9–10
let those who seek to harm me be themselves harmed

Praying for guidance, the psalmist said, "Keep me from the snares which they have laid for me, and the gins [traps] of the workers of iniquity. Let the wicked fall into their own nets, whilst that I withal escape." And we have a metaphor for people seeking to entrap others and ending up victims of their own wiles.

let this cup pass from me
Matthew 26:39
spare me suffering, if you will

When candidates for high public office do everything they can to appear humble except be humble, they are inclined to twist this verse from Matthew to suit their purposes. Thus, when they say, "If this cup should pass from me. . ." they are alluding to the unmentionable, the possibility of losing a nomination or an election. The cup they are talking about is the one they use when drinking at the public trough.

In Matthew "cup" carries a different meaning. Isaiah 51:17 established "cup" as a symbol for suffering, and it is in this sense that Matthew 26 uses the word. Jesus, on the day before his crucifixion, recognized that suffering would shortly befall him. In verse 39, he prayed to be spared while at the same time expressing full submission to God's will: "O my Father, if it be possible, let this cup pass from me: nevertheless not as I will, but as thou wilt." In Jesus' second prayer, verse 42, he reiterated his submission to God's will: "If this cup may not pass away from me, except I drink it, thy will be done."

Quite a different thought from that of the politicians.

See CUP RUNNETH OVER.

let thy words be few
Ecclesiastes 5:2
be more ready to listen than to talk

Sound advice under all circumstances, even though Ecclesiastes in this verse intended specifically to address those who go to pray in the house of God: "Be not rash with thy mouth, and let not thine heart be hasty to utter any thing before God: for God is in heaven: therefore let thy words be few."

Someone is listening to the prayers offered.

let us go up to the mountain
Isaiah 2:2–3
let us receive the word of God

In verse 2 we read, "The mountain of the Lord's house shall be established in the top of the mountains." Then, in verse 3, "Come ye, and let us go up to the mountain of the Lord, to the house of the God of Jacob; and he will teach us of his ways, and we will walk in his paths." Scripture has made people fully aware of mountains in their figurative as well as literal sense. For example, it seems like yesterday, even though it was decades ago, that we heard Martin Luther King, Jr., say on the night before his assassination, "I just want to do God's will. And he's allowed me to go to the mountain. And I've looked over, and I've seen the promised land." The prophetic allusion was to the account of the death of Moses, who ascended Mount Nebo to view the promised land and then died.

let us not be weary in well doing
Galatians 6:9
don't give up working on behalf of others

Your efforts to help others will eventually be rewarded, for such work is the most important of all human enterprises. Those who devote themselves tirelessly to the needs of the less fortunate and the afflicted—consider dedicated social workers, disaster relief workers, Literacy Volunteers, nurses, et al.—are wittingly or not following the counsel Paul gave to the Christian community in Galatia: "Let us not be weary in well doing: for in due season we shall reap, if we faint not." That is, if we don't give up.

The game ain't over till it's over.

For contrast, *see* THEY HAVE SOWN THE WIND.

let us reason together
Isaiah 1:18
all right—I'll give you another chance

People old enough to remember President Lyndon Johnson may recall that he frequently used this line from Isaiah implying that the opinions of all people are worthy and should be heard. But those who knew Lyndon Johnson well understood that what he meant was, Let's talk for a while, but then you had better agree with me. In Isaiah, God had another intention: I'm ready to give an erring Israel another chance, provided that its people renounce hypocrisy and repent. "Come now, and let us reason together, saith the Lord: though your sins be as scarlet, they shall be white as snow; though they be red like crimson, they shall be as wool."

That's known as wiping the slate clean.

let your speech be always with grace
Colossians 4:5–6
how to win friends and influence people

Paul, intent on making a success of the efforts he and his fellow Christians were putting out to convert nonbelievers, advised his followers, "Walk in wisdom toward them that are without, redeeming the time. Let your speech be alway with grace, seasoned with salt, that ye may know how ye ought to answer every man." Don't be put off by "alway." This venerable form, with the meaning of "perpetually," was around for centuries before "always" made its appearance. Of greater interest is the phrase "seasoned with salt." Here Paul was advising that speech becomes more effective when sprinkled with good humor.

Won't we all improve our chances of convincing others if we study how best to respond to every person we meet, as Paul advised?

lick the dust
Psalm 72:9
submit humbly

This metaphor has two modern meanings. Like the current idiom "bite the dust," it means "be killed" and "die." The second modern meaning is "humble oneself" or "grovel." In biblical idiom, the metaphor used in Psalm 72:9 has the latter meaning. Thus, when the psalmist said, "They that dwell in the wilderness shall bow before him; and his enemies shall lick the dust," the intention was clear: They will submit humbly to God.

lift the needy out of the dunghill
Psalm 113:7
help those who need help most

Psalm 113, in praise of a merciful God, cites some of his acts. For example, "He raiseth up the poor out of the dust, and lifteth the needy out of the dunghill." In characterizing the abode of the destitute as dust and dunghill, the psalmist gave Congress and the rest of us two arresting metaphors to bear in mind when we fulfill our duty toward the poor—and when we choose to ignore that responsibility.

Or is it invidious to hope that mere mortals will undertake to do what God does?

lift up mine eyes
Psalm 121:1
I will look to God

Psalm 121 begins with "I will lift up mine eyes unto the hills, from whence cometh my help. My help cometh from the Lord, which made heaven and earth." The mountains and hills of ancient Palestine surely cast their spirit on the people of the Bible, and modern artists and writers reflect a similar sense of awe as they contemplate nature.

light in the darkness
Psalm 112:4
a reward for the worthy

Psalm 112 praises the upright person, who "delighteth greatly" in God's commandments, and enumerates many of the benefits that accrue to those leading blameless lives. In verse 4, we find that "Unto the upright there ariseth light in the darkness," and what could be more welcome?

a light unto my path
Psalm 119:105
divine guidance
See LAMP UNTO MY FEET.

lilies of the field
Matthew 6:28
natural beauties of the universe

William Barrett's novel *Lilies of the Field* provides yet another instance of the help the Bible gives authors in search of appropriate and allusive book titles. So fine a choice was this one that Hollywood moguls accepted it unchanged when they produced a Sidney Poitier movie based on Barrett's book. What's more, the book's theme was not changed in conversion to celluloid: Trust in God for life's necessities. He provides for the birds of the air. He clothes the flowers of the field. And are you not much more important in the scheme than they?

The lilies of the field may be taken to represent all objects of beauty neither planted nor tended by humans. So Matthew 6:28 says, "Consider the lilies of the field, how they grow; they toil not, neither do they spin." And, in verse 29, "Even Solomon in all his glory was not arrayed like one of these."

the **lines are fallen unto me in pleasant places**
Psalm 16:6
I have received good treatment at the hands of God

Those who feel life has been good to them may say along with the psalmist, "The lines are fallen unto me in pleasant places; yea, I have a goodly heritage." In the literal sense the psalmist means, I have been allotted a fair amount of land, as measured off by surveyors' lines. While he was speaking especially of the happiness he found in his relationship with God, he was not unaware that life had been good to him in a material sense. The argument in favor of the latter inference stems from his use of the line metaphor. Poor people don't need surveyors' lines.

Wouldn't it be wonderful if all of us were fortunate enough to own or inherit fertile land?

the **little foxes**
Song of Solomon 2:15
flies in the ointment

Chapter 2 of the Song of Solomon, rich in imagery, has been a mother lode for writers in search of titles. Lillian Hellman called one of her plays *The Little Foxes*; Peter De Vries looked to verse 5 in calling his novel *Comfort Me with Apples*; John Van Druten went to verse 12 for the title of his romantic comedy *The Voice of the Turtle*; and Dalton Trumbo for his 1945 screenplay based on a novel by George Victor followed Victor's lead in verse 15 and came up with *Our Vines Have Tender Grapes*.

Now consider verse 15 in its entirety: "Take us the foxes, the little foxes, that spoil the vines: for our vines have tender grapes." Scholars have long regarded the Song of Solomon as a collection of songs on themes appropriate to marriage festivities. The vines are thought to symbolize a maiden's physical charms—tender grapes indeed—and the little foxes anything that can spoil young love. In Hellman's play, set during the rise of industrialism following the end of the Civil

War, the little foxes are the ruthless new breed of rapacious southerners that arose at that time.
See VOICE OF THE TURTLE.

a **little leaven**
I Corinthians 5:6
a corrupting influence
See A LITTLE LEAVEN LEAVENETH THE WHOLE LUMP.

live by the sword, die by the sword
Matthew 26:51–53
those who hurt others will themselves be hurt

Matthew 26:51 says that when Jesus was about to be arrested, an unnamed disciple standing near Jesus "drew his sword, and struck a servant of the high priest's, and smote off his ear." In the next verse, Jesus stopped him from doing further harm, saying, "Put up again thy sword into his place: for all they that take the sword shall perish with the sword." This account has long been cited both as the ultimate argument for Christian pacifism and as an example of the unrealistic attitude that prayer (verse 53) is mightier than the sword, leaving us with two unanswered questions: Does war ever achieve its promised goal of peace? Do seemingly good ends justify evil means?

Both problems are alive and well today.
See DOUBLE-EDGED SWORD.

a **living dog is better than a dead lion**
Ecclesiastes 9:4
where there's life, there's hope

The text of Ecclesiastes 9 makes plain its writer's view that eventually we all end up dead. Yet verse 4 softens the lesson: "To him that is joined to all the living there is hope: for a living dog is better than a dead lion." Never mind that yours is a dog's life. It's better than death, isn't it? So enjoy life to the extent you can while you still have the chance.

loaves and fishes
Mark 6:41
a metaphor for the help given by God

In church art "the five loaves and the two fishes" symbolize the new age of divine abundance. In Mark 6, Jesus multiplied these scanty provisions of the disciples so they became enough to feed five thousand men. This was the miracle of the loaves and the fishes. A similar miracle, referred to as the multiplication of grain and ascribed to Elisha, is reported in II Kings 4:42–44.

locusts and wild honey
Mark 1:6
the roughest of foods

Locusts and wild honey were not a new diet for those quick to follow nutritional fads; they were the food John the Baptist is said to have eaten. Incidentally, the ascetic John was not the only one who ate locusts. In biblical times, many nomadic people ate them—dried, not fresh.

For contrast, *see* MILK AND HONEY.

looking on a woman with lust
Matthew 5:28
adultery of the eyes

When Jimmy Carter ran successfully for the presidency in 1976, he demonstrated his knowledge of Matthew 5:28:

"Whosoever looketh on a woman to lust after her hath committed adultery with her already in his heart." In the October 1976 issue of *Playboy* magazine, celebrated in its time, Carter was quoted as saying, "I've looked on a lot of women with lust. I've committed adultery in my heart many times." This so-called adultery of the eyes is an example of the intent of Jesus to transfer sinfulness from observable acts to wrong desires. So lust, not adultery alone, is sinful; anger, not violence alone, is sinful. Incidentally, Carter went on in the interview to say of his adultery of the eyes, "This is something that God recognizes I will do—and I have done it—and God forgives me for it."

Good to know this.

loose the bands of Orion
Job 38:31
accomplish the impossible

God, by way of contrasting his majesty with the insignificance of Job, a mere mortal, posed this rhetorical question: "Canst thou bind the sweet influences of Pleiades, or loose the bands of Orion?" We still see the constellation Orion as a hunter wearing a belt and carrying a sword, so in "loose the bands of Orion," the allusion is to the stars that form Orion's belt, or band. And what about the "sweet influences of Pleiades"? According to the ancient Greeks, the first appearance of these stars in the sky each year presaged good sailing. So both metaphors hold up.

Could Job prevent the clustered stars known as the Pleiades from rising, or scatter the stars of Orion? Come now!

the **Lord bless thee and keep thee**
Numbers 6:24–26
the core of a blessing heard in synagogues and churches
   all over the world

From this blessing come the "God bless you" and "Bless you" so often uttered when a friend sneezes or when people take leave of one another. (And when people say "Goodbye," the word they use is a centuries-old contraction of "God be with ye.") While most of us may say such words without giving thought to their original intent, in speaking them we are invoking divine protection or favor for those we love. In Numbers, God gave Moses this form for the blessings of God: "The Lord bless thee, and keep thee: The Lord make his face shine upon thee, and be gracious unto thee: The Lord lift up his countenance upon thee, and give thee peace."

What could be better?

the **Lord gave, and the Lord hath taken away**
Job 1:21
the ultimate expression of resignation supported by
    unshattered faith in God

These are the words uttered so often in the face of devastating loss of family or property. When Job's wife, children, and servants, along with all Job's possessions, were suddenly wiped out by fire and storm, Job fell to the ground and prayed: "Naked came I out of my mother's womb, and naked shall I return thither: the Lord gave and the Lord hath taken away; blessed be the name of the Lord." In orthodox Jewish families, verse 21 is still intoned when a loved one dies.

See SATAN CAME ALSO AMONG THEM.

the **Lord is my shepherd**
Psalm 23:1–2
a profound statement of trust

From beginning to end, this most familiar and beloved psalm resonates in the minds of all who are familiar with it. The Israelites were nomadic shepherds for centuries before settling in Canaan to pursue an agricultural life. But the raising of sheep continued in less fertile parts of the country, and shepherds knew where the best grasses and the most likely sources of water were to be found in a land of long, hot, rainless summers. The shepherds guarded their flocks against wild animals, rounding up strays and giving them comfort. So the metaphor of God as shepherd is readily understandable: "The Lord is my shepherd; I shall not want. He maketh me to lie down in green pastures: he leadeth me beside the still waters."

Theatergoers with some years on them will recall Marc Connelly's marvelous biblical fantasy of the 1930 season, *The Green Pastures*.

lost sheep
Matthew 10:6
those who depart from religious orthodoxy

In this verse from Matthew, Jesus instructed his disciples, who were about to go out to proselytize, "Go rather to the lost sheep of the house of Israel." He was speaking of the common people—regarded as unclean by reason of their occupations, looked down upon by the Pharisees for less than strict observance of God's law, and so the people whom Jesus wanted most to reach. Lost sheep today also include those who deviate from the party line.

What is there about sheep that makes them rich pickings for lasting metaphor? Consider, among others, "black sheep" and "wolves in sheep's clothing." At Yale, of course, we have Rudyard Kipling's whiffenpoofed "poor little lambs who have lost our way. . .little black sheep who have gone astray," echoing Isaiah 53:6, "All we like sheep have gone astray; we have turned every one to his own way." This last is taken as an acknowledgment of the sinfulness of all humanity. In similar fashion, Jeremiah 50:6 relates, "My people hath been lost sheep: their shepherds have caused them to go astray. . .they have forgotten their restingplace." It is clear that the people of Israel, originally nomadic shepherds who well knew the stupidity and waywardness of sheep, were wont to draw on ovine inspiration for appropriate metaphor.

See SHEEP'S CLOTHING.

love is strong as death
Song of Solomon 8:6
maybe

Certainly no garden-variety metaphor for love, yet who can imagine anything as strong as death? In the midst of a long paean to romantic love, or perhaps to God's love for his people, the Song of Solomon gives us, "Love is strong as death; jealousy is cruel as the grave."

Need anyone be reminded that death and the grave continue to bat 1.000 in life's ball game?

love is the fulfilling of the law
Romans 13:10
love of God is essential

The law referred to here is the Ten Commandments, conveyed by Moses to his people. Paul restated most of the commandments, ending with "Thou shalt love thy neighbor as thyself." Then, by way of summary, he said in verse 10, "Love worketh no ill to his neighbor; therefore love is the fulfilling of the law." Law by itself, said Paul, won't work as a means of salvation. Trying to live by its dictates alone leads to despair or excessive pride. Only love for God combined with love for friend and foe and love in all personal relations can make law work.
See LOVE THY NEIGHBOR.

love of money is the root of all evil
I Timothy 6:10
avarice will get you every time
See FILTHY LUCRE.

love thy neighbor
Mark 12:30–31
need one say more?

In verses 30–31 Jesus combined the precept of Leviticus 19:-18, "Thou shalt love thy neighbor as thyself," with that of

Deuteronomy 6:4, "The Lord our God is one Lord," and went on to give the precepts more prominence: "There is none other commandment greater than these." To Hillel (c.60 B.C.–A.D. 9?), an authority on the interpretation of biblical law, is attributed "What you would not have done to yourself, do not do to your neighbor. That is the whole Torah, and all the rest is commentary."

love your enemies
Matthew 5:44
yes, even your enemies

Love of one's neighbor is prescribed in Leviticus 19:16–18 and extended in verse 34 to include foreigners residing in Palestine. But love your enemies? Nothing in Jewish law went as far as Jesus did in Matthew 5:44, a passage from the Sermon on the Mount: "Love your enemies, bless them that curse you, do good to them that hate you, and pray for them which despitefully use you, and persecute you."

Diplomats spend much time debating the banning of chemical warfare, control of nuclear weapons, and the like. Presumably, they will one day get around to discussing love of one's enemies.

Lucifer
Isaiah 14:12
the morning star; more recently, Satan
See HOW ART THOU FALLEN FROM HEAVEN, O LUCIFER.

M

make it plain upon tables
Habakkuk 2:2
read my lips

Habakkuk, a hesitant prophet, had put a question to God. "And the Lord answered me, and said, Write the vision, and make it plain upon tables, that he may run that readeth it." The "tables" were tablets, like those on which the Ten Commandments had been given, and the injunction "that he may run that readeth it" required that the answer be readable at a glance. And what was the answer to be made so plain? Verse 4 supplies it: "Behold, his soul which is lifted up is not upright in him: but the just shall live by his faith." You say you cannot read this at a glance? True, the King James translators were not at their best when they studied this verse in the Hebrew. Its meaning is that those who are evil will not survive, but those who are righteous will, by reason of their faithfulness.

Pass the word.

make light of
Matthew 22:5
treat as of no consequence

In Jesus' parable of the wedding feast, Matthew 22:1–14, the guests who were invited to the wedding of the king's daughter "made light of it, and went their ways, one to his farm, another to his merchandise." That is, they blithely decided not to show up. Too busy with their own petty affairs, they failed to consider how this rejection would affect the king and the young couple.

Be advised, verse 7, that "when the king heard thereof, he was wroth," and the outcome for the no-shows was bloody.

For Luke's account of a remarkably similar parable, but with a less violent ending, *see* HALT AND THE BLIND.

make whole
Mark 5:25–34
cure

In Mark 5, Jesus cured a woman who was afflicted with chronic hemorrhaging. Believing that physical contact with a healer would help her, she touched Jesus' garment while he stood among the crowd. When she said it was she who had done so, Jesus gave her his blessing: "Daughter, thy faith hath made thee whole; go in peace, and be whole of thy plague." And she was well again. The curative effect of faith is a key element in modern theories of faith healing. And faith, to Jesus, was the precondition of healing.

See BARTIMAEUS.

male and female created he them
Genesis 1:27
but did God intend that they not be equal?

In Babylonian writings, the sex element existed before the cosmos was organized, and it served as the primal creative force. In the Old Testament, God is nowhere explicitly associated with either sex. But what are we to think about his human creations? According to the account in Genesis 1:27, male and female humans were created at the same time. But Genesis 2:21–22 gives a different account: The female was made from the rib of the male. Did the author of 1:27 believe that only one pair of humans was created at the beginning, or that numbers of humans were created, as with the animals in 1:24–25? Nothing in 1:27 favors either view, nor does anything in 2:7 or 2:18–23 cast light on the possibility that more than one pair were created at the beginning. Further, in 1:27, where "male and female created he them" first appears, there is no implication of inferior social status for the female or of a wife's subordination to her husband. Genesis 1:27 is a plain statement that God created a sexual differentiation, and the context shows that both sexes were regarded as his special creatures.

Since advocates of male/female equality/superiority can all

quote Scripture to their purpose, the argument continues unabated.

a **man after one's own heart**
I Samuel 13:14
someone whose intent or purpose matches one's own

A presidential candidate who wants a vice president after his or her own heart will look for a running mate among people with comparable views and attitudes. "A man after his own heart" appeared in Scripture when the prophet Samuel broke the bad news that Saul would be replaced as king: "The Lord hath sought him a man after his own heart, and the Lord hath commanded him to be captain over his people, because thou has not kept that which the Lord commanded thee." Saul—not a man after the Lord's own heart—had made the mistake of offering a sacrifice on behalf of the nation's army that only Samuel, the nation's spiritual leader, was empowered to offer.

The king who replaced Saul turned out to be David, who was a man after the Lord's own heart.

man in the image of God
Genesis 1:26–27
like God in essential ways

This idea, given first expression in Genesis 1:26–27, is echoed in Genesis 5:1–3 and 9:1–6. Whether "the image of God" is to be taken literally or as a spiritual abstraction has been much debated by Bible scholars. To some, the literal interpretation seems obvious in 1:27, where God says, "Let us make man in our image, after our likeness." Notwithstanding, many moderns find a spiritual interpretation more congenial.

The Bible as a whole sees humans as distinct from and superior to other creatures, and thus as having been given a share in God's own dignity. Humans also have the possibility of responding to God, of having a relationship with him. They have freedom of choice, self-awareness, personality. Perhaps it is in this sense that mankind was created in the image of God.

man is born into trouble
Job 5:6–7
don't bother to look for trouble—it will find you

A bit of wisdom from Job so often cited that it has become a cliché. Even the most casual reading of our newspapers, which thrive on detailed reports of crimes, misfortunes, and accidents, seems to confirm that too many of us are born into trouble. In the Bible, a well-intentioned friend felt impelled to offer counsel on the source of Job's multiple problems: "Although affliction cometh not forth of the dust, neither doth trouble spring out of the ground; Yet man is born unto [now "into"] trouble, as the sparks fly upward." The precise meaning of this observation, like a great deal of Scripture, is open to interpretation. Is trouble a natural, unavoidable part of life? Do people—Job, for example—bring trouble on themselves? Should they blame others? Should they blame God? We are nowhere near the end of discussion on this one.

Stay tuned. Film at eleven.

manna
Exodus 16:15
a metaphor for God's providence, also given as "manna from heaven"

The Israelites, starving in the wilderness, awoke one morning to find mysterious pellets on the ground. The material they found was manna, and Moses told them, "This is the bread which the Lord hath given you to eat." As explained in Numbers 11:7–8, "The manna was as coriander seed" and after grinding or pounding could be baked into cakes.

manner of man
James 1:22
See BE DOERS, NOT HEARERS ONLY

man of God
I Kings 17:24
a holy person

"Man of God" today may be applied to any—well, almost any—clergyman. In biblical times, a man of God was any devout or holy person, especially a prophet, or in the Christian tradition, a saint. In I Kings, after Elijah had brought back to life the son of a widow, she said to the prophet, "Now by this I know that thou art a man of God, and that the word of the Lord in thy mouth is true."

man of sorrows
Isaiah 53:3
anyone who has suffered loneliness, pain, or profound grief

Isaiah's characterization "He is despised and rejected of men; a man of sorrows, and acquainted with grief" has been interpreted in two ways. Jews see it as a metaphor for the suffering people of Israel, and Christians see it as predictive of Jesus Christ. If the latter interpretation is the correct one, at the very least we can say, Not bad going for Isaiah, which probably was written more than six hundred years before the first books of the New Testament.

man of strife, man of contention
Jeremiah 15:10
one destined to be unpopular

Today we are apt to say of someone that he or she was born into trouble (in Job 5:7, "born unto trouble") with the implication that we are dealing with anything ranging from Peck's bad boy to a felon guilty of terrible crimes. But how did Jeremiah see himself? "Woe is me, my mother, that thou hast borne me a man of strife and a man of contention to the whole earth! I have neither lent on usury, nor men have lent to me on usury; yet every one of them doth curse me." Let's see whether this matter can be put into perspective. Jeremiah had been told by God to serve as bearer of the bad news that his people were in for very hard times, and Jeremiah agonized over his assigned task. It seemed to him he was fated to be unpopular, at times even the object of persecution.

Was Jeremiah a bit paranoid? Consider how long a so-called spokesperson for the White House would last if he or she dared say on TV, "A depression is on the way. Sell dollars. Buy gold!"

See MAN IS BORN INTO TROUBLE.

man shall not live by bread alone
Matthew 4:4
spiritual matters surpass material considerations in
    importance

Applied to the rest of us, this statement encourages active search for something higher in life than mere survival. Jesus had just completed forty days and forty nights of fasting when the devil came to tempt him to turn stones into bread. In rejecting the request, Jesus answered, "Man shall not live by bread alone, but by every word that proceedeth out of the mouth of God." Jesus was quoting Deuteronomy 8:3 almost verbatim: "Man doth not live by bread only, but by every word that proceedeth out of the mouth of the Lord doth man live."

man that is born of woman
Job 14:1–2
everybody

By way of indicating our mortality, the universal human condition, Job said, "Man that is born of a woman is of few days, and full of trouble. He cometh forth like a flower, and is cut down: he fleeth also as a shadow, and continueth not." Given that we are all born of woman and are therefore mortal, is it really consoling to contemplate the fact that every flower will soon be cut down and every shadow will disappear? We can, however, take comfort in reading one of the great poems of world literature, Job 14:1–32.

man upright
Ecclesiastes 7:29
the way we are at birth

Most people start out in life as upright citizens, but somewhere along the line too many of them manage to outsmart
themselves. The writer of Ecclesiastes 7:29 said, "This only
have I found, that God hath made man upright; but they
[humans] have sought out many inventions." While the syn-
tax of this verse may appear anything but straightforward,
there is simple wisdom for all of us here: People need no help
in finding a way to fudge their responsibilities.

the **man whom the king delighteth to honor**
Esther 6:6
a trap for a person too taken with himself

Haman, a powerful member of the court of King Ahasuerus
of Persia, was called before the king. Haman at the time was
plotting to murder Mordecai, a Jew who earlier had saved the
king's life. When Haman arrived, the king asked him, "What
shall be done unto the man whom the king delighteth to
honor?" Haman, certain that the king was speaking of him,
responded at once with a recital of all kinds of extravagant
honors appropriate to such a man. And the king went along
with Haman's ideas—but he rewarded Mordecai, not Haman.
     The moral of the tale is obvious, but too many of us remain
captives of self-pride and forget to listen carefully before
spouting off.

many are called, but few are chosen
Matthew 20:16
many hear the message, but few respond with a
     commitment
See BORNE THE BURDEN AND THE HEAT OF THE DAY.

many as the sand
I Kings 4:20
beyond counting

A section of I Kings 4 concerning the splendor of Israel and the reign of Solomon begins with these words: "Judah and Israel were many, as the sand which is by the sea in multitude, eating and drinking, and making merry." In short, the people of the united kingdoms of Judah and Israel were experiencing good times.

many shall come in my name
Mark 13:6
a condemnation of false messiahs

Jesus was asked by his disciples when the destruction of the Temple would occur and what signs would first be given. Jesus replied, "Many shall come in my name"—many false messiahs, that is—"saying, I am Christ; and shall deceive many." And, Jesus said, "Ye shall hear of wars and rumors of wars."
See WARS AND RUMORS OF WARS.

many that are first shall be last
Matthew 19:30
everything will be put aright

What are seen as injustices on earth will be rectified, according to this proverbial response by Jesus to a question put by Peter: "But many that are first shall be last; and the last shall be first." In Mark 10:31, the line from Matthew is found again, teaching that in the kingdom of God all judgments of worth and evaluations of people will be the reverse of earthly judgments. Those who have passed the test of renunciation and have loyally followed Jesus will rate higher in the eyes of God than those who were great on earth.

So don't give up—it ain't over till the fat lady sings.

many waters cannot quench love
Psalm 42:7
love conquers all
See DEEP CALLETH UNTO DEEP.

mark of Cain
Genesis 4:10–15
a protecting sign

So strongly has Cain impressed himself upon our culture that people are still said to "raise Cain" when they create a disturbance, and the "mark of Cain" is thought to signify a murderer, just as the letter *A* signified adultery in Hawthorne's *The Scarlet Letter*. Genesis 4:10–15 does not support that view of the mark of Cain. Upon his murder of Abel, Cain became the first fratricide, indeed the first murderer of any kind. As punishment, God banished Cain from his homeland, condemning him to a life of wandering. When Cain complained that the punishment was too severe, God put "a mark upon Cain," presumably some kind of tattoo on the forehead. Thus marked, Cain would be recognized from then on as under God's protection and so would not be punished further. No double jeopardy here!

The subsequent use of "mark of Cain" to identify a murderer is nonetheless understandable, since in the New Testament and in the writings of the Christian church fathers, Cain came to represent the forces of evil.

See EDEN *and* MORE THAN I CAN BEAR.

mene, mene, tekel, upharsin
Daniel 5:25
The handwriting on the wall: numbered, weighed, and
    divided—you've had it

And what were the words written on the wall? *Mene, mene, tekel, upharsin*.

To this day, many people recall and respond to the intent of these strange words, and theatergoers with good memories remember a Depression-era show called *Pins and Needles* and one of its songs, "Mene, Mene, Tekel, Upharsin." Daniel 5 tells of a feast given by Belshazzar, king of Babylon, at which these words were written on a wall by a hand not attached to an arm. But what did they mean? No one at the feast knew. Babylonian wise men were called in, but they could not even identify the language in which the words were written. The call went out for Daniel, an Israelite in captivity in Babylon who could interpret dreams and solve riddles. He identified the words as Aramaic and interpreted the message as "numbered, weighed, and divided," meaning that God has numbered Belshazzar's days, weighed him, found him wanting, and divided his kingdom. Rembrandt's painting of this scene makes it clear that all present became greatly agitated—and who wouldn't?

What happened next? The Book of Daniel says that on the very night of the banquet, Belshazzar was slain. And what happened to Babylon? Historians tell us that in 539 B.C., the year of Belshazzar's death, Cyrus, king of Persia, brought Babylon down. Belshazzar was thus the last ruler of Babylon—*mene, mene, tekel, upharsin*.

merchant princes
Isaiah 23:8
wealthy men of commerce
See TYRE, WHOSE MERCHANTS ARE PRINCES.

mess of pottage
a bad bargain

"Mess of pottage" is one of those phrases that do not occur in the Bible yet invariably evoke Scripture when used. In the account of Jacob and his twin brother, Esau (Genesis 25:25–34), Jacob said to Esau, "Swear to me this day; and he sware unto him: and he sold his birthright unto Jacob. Then Jacob gave Esau bread and pottage of lentiles; and he did eat and drink, and rose up, and went his way." So Esau relinquished to Jacob all his rights by birth in exchange for some lentil soup, and a "mess of pottage" stands to this day as a phrase denoting a pittance accepted in return for something of great value.

The word "mess" is of interest. As used here, in a sense not often seen any more, the word denotes a prepared dish of food, generally liquid or partly liquid.

See VOICE IS JACOB'S VOICE.

Methuselah
Genesis 5:26–27
the biblical personification of longevity

And why not? If arithmetic can be trusted, Methuselah died when he was 969 years old. Having begat a son, Lamech, at age 187, Methuselah went on to live another 782 years "and begat sons and daughters." Lamech, who begat Noah, lived a mere 777 years. Whatever else Lamech and Methuselah did is not mentioned in Scripture, but think of how boring it would be to read *Winnie-the-Pooh* aloud to generation after generation of little boys and girls.

For what Noah did with his time, *see* FORTY DAYS AND FORTY NIGHTS.

milk and honey
Exodus 3:8
food aplenty

Milk and honey, delectable items in the diet of the semino-madic Israelites, symbolize the ample provender available in the promised land, a rich and fertile place. Exodus 3:2–3 introduced the memorable burning bush that was not consumed by its own fire. Succeeding verses dealt with God's instructions to Moses concerning his people, who were captive in Egypt. And in verse 8 God said, "I am come down to deliver them out of the hand of the Egyptians, and to bring them up out of that land unto a good land and a large, unto a land flowing with milk and honey." The promised land, of course, was Canaan, later called Palestine. And "land of milk and honey" survives to this day in the English language with its biblical meaning intact but the identity of the land changing from time to time.

See BURNING BUSH, LOCUSTS AND WILD HONEY, PROMISED LAND, *and* SWEETER THAN HONEY.

millstone around one's neck
Mark 9:42
a great weight

In everyday use, a millstone around one's neck is any terribly heavy burden, whether emotional, mental, or financial. The phrase is most often applied to a troublesome friend or family member who can't be shaken off, but in Mark 9:42 a millstone is a heavy circular stone used to grind grain. Jesus said, "Whosoever shall offend one of these little ones that believe in me, it is better for him that a millstone were hanged about his neck, and he were cast into the sea." Anyone so encumbered—recall the phrase "concrete kimono"—and so disposed of would surely end up dead.

In the more sanguine phrase "these little ones," Jesus was referring to all children and adults who had listened to his message.

miserable comforters
Job 16:2–3
with friends like these, who needs enemies?

Three of Job's friends, seeing him suffering, came to offer comfort. But they soon began to accuse him of assorted wrongdoings, including excessive pride and animosity toward God. When Job could listen no longer, he went on the offensive, launching his diatribe with these words: "Miserable comforters are ye all. Shall vain words have an end?"

That's telling them.

molten images are wind and confusion
Isaiah 41:6
ineffectual heathen idols
See GOLDEN CALF *and* THEY HELPED EVERY ONE HIS
NEIGHBOR.

moneychangers
Mark 11:15–17
dealers in currency

Moneychangers earn their livelihood by exchanging currency of one country for that of another. In modern usage, the term is usually pejorative, probably because of the accounts in Mark 11 and Matthew 21 of how Jesus drove the moneychangers out of the Temple. But some of this is a bum rap. In biblical times, in a cosmopolitan city such as Jerusalem, where Roman, Greek, Persian, Syrian, Arabian, and Tyrian money circulated, moneychangers filled an economic need. Especially at the times of major festivals, they would set themselves up for business in the outer court of the Temple to ply their trade among Jewish pilgrims who came to worship from places far away and brought with them foreign coins. The pilgrims were obliged to pay an annual Temple tax of half a shekel, but it had to be paid in certain Tyrian silver coins. The moneychangers exchanged foreign currencies for these coins and charged a fee for their service, which included assuming the risk that the coins they supplied would satisfy Temple authorities.

In Mark 11:15 "Jesus went into the temple, and began to cast out them that sold and bought in the temple, and overthrew the tables of the moneychangers." In verse 17 Jesus said that the house of prayer had been turned into a noisy bazaar, "a den of thieves." Presumably, he would not have objected if the exchange of currency had been carried on less noisily outside the Temple gates.
See DEN OF THIEVES.

more blessed to give than to receive
Acts 20:35
help those who need help
See IT IS MORE BLESSED TO GIVE THAN TO RECEIVE.

more than I can bear
Genesis 4:13
an overpowering emotional burden

Words that may be uttered by anyone who suffers the devastating loss of someone close, particularly of a son or daughter. The phrase is an allusion to the account of Cain's punishment in Genesis 4:12–13. Cain was told by God he had to pay dearly for the murder of his brother, Abel: "A fugitive and a vagabond shalt thou be in the earth. And Cain said unto the Lord, My punishment is greater than I can bear."
    At least God was no hanging judge.
See MARK OF CAIN.

a **mote in the eye**
Matthew 7:3
a trifling fault in another perceived by someone who
    overlooks his or her own greater faults

Matthew 7 begins with Jesus' condemnation of hypocrisy: "Judge not, that ye be not judged." In verse 3 Jesus asked, "Why beholdest thou the mote that is in thy brother's eye, but considerest not the beam that is in thine own eye?" The message is clear: Work on your own faults before offering advice to improve others.

moth and rust corrupt
Matthew 6:19
a metaphor for the futility of putting one's faith in
    worldly goods

In this verse from Matthew, Jesus said, "Lay not up for yourselves treasures upon earth, where moth and rust doth corrupt, and where thieves break through and steal."

mouth of fools
Proverbs 15:2
a source of thoughtless words that can lead to trouble
See A SOFT ANSWER TURNETH AWAY WRATH.

mouths that speak not
Psalm 135:15–17
mouths of idols

The psalmist gives us striking examples of God's wondrous acts but then goes on to tell us that God will one day sit in judgment. And then we had all better watch out. God finds particularly abhorrent the idols of the heathen: "They have mouths, but they speak not; eyes have they, but they see not; They have ears, but they hear not; neither is there any breath in their mouths. They that make them are like unto them; so is every one that trusteth in them." All this by way of reconfirming the Old Testament injunction against making or praying to any type of religious effigy. As Exodus 20:5 decisively says, "Thou shalt not make unto thee any graven image, or any likeness of any thing that is in heaven above."

Clear enough?

much learning doth make thee mad
Acts 26:24
a misconception popular among those of little learning
   who put small store in learning

Paul was arguing his case before Agrippa, king of a Roman administrative district in northern Palestine, who had been consulted by Festus, the Roman governor in Caesarea. Paul took pains to explain his apocalyptic version of Judaism and his own conversion, but Festus understood very little. In frustration, "Festus said with a loud voice, Paul, thou art beside thyself; much learning doth make thee mad."

What Festus meant was that Paul's learning was far beyond the ken of Festus.

See THING NOT DONE IN A CORNER.

multitude of sins
I Peter 4:8
a normal daily quota for too many of us
See CHARITY SHALL COVER THE MULTITUDE OF SINS.

muzzle the ox
Deuteronomy 26:4
let people have a little fun

Deuteronomy teaches a humane lesson: Do not deprive ordinary people of the few pleasures they have that make their lives livable. Since domesticated animals do much for their masters, and can't tell right from wrong, Deuteronomy cautioned against begrudging the dumb creatures an occasional mouthful or two of a farmer's crop: "Thou shalt not muzzle the ox when he treadeth out the corn."

Just so should we not deprive people of harmless enjoyment.

my beloved is mine
Song of Solomon 2:16
love given, love shared

Words describing the joy of love and commitment between man and woman. Yet another entry in the Song of Solomon's lexicon of love: "My beloved is mine, and I am his: he feedeth among the lilies."

See SONG OF SONGS.

N

naked came I out of the womb
Job 1:21
I had nothing when I was born
See LORD GAVE, AND THE LORD HATH TAKEN AWAY.

a **new heaven and a new earth**
Revelation 21:1
a vision of a new and better future

The opening verse of Revelation 21 relates a vision: "I saw a new heaven and a new earth: for the first heaven and the first earth were passed away; and there was no more sea." Alas, the old universe had proven unworthy and unredeemable and had been destroyed by fire. It had given way to an entirely new one, created by God to his own liking, where God would dwell among human beings and the righteous would be granted eternal life.

This, at least, was the vision.

new Jerusalem
Revelation 21:2
the perfect society

According to this visionary verse, "And I John saw the holy city, new Jerusalem, coming down from God out of heaven, prepared as a bride adorned for her husband."

Fresh and clean and beautiful.

new wine in old bottles
Mark 2:22
don't tell people more than they can absorb

A metaphor calling attention to the error of imposing power-ful new practices or principles on people or institutions too old or too set in their ways to withstand the strain. Jesus, perceiving the ideological tension his new teachings were causing within the Judaism prevalent in his time, sought to make his disciples aware of what they were up against. Giving the same message recounted in Matthew 9:17, Jesus in Mark 2 instructed his disciples not to waste effort on trying to force new ways of thinking on those completely wedded to out-moded ideas. The metaphor he used drew on his listeners' knowledge of winemaking: "And no man putteth new wine into old bottles: else the new wine doth burst the bottles, and the wine is spilled, and the bottles will be marred: but new wine must be put into new bottles." And it is true, if not of used wine bottles, then surely of used wineskins—the King James translators did not do well by us here—that they will not be able to withstand the pressure created by fermenting wine.

Mark 2:21 and Matthew 9:16 employ yet another metaphor to offer the same message. In Mark, Jesus said, "No man also seweth a piece of new cloth on an old garment: else the new piece that filled it up taketh away from the old, and the rent is made worse." Like all outstanding metaphors, "new cloth on an old garment" is soundly based and rooted in everyday experience. A newly woven, unshrunk patch will pull away from the edges of old material.

nimrod
Genesis 10:8–9
a hunter

A term today familiar primarily to hunters, denoting an ex-pert or a devotee of the sport. In the midst of the begats of Genesis 10, it is said of Nimrod, here designated the great-grandson of Noah, "He was a mighty hunter before the Lord." That is, he had a great reputation.

no continuing city
Hebrews 13:14
surely there is something better than what we have

Seemingly, the greater the oppression people suffer, the more they hold to the expectation that better times lie ahead. In Hebrews 13:14, the writer has had enough of the materialism and impermanence of the life about him: "Here we have no continuing city, but we seek one to come." He yearned for something better.

the **noise of many waters**
Psalm 93:4
a metaphor for conflicting opinions

The phrase may be applied to opinions expressed on any subject, but particularly on matters vital to the public interest. Consider, for example, the gems of pro-and-con wisdom delivered nightly on radio and TV programs featuring discussions of everything from legalized abortion to capital punishment to gun control to peace formulas for the Middle East. The psalmist tells us God is powerful. Indeed, "The Lord on high is mightier than the noise of many waters, yea, than the mighty waves of the sea."
Hard to match that.

no need of the physician
Mark 2:17
a metaphor characterizing those who live righteous lives

Those who require no advice or assistance may be said to have no need of the physician. Those who do must be given that help. When Jesus was asked why he consorted with "publicans and sinners," he replied, "They that are whole have no need of the physician, but they that are sick: I came not to call the righteous, but sinners to repentance."

Anyone who wishes to help people in need must go where such people can be found. Derelicts frequent Skid Row, not Wall Street.

See FRIEND OF PUBLICANS AND SINNERS.

no peace for the wicked
Isaiah 57:20–21
no rest for those who worship idols

Not a troubling thought for the rest of us, who are, of course, good and law-abiding. But how about the wicked? In verse 3 Isaiah called the idolators within Israel "sons of the sorceress, the seed of the adulterer and the whore." Finally, in verses 20 and 21, he wrote, "The wicked are like the troubled sea, when it cannot rest, whose waters cast up mire and dirt. There is no peace, saith my God, to the wicked."

No wonder so many of us play by the rules.

no place to lay my head
Matthew 8:20
no resting place

"Lay" here means "rest," and a homeless person who says, "I have no place to lay my head" means he is condemned to sleeping not in a proper bed of his own but wherever he can find a temporary resting place. Jesus in this verse was responding to a scribe who offered to go with him as his disciple: "The foxes have holes, and the birds of the air have nests; but the Son of man hath not where to lay his head." Jesus was warning the scribe that life as his disciple would be no bed of roses.

no respect of persons with God
Romans 2:10–11
divine impartiality

Paul explained that God plays no favorites, makes no distinctions between peoples in judging human beings. He brings "glory, honor, and peace to every man that worketh good, to the Jew first, and also to the Gentile." Paul went on to say, "For there is no respect of persons with God."

Are we mortals capable of such impartiality?

no room at the inn
Luke 2:7
no room in your heart for those in need

Even now, with the twentieth century drawing to a close, it appears that in the country that thinks of itself as the most caring of all nations, there is no room at the inn for millions of children or for their parents. Joseph and Mary had journeyed to Bethlehem, Joseph's ancestral birthplace, presumably to register for a Roman census, and Mary was about to give birth. Travel accommodations were not plentiful, and there was no place available for the couple. They had to make do with the corner of a stable. Many a preacher has used the unadorned, poignant statement from Luke, "There was no room for them in the inn," as a parable of the human conscience: Is there room in your heart for a savior or for people in need?

not by might, nor by power
Zechariah 4:6
human might counts for little without spiritual
    commitment

A reminder that we are not solely responsible for whatever success each of us achieves. An angel was asked by the prophet Zechariah to explain a vision in which appeared a golden candlestick with a bowl on it, along with seven lamps, seven pipes, and four olive trees. The angel replied, "This is the word of the Lord unto Zerubbabel, saying, Not by might, nor by power, but by my spirit, saith the Lord of hosts." And who was Zerubbabel? The driving force behind the project to restore the Temple. Thus, one may take the elaborate candlestick to be the Temple, and the message from God to mean that the project was accomplished not by human efforts but by divine power.

At the same time, let us not think that great things can be accomplished on earth without the work of people.

nothing is impossible
Luke 1:36–37
faith can move mountains

With biological clocks ticking away inexorably, women who worry about whether they will ever bear children may find hope in these words. In Luke 1 the angel Gabriel had a fateful conversation with Mary, telling her in verse 31, "Thou shalt conceive in thy womb, and bring forth a son." In verses 36–37, Gabriel related how Mary's cousin Elizabeth, thought to be barren, conceived in her old age. And Gabriel said, "For with God nothing shall be impossible." A similar promise was made to a mother of advanced age in Genesis 18:14—to Sarah, wife of Abraham—and the corresponding words were, "Is any thing too hard for the Lord?" But both Luke and Genesis emphasize that faith is essential.

See also ALL THINGS ARE POSSIBLE.

nothing new under the sun
Ecclesiastes 1:9
everything repeats itself

Anyone who follows the announcements of the U.S. Patent Office or news reports of our rapidly developing sciences must be skeptical of this thought from Ecclesiastes: "The thing that hath been, it is that which shall be; and that which is done is that which shall be done; and there is no new thing under the sun." Continuing the theme of earlier portions of this chapter, verse 9 tells us that all things repeat themselves in nature and in human life, and anything that seems to be new is just a rerun.

Of the thought that there is nothing new under the sun, a commentator said, "And this too is not new."

See VANITY OF VANITIES.

not peace, but a sword
Matthew 10:34
a metaphor for tough measures that must be taken

In this verse from Matthew, Jesus said, "Think not that I am come to send peace on earth: I came not to send peace, but a sword." His intention was to make it plain that his mission would cause tension, struggle, and divisions within families and societies, as well as persecution of his followers.

But the results will be worth all the pain.

number of the beast
Revelation 13:11–18
666

The Book of Revelation was written in a time of real danger for Christians at the hands of the Romans, who regarded Christians as threats to the state religion, that is, the cult of emperor worship. Under Nero (A.D. 37–68) the persecutions became severe. For a Christian, to worship an emperor meant eternal damnation; not to worship an emperor meant persecution and death—but perhaps also a glorious eternal life. To write a tract openly attacking the emperor or the cult was to sign one's own death warrant. The alternative was to write in symbols that only Christian readers would understand. The man named John who wrote Revelation employed a plethora of symbols, most representing satanic Roman forces opposing God, Jesus Christ, angels, and martyrs of the early church. In chapter 13 "the first beast" represents the vicious Emperor Nero, but it also symbolizes the Antichrist of early Christian belief. "The second beast," John wrote, caused all who wished to engage in business to be marked on the forehead or the right hand. This mark was "the name of the beast, or the number of his name." And that number is given as "six hundred threescore and six," or 666.

John seems almost to have challenged his readers to decipher his intention in using this number. Undoubtedly, some were able to interpret his meaning correctly at the time, but since then much effort has gone into recapturing it, and many people have claimed to have the correct answer to the riddle. The current best guess is that since 777 was considered a perfect and holy number in its time, 666 must have been its opposite—the incarnation of wickedness.

The number 666 appeared in news reports when Ronald Reagan and his wife were preparing to leave the White House. The press reported that 666 was the street address of the house in California to which the Reagans would move, and that Mrs. Reagan arranged to have it changed to 668. So the "number of the beast" lives on—as a symbol to be taken seriously by some and as the title of one of Robert Heinlein's many novels.

And numerologists and astrologers thrive.

of making many books there is no end
Ecclesiastes 12:12–13
book learning doesn't give us all the answers

Not a motto to be emblazoned on a publisher's walls, not the plaintive cry of a college librarian with budget strained to the utmost, but the complaint of someone who has read long and hard and finally come to understand that study alone does not yield solutions for all of life's problems: "Of making many books there is no end; and much study is a weariness of the flesh."

Omar Khayyam, as translated by Edward FitzGerald, also understood the futility of the search for understanding life's profoundest mysteries:

Myself when young did eagerly frequent
Doctor and Saint, and heard great argument
About it and about: but evermore
Came out by the same door wherein I went.

of the earth, earthy
I Corinthians 15:47
coarse, unrefined

Basic to Paul's concept of resurrection was the distinction the apostle drew between the first Adam, who died, and the one he called the second Adam, Jesus, who was resurrected: "The first man is of the earth, earthy: the second man is the Lord from heaven." The first Adam, formed of the dust of the earth (Genesis 2:7), initiated an earthy order of humanity. The risen

Jesus Christ initiated a new order characterized by a spiritual body distinct from man's earthly body.

See THE LAST ADAM.

oh that mine adversary had written a book
Job 31:35
if only I knew just what I am being accused of!

The classic complaint of anyone who stands accused by voices unidentified, by leakers of information willing to be quoted without attribution, by unnamed witnesses cited in secret FBI reports. Job, in a final outburst, repeated a wish he had expressed previously—to be heard in a fair trial in the court of last appeal before an equitable divine judge: "Oh that one would hear me! behold, my desire is, that the Almighty would answer me, and that mine adversary had written a book." What Job meant by "book" was a detailed indictment, written or spoken openly. He wanted to know the sins of which he had apparently been accused and convicted without a hearing, the sins that had brought down on him the severe testing he was undergoing.

Seems only fair.

olive branch
Genesis 8:11
a symbol of peace

Anyone who holds out an olive branch—an uxorious husband peeking timorously from the doghouse, the leader of a nation at war, or the like—is seeking peace. In Genesis 8:4–11, while the waters of the great flood were receding, Noah's ark waited "upon the mountains of Ararat." And after forty days, Noah sent out a raven and a dove to find out whether the flood had subsided sufficiently for his family to leave the ark. It had not. But seven days later, when he repeated the experiment with the dove, the bird returned and "Lo, in her mouth was an olive leaf pluckt off: so Noah knew that the waters were abated from off the earth." He also knew the Lord had not forgotten him.

By the fourteenth century, the olive leaf had begun to be replaced in writing and art by the olive branch, and peace had yet another symbol.

See FORTY DAYS AND FORTY NIGHTS.

one event happeneth to them all
Ecclesiastes 2:14–15
in the end we all die

We read in Ecclesiastes 2:14–15, a meditation on death, that all people meet a common fate: "One event happeneth to them all." And then we read, "As it happeneth to the fool, so it happeneth even to me; and why was I then more wise?" After death, the wise person is remembered no longer than the fool.

Thomas Gray, an eighteenth-century English poet who knew his Ecclesiastes, gave us a similar insight in these admirable lines from "Elegy Written in a Country Churchyard":

The boast of heraldry, the pomp of pow'r,
And all that beauty, all that wealth e'er gave,
Awaits alike the inevitable hour:
The paths of glory lead but to the grave.

See ALL THINGS COME ALIKE TO ALL, HOUSE APPOINTED FOR ALL LIVING, THREESCORE AND TEN, *and* TO EVERY THING THERE IS A SEASON.

one generation passeth away
Ecclesiastes 1:4
people have only a finite amount of time on earth
See VANITY OF VANITIES.

one that feared God
Job 1:1
a person in proper awe of God

We learn from Job that to fear God is to stand in awe of God and from that emotion gain the power to avoid evil. The Book of Job opens with one of those marvelously simple sentences that get us right into the middle of things: "There was a man in the land of Uz, whose name was Job; and that man was perfect and upright, and one that feared God, and eschewed evil." This man of integrity lived prosperously, unaware that he was being set up by Satan for sore testing by calamity and disaster.

Just wait.

See SATAN CAME ALSO AMONG THEM.

our daily bread
Matthew 6:11
the food needed to sustain life

In a prayer Jesus taught his disciples, now called the Lord's Prayer, verse 11 says, "Give us this day our daily bread." Bread, the most essential of foods, here is taken to symbolize all necessary food. Yet it must be understood that the prayer asks for day-to-day necessities—not for a guaranteed lifetime supply or for luxuries—as is made clear in Matthew 6:25–33.

our days upon earth are a shadow
Job 8:9
we don't live long enough to learn all the mysteries of existence

By way of affirming God's justice, Job's friend tells him, "For we are but of yesterday, and know nothing, because our days upon earth are a shadow."

our refuge and strength
Psalm 46:1
God

Martin Luther's famous hymn "Ein' Feste Burg," known in English as "A Mighty Fortress Is Our God," was inspired by this verse from Psalm 46, which says in full, "God is our refuge and strength, a very present help in trouble." So God provides a refuge for the lonely, the troubled, the insecure in all kinds of disasters.

out of the depths
Psalm 130:1
a bitter cry of wretchedness

These opening words of the psalm (in Latin, *de profundis*) initiate a call by the psalmist for divine redemption of Israel: "Out of the depths have I cried unto thee, O Lord." In Roman Catholic ritual, these words form part of the burial service.

Oscar Wilde used *De Profundis* as the title for an essay of confession and reminiscence, written while he was in prison but not published until 1905, five years after he died.

out of the mouths of babes
Psalm 8:2
comes praise of God

Doting parents, know what you are about when using "out of the mouths of babes" to express wonder at the simplicity and directness of your small children, who may appear wise when speaking of serious matters. Psalm 8:2 says, "Out of the mouth of babes and sucklings hast thou ordained strength because of thine enemies, that thou mightest still the enemy and the avenger." The Hebrew text here is confused and confusing. What the psalmist probably meant was that even children can recognize and praise God's greatness.

ox to the slaughter
Proverbs 7:22
a metaphor for a person acting without regard for
   consequences

And the result too often is deep trouble.

By way of lecturing on the desirability of sexual continence
outside marriage, Proverbs 7 describes the seduction of an
unwary man by a loose woman, described as wearing "the
attire of an harlot." In the preceding verses, the woman invited a stranger to go home with her, saying her husband was
out of town: "Come, let us take our love until the morning:
let us solace ourselves with love." And what was his response?
"He goeth after her straightway, as an ox goeth to the slaughter, or as a fool to the correction of the stocks."

How did things turn out for him? Not to put too fine a point
on the matter, verse 27 says, "Her house is the way to hell,
going down to the chambers of death."

O ye of little faith
Matthew 8:26
a way of chiding the irresolute

When the disciples begged Jesus to save them from a sudden
storm that was battering their ship on the Sea of Galilee, he
replied, "Why are ye fearful, O ye of little faith?" The account
of this incident in verses 23–27 is taken as a commentary on
the helplessness of those who do not put their entire trust in
God in the face of storms both literal and figurative.

P

painted woman
II Kings 9:30
a prostitute
See JEZEBEL.

pale horse
Revelation 6:8
a metaphor for approaching death

The Revelation of John, last book of the New Testament, is also known as the Apocalypse, a term deriving ultimately from a Greek word for "uncovering," or "revelation." A vision of four horses, each of a different color, and their riders—in modern English referred to as the Four Horsemen or the Four Horsemen of the Apocalypse—is recounted in Revelation 6:2–8. The riders personify the four major plagues of mankind: war, famine, pestilence, and death. Verse 8 begins with an enduring spine-chiller: "And I looked, and behold a pale horse: and his name that sat on him was Death, and Hell followed with him."

No wonder Helen MacInnes entitled one of her novels of espionage *Ride a Pale Horse*, and Katherine Anne Porter used "Pale Horse, Pale Rider" as the title of her story about love during an outbreak of deadly influenza. Sports fans of long memories will recall the Notre Dame football team of 1924, whose backfield was dubbed the Four Horsemen of Notre Dame by sportswriters because it struck fear in the opposing teams.

they **parted his garments, casting lots upon them**
Mark 15:24
gambled for possession of Jesus' clothing

After Jesus asked forgiveness for the soldiers whose job it was to carry out the crucifixion, as related in Luke 23:34, they divided his garments into shares to gamble for the various items that would become their booty. What was Jesus wearing that could have interested them—cloak, tunic, loincloth, sandals? Consider the irony in the account given in Mark 15: "And when they had crucified him, they parted his garments, casting lots upon them, what every man should take." All that Jesus meant to the few soldiers present was a chance to roll dice and win some used clothing. Now we know the reason why Jesus said, "Father, forgive them; for they know not what they do."

the **parting of the way**
Ezekiel 21:21
where a choice must be made between courses of action

The metaphor calls to mind the point where a road, or way, divides and branches off in different directions, so we are not surprised when friends or married couples use these words in a narrow, and sad, sense. In Ezekiel, Nebuchadnezzar had to make up his mind on a tough choice that faced him: Should he attack Judah first or Ammon first? "For the king of Babylon stood at the parting of the way, at the head of two ways." So, like many leaders of his time, he decided to "use divination: he made his arrows bright, he consulted with images, he looked in the liver." The word "images" may be taken to mean Nebuchadnezzar's gods, and "arrows" the knives used in animal sacrifice. But how about "looked in the liver"? Haruspicy—that is, divination by examination of the entrails of a bird or animal killed in sacrifice, particularly its liver—was popular at the time. Whatever the signs were, the king read them as indicating that the kingdom of Judah had lost the toss. Having made his decision, Nebuchadnezzar promptly attacked, and Judah fell.

Maybe divination beats computer modeling when it's time to make an important decision.

passing the love of women
II Samuel 1:26
more profound than sexual love

The friendship of David and Jonathan has given us a memorable expression for love of close friends for one another. Apprised of the death in battle of his closest friend, David lamented: "I am distressed for thee, my brother Jonathan: very pleasant thou hast been unto me: thy love to me was wonderful, passing the love of women."

Passover
Exodus 12:13
a week-long Jewish festival commemorating the exodus from Egypt

The name of the festival, in Hebrew *pesach*, meaning "pass over," alludes to the sparing of the Israelites from the final plague brought upon their oppressors. The firstborn children of Egyptian families were killed by the angel of death, but the angel passed over the homes of the Israelites, sparing their children. In Exodus 12:14–15, God said, "And this day shall be unto you for a memorial; and ye shall keep it a feast to the Lord throughout your generations....Seven days shall ye eat unleavened bread." Ever since, orthodox Jews during Passover have eaten matzoth and eschewed bread.

pass over Jordan
Joshua 3:14
reach the promised land

Joshua, who soon would lead the Israelites in conquest of the promised land, had first to see them safely across the Jordan River, that is, "pass over Jordan." To this day, spirituals such as "Deep River" and "Swing Low, Sweet Chariot" express a longing for freedom, whether on this earth or in an afterlife. And the River Jordan figures prominently in many of these songs. In this context, it serves as the Christian equivalent of the River Styx of classical mythology.

pass under the rod
Ezekiel 20:37–38
come under close scrutiny

It was the practice among shepherds to use their staffs, or rods, in counting sheep at day's end, and while the animals passed under the rod the shepherds would also inspect them for signs of injury or disease. And this is the metaphor used in Ezekiel to describe what God planned to do with his people. While the Israelites were in captivity in Babylon, Ezekiel heard the word of God offering hope for their release from captivity and return to their homeland. But while the news was welcome for most of the Israelites, it wasn't for others: "I will cause you to pass under the rod, and I will bring you into the bond of the covenant: And I will purge out from among you the rebels, and them that transgress against me." So those who passed under the rod successfully would be back in the fold, their bond with God renewed, but those who failed would not be permitted to enter the land of Israel.

the **peace of God which passeth all understanding**
Philippians 4:7
the peace attained only by true believers

Peace between nations is achieved by the efforts of men and women. But what about peace of mind and the peace of God? Paul, approaching the close of his epistle to the Philippians, called attention to the deep serenity of true believers, who know God is with those who put their trust in him: "And the peace of God, which passeth all understanding, shall keep your hearts and minds through Jesus Christ." For "passeth," read "transcends" or "is too great for."

Meanwhile, propagandists and advertising writers, whose

effort also passeth all understanding, try daily to outdo one another in competing for control of people's hearts and minds.

peace when there is no peace
Jeremiah 6:14
deceitful talk intended to mislead
See SAYING, PEACE, PEACE; WHEN THERE IS NO PEACE.

pearls before swine
Matthew 7:6
effort misspent on preaching to hostile audiences

People who cast pearls before swine are wasting time and effort by offering something of quality to those who are unable to appreciate it. "Pearls before swine" is a colorful and lasting metaphor too often muttered by self-important and self-pitying university lecturers who spend too few hours a week—and too few weeks a year—setting their pearls of wisdom before too many of what they perceive to be wretched, unappreciative students.

Jesus said to his disciples, "Give not that which is holy unto the dogs, neither cast ye your pearls before swine, lest they trample them under their feet, and turn again and rend you." The pearls may be thought of as the joys found in God's kingdom, the swine as unclean creatures (their meat was forbidden to Jews), incapable of appreciating such joys. Thus, Jesus was saying, Don't waste time trying to reach those who are unreceptive or hostile.

There are plenty of others eager to hear your message.

Peter
one of the twelve apostles and the most prominent in the gospels
See UPON THIS ROCK.

Pharisees

A Jewish group that promoted rigorous observance of religious practices as a means of expressing spirituality, human compassion, and human dignity. Some people have thought of the Pharisees as less than admirable, but modern scholarship has done much to modify this image.

See SCRIBES AND PHARISEES.

Philistines

Judges 14:1
a warlike people in conflict with their Israelite neighbors

Today, "philistine" is a contemptuous epithet for materialistic people deficient in cultural interests and aesthetic values. This extended meaning of the term appears to have originated in seventeenth-century Jena, a German university town where students used the word *Philister* to denote the townspeople, whom they considered outsiders lacking in culture. *Philister*, of course, means Philistine.

The biblical Philistines settled on the southern coast of Palestine about the time when the Israelites were wandering in the desert. They were one of the so-called sea peoples, who came about 1200 B.C. from the area of the Aegean basin to that of the eastern Mediterranean in search of a homeland. By reason of their superior Iron-Age weapons and their more fertile land, the Philistines were able to oppress the Israelites for 150 years until they were finally defeated by King David. Intermarriage with Philistines was excoriated by the Israelites, who detested the uncircumcised worshipers of fertility gods.

physician, heal thyself

Luke 4:23
take care of your own problems before you dare tell anyone else how to behave

As related in Luke 4:16–30, Jesus encountered a mood of suspicion among the congregants while reading from Scripture at a synagogue in Galilee, his hometown. He chided them saying, "Ye surely will say unto me this proverb, Physician, heal thyself"—implying that Jesus was himself in need of help—and then went on in the same rhetorical vein, "Whatsoever we have heard done in Capernaum, do also here in thy country." Finally, Jesus added yet another proverb: "Verily I say unto you, No prophet is accepted in his own country." This last reflected his experience in Capernaum, in Galilee, where he had lived. There he had healed, taught, and performed exorcisms yet felt rejected by the local folk.

See NO NEED OF THE PHYSICIAN *and* PROPHET WITHOUT HONOR.

pillar of cloud, pillar of fire
Exodus 13:21–22
metaphors for God as guide and protector

In leading the children of Israel out of Egypt, God "went before them by day in a pillar of a cloud, to lead them the way; and by night in a pillar of fire, to give them light."

pillar of salt
Genesis 19:26
an enduring epithet for Lot's wife

It recalls her disobedience of God's instruction and serves as a warning to anyone who considers flouting the word of God. Lot, his wife, and their children, in accordance with God's instruction, were in the act of fleeing the sinful cities of Sodom and Gomorrah. Unfortunately, Lot's wife disobeyed God's command not to look back while the family was making its way out of town: "But his wife looked back from behind him, and she became a pillar of salt." In Luke 17:31–32 Jesus, warning his disciples of the momentous events that would accompany the appearance of the Son of man, gave a similar instruction to his disciples: "He that is in the field, let him likewise not return back. Remember Lot's wife." He was not issuing a literal warning to them. Rather, Jesus was teaching the folly of wasting one's time regretting a life being left behind while ignoring the better life that lay ahead.

Incidentally, tourists visiting the southern end of the Dead Sea area still find upright columns of rock salt there.

See SALT OF THE EARTH *and* SODOM AND GOMORRAH.

plow with my heifer
Judges 14:18
use information obtained unfairly

This metaphor is found in the sentence "If ye had not plowed with my heifer, ye had not found out my riddle," spoken by Samson to his bride's countrymen. The context of the metaphor is this: Samson posed a difficult riddle that turned out to have fateful consequences for thirty young countrymen of Samson's bride who were guests at the couple's wedding festivities. When the thirty could not themselves solve the riddle within the stipulated time of seven days, they took unfair advantage of Samson's young wife, pressing her until she revealed the solution—and just under the deadline.

"Heifer" has served in the past as a figurative term for "wife" and is now occasionally used as a slang term for "woman" or "girl." In our enlightened time, of course, it is used almost exclusively to denote a cow in its second year of life that has not yet produced a calf.

For more of the story, *see* SMOTE THEM HIP AND THIGH *and* SWEETER THAN HONEY.

the **poor are always with us**
Mark 14:7
there will always be poor people who need assistance

Quoting out of context, the cynical may use "the poor are always with us" to suggest that indifference to the plight of the poor is acceptable and realistic. In context, the statement means that the poor are an omnipresent problem, and there will be continuing opportunities to help them. In Mark 14 Jesus' disciples expressed indignation over what they saw as a wasteful act: A woman had poured an expensive ointment over Jesus' head, which they thought might better have been sold and its proceeds given to the poor. Jesus, aware of the dreadful fate awaiting him, said to his disciples, "For ye have the poor with you always, and whensoever ye will ye may do them good: but me ye have not always." So Jesus was far from indifferent to the plight of the poor—who would always need help—but saw the anointment as a ritual of remembrance of Jesus alive that would never again be performed.

See GRIND THE FACES OF THE POOR.

Potiphar's wife
Genesis 39:7–23
a seductress

This term is applied especially to a married woman who leads on a man other than her husband, in particular to a woman who cries foul after being spurned by the man toward whom she has made sexual advances. Joseph was sold by his envious brothers to merchants who took him in their caravan to Egypt, where he was resold as a slave to Potiphar, captain of the Pharaoh's guard. While Joseph was working as Potiphar's household steward, "It came to pass. . .that his master's wife cast her eyes upon Joseph; and she said, Lie with me." He turned her down, but that was not the end of the story. Day after day she tried her luck, and still no dice. Joseph, "a goodly person," knew better. But one day, while the house was otherwise empty, "She caught him by his garment, saying, Lie with me; and he left his garment in her hand, and fled, and got him out." When Potiphar returned, his wife accused Joseph of sexual assault and used his garment as proof. Joseph went to the clink, but in time was able to find a way out.

pottage
Genesis 25:30
soup
See MESS OF POTTAGE.

potter's field
Matthew 27:7
a burial place for strangers and the friendless poor
See THIRTY PIECES OF SILVER.

the **powers that be**
Romans 13:1
those in control

This is still a commonly heard characterization of people or institutions in the catbird seat. In writing of "the powers that be," Paul had in mind the Roman Empire, and he recognized that the apostles had some reasons to be grateful to their temporal rulers.

But read on: "Let every soul be subject unto the higher powers. For there is no other power but of God: the powers that be are ordained by God." Now we understand why Paul counseled obedience to governing authorities. He held that all authority comes from God, and those in positions of authority have been put there by God. In so writing, Paul was reflecting the traditional and widely held ancient view of the authority of governments. To Paul, if any change were needed, God could be counted on to initiate that change. Paul, it should be remembered, was a first-century man writing for his contemporaries, not for twentieth-century readers.

That rulers were ordained by God led eventually to the notion of the divine right of kings and, for Charles I of England, to the executioner's block.

price far above rubies
Proverbs 31:10–31
priceless

Proverbs 31:10 poses an interesting question: "Who can find a virtuous woman? for her price is far above rubies." When we read further, it becomes clear that a woman who meets all the specifications of such a woman would certainly be worth the price and more. The virtuous woman is not only completely trustworthy, but she arises "while it is yet night" to prepare food for the entire household, plants and cares for a vineyard, spins yarn, helps the poor, and much more. Incidentally, "Her candle goeth not out by night." So she works without stopping almost around the clock. What is her husband doing all this while? "He sitteth among the elders of the land." Small wonder it would be hard to find a woman who meets these ancient specifications.

If women take offense at being compared with rubies, Job 28:18 offers some comfort: "The price of wisdom is above rubies," and Proverbs 31:10 says the price of a virtuous woman is far above rubies.

pride goes before a fall
Proverbs 16:18
a warning for those who hold too high an opinion of themselves

When we wish to criticize someone for falling prey to overweening self-esteem—pride, after all, is the first of the seven deadly sins—we have no better recourse than to invoke Proverbs: "Pride goeth before destruction, and an haughty spirit before a fall."

So watch out.

See WHOSOEVER SHALL EXALT HIMSELF.

prisoners of hope
Zechariah 9:12
an epithet for the Jewish people

"Prisoners of hope" appears in a message from God promising the Jews they will be returned from the Diaspora to their homeland: "Turn ye to the strong hold, ye prisoners of hope: even to day do I declare that I will render double unto thee."

Incidentally, the reader should not be surprised to find the word "stronghold" as two words here (just as the word "today" appears as "to day" so often in the King James Version). As a phrase in English since long before the seventeenth century, "strong hold" meant a fortified defense position in warfare, still a principal meaning of today's "strong-hold." "Hold" or "strong hold" also had the meaning of a place of refuge, the sense intended in the verse from Zechariah. "Stronghold" began to appear in the seventeenth century, but "strong hold" and "strong-hold" held out determinedly in the work of some writers for at least two more centuries.

For another example of how a phrase can become a single word, see HELPMEET.

prodigal son
Luke 15:13
one who has left home and wasted his inheritance

This term owes its enduring life to Jesus' parable of the prodigal son in Luke. A younger son has asked his father to give him in advance "the portion of goods that falleth to me," that is, the share of his father's estate that one day will be his. Granted the request, the son "gathered all together, and took his journey into a far country, and there wasted his substance with riotous living."

For the rest of the story, *see* FATTED CALF.

promised land
Genesis 12:1–8
heaven or a place of ultimate happiness

Though not occurring in Scripture, this phrase denoting the final realization of one's hopes or dreams is so firmly entrenched in English that many believe the words as well as the idea to be of biblical origin. In Genesis 12:1–8 God instructed Abraham to leave Ur of the Chaldees with his family and flocks and head for a land God would show him. God promised to make a great nation of Abraham's descendants, one that would be a blessing to all nations, and to give those descendants the land of Canaan as a homeland, with boundaries spelled out in Genesis 15:18 as extending "from the river of Egypt unto the great river, the river Euphrates."

Modern geographers are more inclined to site Canaan on the Mediterranean coast west of the Jordan River from Syria to the border of Egypt.

Henri Frédéric Amiel, a nineteenth-century Swiss poet and philosopher, is said to have remarked that "the Promised Land is the land where one is not." A sage observation.

See MILK AND HONEY.

prophet without honor
Mark 6:4
an inspired but unrecognized thinker

This phrase survives to describe any of the great scholars and artists who have had to go abroad to gain the recognition they deserved. Jesus, commenting in Mark 6:4 on the frosty reception given him by skeptical villagers when he visited Nazareth, his hometown, said, "A prophet is not without honor, but in his own country, and among his own kin, and in his own house."

Yes, even in his own house.

publicans and sinners
Matthew 11:19
tax collectors and reprobates
See FRIEND OF PUBLICANS AND SINNERS.

publish it not in the streets of Askelon
II Samuel 1:20
don't spread the news around
See TELL IT NOT IN GATH.

put not your trust in princes
Psalm 146:3
trust in God

Sound advice for modern times, when elected leaders, civil servants, captains of industry, even giants of Wall Street have been known to fail us. The psalmist said, "Put not your trust

in princes, nor in the son of man, in whom there is no help."
(Here "son of man" means "human being," as it nearly always
does in the Old Testament.)

Where then to put one's trust? Verse 5 provides the answer: "Happy is he that hath the God of Jacob for his help,
whose hope is in the Lord his God."

put off thy shoes from off thy feet
Exodus 3:5
a little respect, please

God spoke to Moses from the midst of a bush that burned and
yet was not consumed by the flame: "Draw not nigh hither:
put off thy shoes from off thy feet, for the place whereon thou
standest is holy ground. Moreover he said, I am the God of
thy father, the God of Abraham, the God of Isaac, and the
God of Jacob."

It is not said whether Moses did remove his shoes, but
Muslims to this day do so before entering a mosque.

For what Moses did, *see* BURNING BUSH.

putting out the fleece
Judges 6:36–40
a means of divination

In biblical times, various ways of divining God's will were
practiced. The most prominent was the casting of lots, probably marked stones and therefore suggesting the throwing of
dice. Gideon, before doing battle with the invading Midianites, wanted to determine whether it was God's will that he
lead the Israelites. So he sought a sign from God, saying, "I
will put a fleece of wool upon the floor; and if the dew be on
the fleece only, and it be dry upon all the earth beside, then
I shall know that thou wilt save Israel by mine hand, as thou
hast said." On the next morning, when Gideon squeezed the
fleece, out came enough water to fill a bowl, and the ground
around it was dry. But he sought one more sign from God.
Again putting the fleece upon the floor, he said that if this
time the fleece was dry but the ground around it had dew on

it, he would be convinced. Everything worked out, and Gideon knew God's will.

A practice called "putting out the fleece" is still seen occasionally among evangelical and fundamentalist Christians when they are about to launch a new program or dedicate their lives to serving God. The fleece today is some token other than the wool of a sheep. For example, a student considering whether to enter the ministry might pray, "Lord, if three people urge me to become a minister within the next three days, I will know that it is your will for me."

For the outcome of Gideon's battle with the Midianites, *see* GIDEON'S ARMY.

quit yourselves like men, and fight
I Samuel 4:9
let's win this one for the Gipper

A leader of the Philistines gave a pep talk to his fighting men, who showed every sign of being terrified by the approach of a stirred-up army of Israelites. The Israelites were carrying into battle with them the famed ark of the covenant, whose presence was thought to make victory a sure thing. To allay the soldiers' fears, the Philistine leader said, "Be strong, and quit [acquit] yourselves like men, O ye Philistines, that ye be not servants unto the Hebrews, as they have been to you: quit yourselves like men, and fight." The Philistines rose to the occasion, routed the Israelites, and captured the ark. It would not be returned to Jerusalem until the reign of David.

See also GLORY HAS DEPARTED FROM ISRAEL.

quiver full
Psalm 127:5
a marvelous metaphor for a large and happy family

Referring to children and the blessings they bring, verse 5 says, "Happy is the man that hath his quiver full of them." In biblical times, quivers were familiar to all males, for bows and arrows were normally carried by nomads and hunters. But how many arrows—in this case, how many children—constitute a full quiver? The disconcerting answer is that, depending on the intricacy of the arrowheads, a quiver in biblical times might hold as many as twenty arrows.

Ouch!

See BE FRUITFUL AND MULTIPLY.

R

---

the race is not to the swift
Ecclesiastes 9:11
good people do not always seem to be treated fairly

This insight is not intended for improvers of the breed, who are well advised to bet on speed when thoroughbreds are on their way to the starting gates. (Didn't Damon Runyon tell us that the race might not be to the swift, nor the battle to the strong, but that's the way to bet?) Rather, "the race is not to the swift" is intended for men and women of great ability who end up receiving a smaller portion of life's bounties than they think they should. According to the writer of Ecclesiastes, "The race is not to the swift, nor the battle to the strong, neither yet bread to the wise, nor yet riches to men of understanding, nor yet favor to men of skill; but time and chance happeneth to them all."

But could the writer have foreseen the day when baseball players, tennis stars, writers of best-sellers, and the like would be rewarded with millions of dollars a year? For the rest of us, who cannot throw a mean slider, rush to the net with aplomb, or keep readers riveted through 800 pages of heaving bosoms, the wisdom of Ecclesiastes had best be heeded: Do not expect life's rewards to be handed out rationally or justly.

That's just the way it is.

Rachel weeping for her children
Jeremiah 31:15
maternal grief

Jeremiah reported that the Lord told him a lamentation had been heard "and bitter weeping; Rahel weeping for her children refused to be comforted for her children, for they were not." That is, her children were dead. The children Rachel wept for were the descendants of her son Joseph, the tribes

200

of his sons Ephraim and Manasseh. These were the chief tribes of the Northern Kingdom of Israel, which were defeated by the Assyrians in 722 B.C. and dispersed in captivity around the Assyrian empire. God, reported Jeremiah, said that Rachel need weep no more, because they one day would return—and they did, but not as a political entity. Nevertheless, the image of a mother weeping for her children—whether her name be spelled "Rachel" or "Rahel"—haunts readers even to this day.

See MAN OF STRIFE, MAN OF CONTENTION.

raise the poor out of the dust
Psalm 113:7
give them a place to rest their heads
See LIFT THE NEEDY OUT OF THE DUNGHILL.

reap the whirlwind
Proverbs 11:29
troublemakers will get what's coming to them
See THEY HAVE SOWN THE WIND.

rejoice in thy youth
Ecclesiastes 11:9
good advice for young people

Enjoy yourself while you're at your best: "Rejoice, O young man, in thy youth; and let thy heart cheer thee in the days of thy youth, and rejoice in them all." Life will indeed not seem as sweet when you get older, so take counsel from Ecclesiastes.

See DAYS OF THY YOUTH.

rejoice with the wife of thy youth
Proverbs 5:18–19
a prescription for a happy marriage

Husbands: Be ever faithful and ardent in marriage; look not elsewhere. "Rejoice with the wife of thy youth. Let her be as the loving hind and pleasant roe; let her breasts satisfy thee at all times; and be thou ravished always with her love."

remember Lot's wife
Luke 17:32
obey God and don't look back at the life you've left behind
See PILLAR OF SALT.

render to Caesar
Mark 12:17
obey civil authority

Asked whether it was lawful to give tribute to Caesar, Jesus answered, "Render to Caesar the things that are Caesar's, and to God the things that are God's." Jesus was not discussing church-state relations. He was counseling acceptance of tax burdens imposed by relentless and powerful secular authorities. In speaking of "the things that are God's," he made it clear that the greater duty was to God.

Frederick Wilhelm I of Prussia is reported to have said, "Salvation is of God. Everything else is my affair."

repent in dust and ashes
Job 42:5–6
eat crow, eat humble pie—take your pick

After listening carefully to everything God had to say, Job finally understood his presumptuousness in challenging the Lord: "I have heard of thee by the hearing of the ear: but now mine eye seeth thee. Wherefore I abhor myself, and repent in dust and ashes." Job had learned that falling into the hands of God can be a terrible experience, yet Job could reflect that God had addressed him directly!

Jonathan Edwards, the eighteenth-century clergyman, knew how to scorch his New England parishioners with visions of hellfire. Using Hebrews 10:31 as the text for his sermon "Sinners in the Hands of an Angry God," Edwards thundered, "It is a fearful thing to fall into the hands of the living God."

As Job had discovered.

the **rich hath many friends**
Proverbs 14:20
why do we behave like sycophants in the presence of the rich?

Wisdom from Proverbs casting humanity in a bad light: People cluster about those who have a great deal of money and hang upon their every word, at the same time avoiding those who have little. This observation is found in 14:20 as "The poor is hated even of his own neighbour; but the rich hath many friends"; in 19:4 as "Wealth maketh many friends; but the poor is separated from his neighbour."

Sad but true.

rivers of Babylon
Psalm 137:1–6
a symbol for a place in which one feels estranged

"By the rivers of Babylon, there we sat down, yea, we wept when we remembered Zion." So begins one of the most poignant laments in world literature, which includes the resolve, "If I forget thee, O Jerusalem, let my right hand forget her cunning. If I do not remember thee, let my tongue cleave to the roof of my mouth." These verses portray the mood of the Jews in their Babylonian captivity, expressing loyalty to God and exquisite longing for their homeland. Unashamed, they wept.

See HANGED OUR HARPS UPON THE WILLOWS.

a **rock higher than I**
Psalm 61:2
a metaphor for safety and stability

Psalm 61 is the prayer of a fearful or insecure person in need of God's protection. Seeking refuge from his condition, the psalmist acknowledges that he cannot find it on his own: "Lead me to a rock that is higher than I."

rock of ages
Isaiah 26:4
an epithet for Christ

This enduring epithet for Christ as the unshakable foundation, made familiar in English in the hymn "Rock of Ages," draws on Isaiah 26:4: "Trust ye in the Lord forever: for in the Lord JEHOVAH is everlasting strength."

"Everlasting strength" is the translation used in the King James Version for a Hebrew phrase that means "rock of ages."

See SHADOW OF A GREAT ROCK.

rock solid
built to last

Small wonder insurance companies and banks exploit this image. In Matthew 7:24–27 Jesus related the parable of the wise man who built his house on a rock: "The floods came, and the winds blew, and beat upon that house; and it fell not: for it was founded upon a rock." An apt figure, for ancient Palestine was a land whose weather would change suddenly from long dry spells to periods of rain, sometimes heavy. When the rains did come, dry watercourses would be transformed into raging rivers. Thus, Jesus' listeners understood his contrast of the wise man who "heareth these sayings of mine and doeth them," and the foolish man "which built his house upon the sand."

root of all evil
I Timothy 6:10
where all trouble begins

One of the most frequent misquotations from the Bible holds that money is the root of all evil. But verse 10 actually says in full, "For the love of money is the root of all evil: which while some coveted after, they have erred from the faith, and pierced themselves through with many sorrows." And the preceding verse, less widely known, says, "They that will be rich fall into temptation and a snare, and into many foolish and hurtful lusts, which drown men in destruction and perdition."

The idea that avarice leads inevitably to moral decay was widely held in the Hellenistic world. For example, the Greek ascetic philosopher Diogenes, fourth century B.C., the man whom Seneca described as living in a tub and who is popularly recalled as going about with a lantern in daylight in fruitless search for an honest person, is credited with "The love of money is the mother-city of all evils."

See FILTHY LUCRE *and* GOD AND MAMMON.

rose of Sharon
Song of Solomon 2:1
a metaphor for a young woman of great beauty

"I am the rose of Sharon, and the lily of the valleys," sings the maiden at the start of a lyrical dialogue with her lover. Little is known for certain about this rose that grew in Sharon, the fertile coastal plain of north-central Palestine, except that it was not a rose and that it bore no resemblance to the tree we call rose of Sharon. Some scholars suggest that the biblical flower may have resembled the crocus.

"Lily of the valley" in the King James Version is a translation of *lilium convallium* in the Latin of the Vulgate, a literal translation of the original Hebrew phrase.

rumors of wars
Matthew 24:6
tumult accompanying the clash of arms; reports
      circulating without clear evidence of their validity
See WARS AND RUMORS OF WARS.

a **rushing mighty wind**
Acts 2:2
a sound from heaven
See UNKNOWN TONGUE.

the **rushing of mighty waters**
Isaiah 17:12
a metaphor suggesting a powerful natural force that
   sweeps along everything in its path

In Isaiah, the phrase may allude to the mighty Assyrian military force. Yet Isaiah prophesied that God would deal with it, just as he would withstand everything directed against his people: "Woe to the multitude of many people, which make a noise like the noise of the seas; and to the rushing of nations, that make a rushing like the rushing of mighty waters." This passage recalls Psalm 93:4, "The Lord on high is mightier than the noise of many waters, yea, than the mighty waves of the sea."

S

the **sabbath was made for man**
Mark 2:27
a challenge to the letter of the law

In Exodus 20:8, the sabbath day—*shabbath* is a Hebrew word meaning "cease, desist"—was divinely provided for people's regular respite from work. As time went by, interpreters of the law came up with increasingly restrictive sabbath work prohibitions, and by the first century A.D. the definition of work had been extended to include work done in healing and anything that resembled the act of harvesting. In Mark 2, Jesus' disciples, finding themselves hungry on the sabbath, picked grain to eat while passing through a field. For this action they were challenged by the Pharisees. Jesus defended the disciples, citing David's action in feeding himself and his followers when they were hungry by taking loaves of bread intended as offerings to God. Jesus concluded his argument by saying in verse 27, "The sabbath was made for man, and not man for the sabbath." In enunciating this principle, Jesus was challenging head-on the entire Pharisaic interpretation of the law.
See I WAS BLIND, NOW I SEE *and* SCRIBES AND PHARISEES.

sackcloth and ashes
Daniel 9:3
a metaphor for penitence and contrition

To this day, a penitent or contrite person, and particularly a person in mourning, may be said to be wearing sackcloth and ashes. Daniel, expressing profound humility, said, "I set my face unto the Lord God, to seek by prayer and supplications, with fasting, and sackcloth, and ashes." Sackcloth was a coarse

207

dark haircloth used in making sacks. It was the Hebrew custom during a period of penitence or mourning to wear garments made of this cloth and to daub ashes on them.

Some ascetics and penitents long after biblical times wore hair shirts—extremely uncomfortable next to the skin—as a sign of humility. Today, unkind observers may say disparagingly of a person who habitually chooses to suffer needlessly and publicly, "He wears a hair shirt."

Sadducees

A party within Judaism in biblical times, centered in Jerusalem, that consisted primarily of priests and wealthy people. It was the Sadducees who controlled the Temple. Incompletely described in the Bible, they differed from the Pharisees chiefly in their rejection of the oral tradition, the coming of a Messiah, and belief in a life after death. The Sadducees were among the opponents of Jesus and played a major role in the events leading to his crucifixion.

See SCRIBES AND PHARISEES.

salt of the earth
Matthew 5:13
anyone or any group considered tops

To this day we pay a fine compliment when we refer to someone as the salt of the earth, as Jesus did in Matthew 5:13 when he said to his disciples, "Ye are the salt of the earth." Salt was not something to be taken for granted in biblical times. Rather it was an important commodity. Besides imparting zest to what otherwise would have been bland nourishment, salt was essential in preserving food.

For another use of salt, *see* LET YOUR SPEECH BE ALWAYS WITH GRACE.

Samaritans
residents of the district of Samaria
See GOOD SAMARITAN.

the **same yesterday, and to day, and for ever**
Hebrews 13:8
true consistency

Employing one of the most memorable phrases of the New Testament, Hebrews 13 begins, "Let brotherly love continue." It then goes on to counsel upright behavior toward all and careful attention to the words of church leaders. In verse 8, the writer calls attention to the timeless Jesus who abides unchanging: "Jesus Christ the same yesterday, and to day, and for ever."

That is, not here today and gone tomorrow.
See BROTHERLY LOVE.

Satan
an adversary, a tempter, the prince of the devils

When we speak of Satan today we almost always mean the devil, but 'twas not always thus. The Hebrew word *satan* has the literal meaning of "adversary," an appropriate term in the Old Testament, where Satan was portrayed as a member of God's court in heaven with the function of acting as accuser and prosecuting attorney against humans brought before God. In later Jewish writings, Satan became a tempter to sin, attacker of humans, and prince of the devils. In the New Testament, for example in Matthew 4 and Luke 11, he was the incarnation of evil, responsible for all misfortune and ruling over demonic forces opposed to God. It was in the latter role that Jesus saw Satan, as did Martin Luther, who once threw an inkpot at him.
See SATAN CAME ALSO AMONG THEM.

Satan came also among them
Job 1:6–12
watch what you say—someone may be listening

Satan, empowered to "go to and fro in the earth" and report back as necessary, stood ready to accuse persons of wrong-doing, hypocrisy, and the like. Thus, "There was a day when the sons of God came to present themselves before the Lord, and Satan came also among them." And, when Satan comes, trouble is just around the corner, as Job soon found out. Satan told God that Job appeared to be "a perfect and upright man, one that feareth God, and escheweth evil." And why not, said Satan: "Thou hast blessed the work of his hands, and his substance is increased in the land. But put forth thine hand now, and touch all that he hath, and he will curse thee to thy face." In short, isn't it easy for people to observe all the rules when things are going well for them? But see what happens when hard times arrive.

Sure enough, God gave Satan the green light to try Job to the extent that he wished. And the rest, as they say, is history.

See LORD GAVE, AND THE LORD HATH TAKEN AWAY *and* SATAN.

Saul hath slain his thousands, and David his ten thousands

I Samuel 18:7

a great put-down: you're pretty good, but you're only half the man he is

As David grew in King Saul's esteem, so also did David's popularity increase among the people. And Saul became increasingly envious of David. The situation wasn't helped a bit when women from all over Israel turned out to greet David with singing and dancing on the occasion of his return after a great victory over the Philistines: "And the women answered one another as they played, and said, Saul hath slain his thousands, and David his ten thousands."

In the next verse we learn that "Saul was very wroth." He could read the handwriting on the wall—David was sure to replace Saul one day soon.

See HANDWRITING ON THE WALL.

saying, peace, peace; when there is no peace

Jeremiah 6:14

a shallow prediction or proclamation intended to mislead or mollify

Jeremiah, prophesying the invasion of Jerusalem, related the Lord's dissatisfaction with Israel. God accused the people from the highest to the lowest of covetousness and false dealing. And he accused their prophets and priests of deceitful talk, of "saying, Peace, peace; when there is no peace." These same words are employed in Ezekiel 13:10 and 16, again by way of condemning false prophets.

Those old enough to remember the period just before World War II, and those who have read histories of that time, recall with sadness Neville Chamberlain's promise of "peace in our time" (evoking "Give peace in our time, O Lord," a versicle from *The Book of Common Prayer*). But we don't have to go to British prime ministers for modern examples of saying peace, peace, when there is no peace. How many times during the Vietnam War did Americans hear spurious claims from their leaders that victory lay just ahead, that there was light at the end of the tunnel?

It seems humanity has long had a penchant for papering over the realities of a dire situation.

scapegoat
Leviticus 16:7–22
an unwitting victim

In modern English a scapegoat is an innocent person or group made to bear blame for others and to endure punishment in their place. The account in Leviticus is of an annual Temple rite in which offerings were made of various animals, including two goats. The high priest would draw lots to determine which goat would be the Lord's goat and which would be the scapegoat. It was to the latter that the high priest would transfer his own sins and the sins of all the people. The Lord's goat would then be sacrificed as an offering to God, and the scapegoat, unwittingly burdened with the sins of all the people, would be turned loose—or be allowed to escape—in the wilderness.

Combining "scape," a form of "escape," with "goat," early English translators invented a word that has survived through the centuries. Yet one cannot leave this subject without wondering whether the Lord's goat was actually better off than the scapegoat.

scarlet woman
Revelation 17:1–6
a prostitute or a notoriously licentious woman

In a vision, John saw a woman "arrayed in purple and scarlet color, and decked with gold and precious stones and pearls, having a golden cup in her hand full of abominations and filthiness of her fornication: And upon her forehead was a name written, MYSTERY, BABYLON THE GREAT, THE MOTHER OF HARLOTS AND ABOMINATIONS OF THE EARTH. And I saw the woman drunken with the blood of the saints, and with the blood of the martyrs of Jesus." The woman in John's vision is generally believed to have been an allusion to pagan Rome. Over the centuries—people being what they are—some ill-tempered Protestants have termed the Roman Catholic Church "the scarlet woman," even "the scarlet whore." And, not unexpectedly, some Catholics have behaved no better in applying opprobrious epithets to Protestant churches.
See BABYLON.

scribes and Pharisees
Mark 2:16
groups that practiced strict orthodoxy

Understanding of the phrase "scribes and Pharisees" has relied heavily on its use in Mark 2, which describes the opposition of these groups to the activities of Jesus. Scribes, in biblical times the scholars and teachers of Jewish law and tradition, played an honorable role analogous to that of modern professors of constitutional law. The Pharisees were members of a Jewish group that believed in the oral tradition—which included belief in an afterlife and the coming of a Messiah—as well as in the law of Moses and in strict adherence to prescribed religious practices. Inevitably, their insistence on rigorous observance of ritual was considered to have led to new and hampering restrictions in Jewish law, fostering attention to details of religious life rather than reverence for principles. Not surprisingly, Jesus encountered antagonism in many Pharisees of harsh disposition, who felt he went beyond the law in acting on his own authority.

Because of this opposition to Jesus, in the course of time "pharisee"—that's a small *p*—came to have its present meaning of a self-righteous, hypocritical person.

See STRAIN AT A GNAT, SWALLOW A CAMEL.

seasoned with salt
Colossians 4:5
salted with wit
See LET YOUR SPEECH BE ALWAYS WITH GRACE.

the **second mile**
Matthew 5:41
more than is required
See TRAVEL THE SECOND MILE.

see eye to eye
Isaiah 52:8
agree; see God directly

When people today see eye to eye on a subject, they think alike, are of one mind—at least in regard to that subject. But Isaiah, a visionary, intended to be taken quite literally when he wrote, "Thy watchmen shall lift up the voice; with the voice together shall they sing: for they shall see eye to eye, when the Lord shall bring again Zion." So just as in Exodus 33:11 "the Lord spake unto Moses face to face, as a man speaketh unto his friend," the watchmen on the tower of Jerusalem will see the Lord eye to eye, so near to them will he be when he restores Zion to its past glory.

And the romantics among us, longing for a miraculous time, one day will say along with Wordsworth (although he had secular events in mind in "The Prelude"):

Bliss was it in that dawn to be alive,
But to be young was very heaven!

seek, and ye shall find
Matthew 7:7
keep at it

Advice today given the young and not-so-young when they despair of ever achieving anything: Keep on trying; no matter how grim things look, all doors are not closed to you. Jesus instructed his disciples in this verse, "Ask, and it shall be given you; seek, and ye shall find; knock, and it shall be opened unto you." That is, your prayers will be answered, for God will always respond to the need expressed. But is the answer to prayer always the one we seek? Not so. Jesus never tried to use God's power for his own advantage, nor did he say that every wish would be gratified.

see through a glass, darkly
I Corinthians 13:12–13
perceive imperfectly

Today, when a situation is not entirely clear, we may say it is seen through a glass darkly. For "glass" read "mirror," since in biblical times mirrors were made of polished bronze or other metal. The reflections they gave were uncertain, sometimes baffling.

Paul wrote, "For now we see through a glass, darkly; but then face to face: now I know in part; but then shall I know even as also I am known." He was speaking of humanity's imperfect understanding of God, a mystery, yet useful as guidance for living. Paul promised the faithful that in the fullness of time more complete knowledge, greater illumination, would surely be available. The chapter concludes, "And now abideth faith, hope, and charity, these three; but the greatest of these is charity." So, lacking a perfect understanding of God, Christians must rely on these three virtues to sustain them: *faith* in the love of God, *hope* that God's promises will be fulfilled, and *charity* or love for one's fellow humans.

Sennacherib
II Kings 18 and 19
a king of Assyria whose military force at one time
    overwhelmed Judah and all neighboring countries

separate the sheep from the goats
Matthew 25:32
tell the good guys from the bad guys

Jesus said, "He shall separate them one from another, as a shepherd divideth his sheep from the goats." The metaphor was not based on the relative desirability of goats and sheep, since both were crucial in the agricultural economy. Jesus was alluding to the fact that Palestinian sheep were white and goats dark brown, which made identification easy even in poor light. So Jesus' message was that when the time comes to judge the people of the world, it will be easy to distinguish good people from bad.

John Simon, the acerb theater critic expert in use of the English language who regularly separates good plays from bad for his readers, used the title *Sheep from the Goats* for a collection of his literary essays.

serve two masters
Matthew 6:24
be faithful to disparate goals and programs—an
    impossibility
See GOD AND MAMMON.

set one's nest on high
Habakkuk 2:9
act superior to others

The prophet cautioned the unrighteous—as well as the rest of us—not to seek prideful security by chasing after wealth and station in less than honorable ways: "Woe to him that coveteth an evil covetousness to his house, that he may set his nest on high, that he may be delivered from the power of evil!"

Penthouse dwellers and ye who live in expensive condos—heed the words of Habakkuk.

set thine house in order
II Kings 20:1
make all necessary final arrangements

It is time to get control of your affairs, draw up a will, clear up any unfinished business: "Set thine house in order; for thou shalt die, and not live." This is what the prophet Isaiah told King Hezekiah of Judah when Hezekiah was "sick unto death." Notice that Isaiah was emphatic: Not only would the king die, but he would not live. How's that for laying it on the line?

seven years of plenty
Genesis 41:29–30
good times

Economists, those infallible observers of the cyclical nature of boom and bust, as well as hard and soft landings, find their paradigm in these verses from Genesis, and observant consultants to modern governments take notice of them as well. The Pharaoh in the time of Joseph had a dream that proved difficult to interpret—seven fat cows were thriving in the pasturelands along the Nile, but seven gaunt cows moved in and consumed the fat ones. This was an extraordinary feat for herbivorous animals, but that's what the dream showed, and the call went out for Joseph, who was good at dream interpretation. He solved the puzzle: "Behold, there come seven years of great plenty throughout all the land of Egypt; And there shall arise after them seven years of famine." Like any good consultant, Joseph went on to propose a solution: Choose an overseer, an agricultural czar, whose job it will be to see that

Egyptian granaries are filled in the seven years of plenty so no one will go hungry during the seven years of famine.

And who was appointed overseer? Joseph, of course.

the **shadow of a great rock**
Isaiah 32:2
a metaphor for anything substantial and dependable for reviving body and spirit

The prophet Isaiah depicted an ideal social order based on justice, in which the ruling princes would be "as an hiding place from the wind, and a covert from the tempest; as rivers of water in a dry place, as the shadow of a great rock in a weary land."

See ROCK SOLID.

the **shadow of thy wings**
Psalm 17:8–9
a metaphor for complete, comforting protection

Consider the unfailing attention given eggs and newly hatched birds by their mothers. Who among us does not need such comfort from time to time? In Psalm 17, the poet wrote, "Keep me as the apple of the eye, hide me under the shadow of thy wings, From the wicked that oppress me, from my deadly enemies, who compass me about." The avian locution appears in modified form elsewhere in Scripture. For example, Psalm 61:4 and Ruth 3:12 speak of "the shelter of thy wings," and Matthew 23:37 offers "as a hen gathereth her chickens under her wings."

See also APPLE OF ONE'S EYE.

Shadrach, Meshach, and Abednego
Daniel 3:12–30
exemplars of unshakable faith

Shadrach, Meshach, and Abednego—friends of Daniel and soon to become symbols of willingness to undergo martyrdom rather than forsake their faith—lived along with Daniel as exiles in Babylon at the court of King Nebuchadnezzar. When the king ordered that the three men be cast into a fiery furnace for refusing to worship a golden idol, the order was carried out. But Shadrach, Meshach, and Abednego were not burned at all. An angel, described as "like the Son of God," was reported to be with them in the intense flames. The king, hearing this, called out to the steadfast trio, and they emerged without a "hair of the head singed."

The king, astute enough to recognize *force majeure* when he saw it, promptly acknowledged the power of the Hebrew God and pardoned Shadrach, Meshach, and Abednego.

See also LAW OF THE MEDES AND PERSIANS.

shed blood
Genesis 9:6
do someone in

This all-too-common verb phrase, in Genesis meaning "destroy human life by violent means," appears in a biblical verse of fateful portent: "Whoso sheddeth man's blood, by man shall his blood be shed: for in the image of God made he man." And it is God who is uttering these words. As one might anticipate, verse 6 is often cited in defense of capital punishment for those convicted of murder.

See EYE FOR EYE, TOOTH FOR TOOTH.

sheep from the goats
Matthew 25:32
telling good from bad
See SEPARATE THE SHEEP FROM THE GOATS.

sheep's clothing
Matthew 7:15
disguise

Folklore has it that wolves will don the skin of dead sheep in order to gain entry into a flock and kill additional sheep. Whether true or not, connivers termed "wolves in sheep's clothing" hide their true intentions in order to fleece their victims. In turn, these innocents are said to be led like "lambs to the slaughter." In Mark 13:4–8 Jesus warned his disciples that the appearance of false messiahs would presage the coming of a radically different world order. In Matthew 7:15 he warned, "Beware of false prophets, which come to you in sheep's clothing, but inwardly they are ravening wolves."

A timely warning in the age of hard-sell political, commercial, religious, and investment pitchmen, especially those with the powerful instruments of telemarketing and television at their service.

See LAMB TO THE SLAUGHTER.

shibboleth
Judges 12:6
a catchword

We use "shibboleth" most often today to denote a catchword or slogan—often representing a worn-out or discredited doctrine. Two of the most common shibboleths still vibrant in the United States are "pro-choice" and "pro-life," which are too often known to generate violent responses in people of the opposite persuasion. In Judges 12:6 "shibboleth" denotes a use of language that distinguished one group of people from another. The Hebrew word *shibboleth*, with various meanings—"stream," "flood," and "ear of wheat"—was employed as a password by Gileadite soldiers under the command of Jephthah, who lay in wait for the Ephraimites at a ford on the river Jordan. The Gileadite sentries could tell immediately whether someone they challenged to give the password was an Ephraimite, because the Ephraimites could not make the "sh" sound. When the sentries heard "sibboleth" instead of "shibboleth," they knew they were dealing with an enemy.

Alas, things didn't go well for the Ephraimites: "There fell at that time of the Ephraimites forty and two thousand." Modern scholars think this number was grossly exaggerated, but it is clear that speech therapists could have made out like bandits in the world of the Bible.

See BALM IN GILEAD.

ships of Tarshish
I Kings 10:22-23
carriers of rich cargoes

The ships of Tarshish, large vessels plying the Mediterranean, brought luxuries to Solomon's capital, Jerusalem: "Once in three years came the navy of Tharshish, bringing gold, and silver, ivory, and apes, and peacocks. So king Solomon exceeded all the kings of the earth for riches and for wisdom." The place here called Tharshish is more commonly known as Tarshish, and its precise location remains uncertain. It may have been in Spain or on the east coast of Africa.

signs of the times
Matthew 16:3
indications of current trends

"Signs of the times" occurs in a passage that begins as a discussion of weather forecasting. Jesus, challenged by the Pharisees and Sadducees to produce a "sign from heaven," a portent to prove his authority, launched his response with, "When it is evening, ye say, It will be fair weather: for the sky is red." After continuing in this meteorological vein for a while, Jesus said, "Ye can discern the face of the sky; but can ye not discern the signs of the times?" And there the discussion ended.

Jesus had made it clear that people clever enough to predict weather should be capable of reading moral signs as well.

silver cord
Ecclesiastes 12:6
a strong tie
See GOLDEN BOWL.

sing for joy
Job 29:13
show delight

Most of us now are inclined to jump rather than sing for joy, but "sing" is the word used in verse 13, and "joy" is so rarely encountered in this book of man's troubles that it must not go unnoticed. It happened this way. Job was looking back nostalgically at his earlier, happier days—happier because he had the respect of the town elders as well as the young and because he helped the poor, the orphans, and the widows. Recalling his acts of generosity, Job said, "I caused the widow's heart to sing for joy." An entirely creditable achievement when we consider that widows in biblical times had no rights of inheritance and usually had to depend on charity.

A reminder: Acts of charity still have the potential for causing people's hearts to sing—or jump—for joy. Many widowers as well as widows living their last years in virtual solitude would welcome a visit from a Job or any other kindly person—anytime.

six things doth the Lord hate
Proverbs 6:16–19
watch out for these

Excellent counsel from Proverbs: "These six things doth the Lord hate; yea, seven are an abomination unto him: A proud look, a lying tongue, and hands that shed innocent blood. An heart that deviseth wicked imaginations, feet that be swift in running to mischief. A false witness that speaketh lies, and he that soweth discord among brethren." So even though the six turned out to be seven, this is surely an observation to be taken seriously.

the **skin of one's teeth**
Job 19:20
the narrowest of margins

Everyone who has ever managed to squeak through a difficult college course knows what it means to make it by the skin of one's teeth. And the metaphor is applied regularly to a host of other narrow escapes from disasters large and small. Job, in the midst of a long complaint about how difficult life was for him, cried out in verse 20, "My bone cleaveth to my skin and to my flesh, and I am escaped with the skin of my teeth."

Thorton Wilder in his play *The Skin of Our Teeth* showed us how humanity has managed time after time since Creation to avoid disaster by the skin of its teeth—thus far at least. Let's see whether our streak of dumb luck will continue unbroken. Greenhouse effect. Ozone layer. Nuclear waste. Unauthorized releases to the atmosphere. PCBs. Fluorocarbons. Air pollution. Oil spills. Soil contamination.

the **sleep of a laboring man is sweet**
Ecclesiastes 5:12
do a day's work, sleep like a baby

By way of advising humanity on how to achieve peace of mind, Ecclesiastes 5 tells us that those who do an honest day's work will never have to buy sleeping pills. In verse 12 we learn of the cares that come with wealth: "The sleep of a laboring man is sweet, whether he eat little or much: but the abundance of the rich will not suffer him to sleep." Whether "abundance" here applies to a rich and more than ample diet or to wealth and the easy living that is its concomitant we do not know, but for the importance of sleep we go to Shakespeare's *Macbeth*, where innocent sleep is called "chief nourisher in life's feast."

For another view of sleep *see* WHEN DEEP SLEEP FALLETH UPON MEN.

slippery places
Psalm 73:18
conditions conducive to moral or ethical tumbles

This metaphor is most apposite when discussing people who are given the opportunity to achieve wealth or power through less than ethical means. Consider government officials elected on promises to eliminate corruption and soon sent to prison because they added to the corruption instead.

Psalm 73 begins in a mood of resentment against the prosperity of the wicked. The psalmist asks whether God really cares about how people spend their lives. On visiting the Temple, however, he comes to realize that evil people will ultimately slip and get what's coming to them. He is talking about "the ungodly, who prosper in the world; they increase in riches." He says that God has set them up for a mighty fall: "Thou didst set them in slippery places: thou castedst them down into destruction."

And that's why surety bonds were born.

See AS A DREAM WHEN ONE AWAKETH *and* PRIDE GOES BEFORE A FALL.

the **small dust of the balance**
Isaiah 40:15
an infinitesimal amount
See DROP OF A BUCKET.

smell battle from afar
Job 39:19–25
praise for a war-horse, human or equine

God cited his many acts of creation by way of challenging Job to match them with his own accomplishments and capabilities. Speaking of the horse, God described its speed and bravery in battle: "He saith among the trumpets, Ha, ha; and he smelleth the battle afar off, the thunder of the captains, and the shouting." Could Job create such a creature?

Job stood mute.
For more of God's challenges, *see* LOOSE THE BANDS OF
ORION.

smoke in my nose
Isaiah 65:5
a source of constant annoyance
See HOLIER THAN THOU.

smoother than butter
Psalm 55:21
ingratiatingly polite

To this day we disparage anyone of whom we say, "His words
are smoother than butter." We also "butter people up" and
describe hypocrites and sweet-talkers as "oily." Why this
derogation of saturated fats? After all, most of us never heard
of cholesterol until a few years ago. The metaphorical use of
butter and oil appears to have had its origin in this verse from
Psalms. Complaining about a former friend, the psalmist said,
"The words of his mouth were smoother than butter, but war
was in his heart: his words were softer than oil, yet were they
drawn swords."
A classic characterization of a hypocrite.

smote him under the fifth rib
II Samuel 2:23
did him in

Modern readers rarely encounter the verb "smite" in any
form except "smitten" and then, it would seem, only when
struggling through less than inspiring love poetry or bad
fiction. Scripture, by contrast, makes frequent use of all the
"smites" and in a more violent sense. In II Samuel, Abner, a
commander in Saul's army, failed to persuade young Asahel,
a brother of one of David's generals, not to take him on in
combat. Finally, regretting what he knew he had to do, Abner

went at him: "Wherefore Abner with the hinder end of the spear smote him under the fifth rib, that the spear came out behind him; and he fell down there, and died in the same place." Bloody enough for you? Soon enough, in verse 27, Abner himself suffered the same fate at the hands of Asahel's brother: "Joab smote him there under the fifth rib, that he died, for the blood of Asahel his brother."

These fellows really had a thing about smiting under the fifth rib, the location of which most modern translators interpret as "in the belly" and some as a euphemism for "in the groin." In any case, such blows are sufficient to do someone in, whether literally or figuratively.

smote them hip and thigh
Judges 15:8
clobbered them

An extreme act of revenge for the taking of a wife's life has given us a vivid metaphor for devastating retribution: smite someone hip and thigh. The Philistines had put Samson's wife and her father to the torch, so Samson, the Israelite strongman, took vengeance against the Philistines. "He smote them hip and thigh with a great slaughter," meaning he made mincemeat of every Philistine within reach. Somewhat later—read on in Judges—Samson did it once again, on that occasion wielding the fabled jawbone of an ass.

For background information, *see* PLOWED WITH MY HEIFER.

Sodom and Gomorrah
Genesis 18:20
the twin Sin Cities

Sodom and Gomorrah were the inhospitable and immoral cities God destroyed "because their sin is very grievous." Genesis 19:4–9 describes attempts at sexual attacks on angels in disguise and on Lot's daughters as examples of the immorality prevalent in Sodom.

The word "sodomy" stands as a memorial to one of these

cities. "Gomorrahy" doesn't seem as mellifluous for this broadly interpreted act of sexual misconduct.

See PILLAR OF SALT.

song of songs
Song of Solomon 1:1
joyous verses in celebration of love

Chapter 1 of the Song of Solomon begins, "The song of songs, which is Solomon's." (Song of Songs is a translation of the Hebrew title of the book we call Song of Solomon.) What follows in the rest of the chapter and throughout the remaining seven chapters constitutes a marvelous collection of pastoral lyrics. The verses, many of them erotic, are addressed to lovers and are believed by some scholars to have been intended for use in the typical week-long celebration of a wedding.

Son of God
Mark 15:39
the ultimate term for Jesus Christ

"Son of God" replaced "Son of man" and "Messiah" as the early church broke from Judaism and moved into the Roman-Hellenistic world with a message of salvation. In the verse from Mark, it was a Roman centurion standing guard at the crucifixion who said, "Truly this man was the Son of God."

sons of Belial
I Samuel 2:12
an epithet for nasty people, more narrowly for ungodly men

Elsewhere, "sons of Belial" is given as "men of Belial." The verse from I Samuel says in its entirety, "Now the sons of Eli were sons of Belial; they knew not the Lord." Sin enough. But the chapter goes on to recite some of these bozos' tricks, and we are not surprised on reaching verse 17 to find, "Wherefore the sin of the young men was very great before the Lord."

Incidentally, Belial is also associated with women, in "daughter of Belial," I Samuel 1:16, where the phrase may be taken as an epithet for a worthless woman.

So who is Belial? Satan, or the personification of evil. In Hebrew, the word we transliterate as "belial" means "wickedness" or "worthlessness."

sounding brass or tinkling cymbal
I Corinthians 13:1
empty words—sound without melody or meaning

Paul, opening a discourse on love of God and fellow men, wrote to his church in Corinth: "Though I speak with the tongues of men and of angels, and have not charity, I am become as sounding brass, or a tinkling cymbal." That is, unless inspired by the spirit of love, people's words—no matter how eloquent—and ecstatic speaking in tongues can have no more value than the meaningless sounds made by temple musical instruments. Words uttered without love, that great gift of the spirit, are but noise and will avail us nothing.
See UNCERTAIN SOUND.

the **sound of his master's feet**
II Kings 6:32
trouble on the way
See IS NOT THE SOUND OF HIS MASTER'S FEET BEHIND HIM?

sour grapes
Ezekiel 18:2
a metaphor for disavowed responsibility

Whether we first encountered "sour grapes" in Ezekiel, Jeremiah, Aesop, or La Fontaine, the efficacy of this fine phrase is proved over and over again, enabling us forever to derogate people feigning disdain for something they do not or cannot have. That is what Aesop and La Fontaine taught us. But read on.

The prophet Ezekiel—and Jeremiah 31:29—used "sour

grapes" in a different sense. In 18:1–4 Ezekiel challenged the orthodox view of the time that the group—family, clan, nation—was responsible for the wrongdoing of its members. He chided the members for using the proverb "The fathers have eaten sour grapes, and the children's teeth are set on edge." Don't blame your troubles on something your fathers did, said Ezekiel. You're not being punished for your fathers' sins, but for what you yourselves are doing or are not doing. You are charging God with an injustice. God is just, and all souls are his. So verse 4 says, "The soul that sinneth, it shall die."

Thus, the responsibility for errant behavior is here placed directly on the sinner, and that's something to think about.

spare the rod and spoil the child
Proverbs 13:24
counsel for parents

Good advice from Scripture not to allow childish faults to go unnoticed and unreproved, in this verse from Proverbs given as, "He that spareth his rod hateth his own son: but he that loveth him chasteneth him betimes."

Who needs Dr. Spock?

speaking in tongues
I Corinthians 14:6
ecstatic speech
See UNCERTAIN SOUND.

speak to the earth
Job 12:8
don't tell me what I already know

In saying "Speak to the earth, and it shall teach thee; and the fishes of the sea shall declare unto thee," Job was reproving his friends for stating the obvious. All God's creations—large and small—know the great things he has done.

the **spirit is willing, but the flesh is weak**
Matthew 26:40–41
I would like to but I can't

Moderns finding themselves unable to persist in some form of desirable regulation of their lives—dieting, abstinence from liquor, or the like—invoke this line from Matthew as an excuse for personal weakness. It had its origin in a much more serious time in the life of Jesus, when he knew that death was near. Seeing that three of his disciples were unable to remain awake and give him human support in his dark hour in Gethsemane, Jesus said to Peter, "What, could ye not watch with me one hour? Watch and pray, that ye not enter into temptation: the spirit indeed is willing, but the flesh is weak."
See GETHSEMANE.

spreading like a green bay tree
Psalm 37:35
a marvelous metaphor for a grasping, prideful person

The psalmist counseled that God protects the faithful against depredation by the wicked: "I have seen the wicked in great power, and spreading himself like a green bay tree." The fragrant leaves of the bay tree symbolize distinction and prosperity. For this reason, the metaphor is appropriate for the arrogantly rich and powerful, just the kind of people many enjoy looking down on. Wouldn't you know it, before long "the wicked in great power spreading himself like a green bay tree" got his comeuppance.
Louis Bromfield in 1924 published his first novel under the title *The Green Bay Tree*, and playwright Mordaunt Shairp used the same title for his 1932 comedy.

the **stars in their courses**
Judges 5:20
a metaphor for the fundamental laws that govern the world

The stars are claimed by astrologers to have overwhelming influence on the lives of people, even on the lives of government officials. Against the stars in their courses, even the evil cannot hope to prevail. Sisera, in the Song of Deborah, Judges 5, commanded nine hundred chariots of Canaanites in a great battle with a lesser force of Israelite foot soldiers. God, intervening on behalf of his outnumbered people, caused a torrential rainstorm to fall and turn the battlefield into a quagmire. Sisera's chariots soon bogged down, and the Israelites quickly closed in on their enemies. As verse 20 says, "They fought from heaven; the stars in their courses fought against Sisera." Thus were the Canaanite forces destroyed.

Men seem always more eager to do battle when they believe their god or the stars will assist them.

the **stars of heaven shall fall**
Mark 13:32
the day of judgment
See THAT DAY AND THAT HOUR KNOWETH NO MAN.

stars sang together
Job 38:7
in joy, that is

Not young love's hyperbole but a characterization of the moment of Creation, found in the famous chapter in which God replied to Job, "When the morning stars sang together, and all the sons of God shouted for joy."
See SING FOR JOY.

stiff-necked
Psalm 75:5
haughty

A metaphor applied today to an obstinate or haughty person, and well established in English by the time the King James Version appeared. Jews, accused many times by God of being stiff-necked (Isaiah 48:4 calls attention to this condition in "thy neck is an iron sinew"), consider obstinacy and haughtiness a sin and ask forgiveness for this sin in the Yom Kippur service.

One among many biblical uses of "stiff-necked" is found in Psalm 75:4–5: "I said unto the fools, Deal not foolishly: and to the wicked, Lift not up the horn: Lift not up your horn on high: speak not with a stiff neck." The word "horn" requires explanation. In biblical use a horn symbolizes power, and "lift up the horn" means "exalt oneself." Although "lift up the horn" is no longer heard, we speak to this day of "pulling in one's horns" or "drawing in one's horns," with the meaning of restraining oneself or retreating.

a **still small voice**
I Kings 19:11–13
the gentle voice of God

Once Jezebel's priests of Baal had been routed, the prophet Elijah fled from the wrath of Jezebel into the wild Sinai peninsula, where he experienced great winds, earthquake, and fire. In the Bible, such manifestations are conventional preludes to a theophany, that is, to an appearance of God to a human being: "And after the earthquake a fire; but the Lord was not in the fire: and after the fire a still small voice." When Elijah heard it, he stood in the entrance to the cave where he had taken shelter, "And, behold, there came a voice unto him, and said, What doest thou here, Elijah?"

Elijah knew he was hearing the voice of God, and the rest of us acquired a marvelous characterization of that voice. Small wonder that John and Janet Wallach used the title *Still Small Voices* for their recent book about people who live in troubled areas of modern Israel.

See JEZEBEL.

stolen waters are sweet
Proverbs 9:17–18
as is forbidden fruit

This guileful metaphor is intended to expose the weakness of the unwary. In the verses from Proverbs, the reader is warned against consorting with a prostitute, who may entice pass-ersby with "Stolen waters are sweet, and bread eaten in secret is pleasant." The righteous man so cajoled "knoweth not that the dead are there; and that her guests are in the depths of hell."

Just say no.

a **stone of stumbling**
Isaiah 8:13–14
an obstacle; an instance of being hindered

Consider all the headlines written about people tripped up by political and personal scandal, preachers who ignore their own preachings, athletes whose drug habits come to light. All such people have stumbled on a stone of stumbling, a stum-bling block if you will, as in Ezekiel 3:20, for example: "When a righteous man doth turn from his righteousness, and com-mit iniquity, and I lay a stumbling-block before him, he shall die."

God instructed Isaiah to rouse his people by warning them: "Sanctify the Lord of hosts himself; and let him be your fear, and let him be your dread. And he shall be for a sanctuary; but for a stone of stumbling and for a rock of offense to both the houses of Israel, for a gin and for a snare to the inhabi-tants of Jerusalem." Isaiah's "gin," of course, was not the familiar beverage, but an old word meaning "snare."

Even so, who can deny that modern gin, mismanaged, can become a stone of stumbling?

See LET THE WICKED FALL INTO THEIR OWN NETS.

stones would cry out
Luke 19:40
it's useless to try to suppress the truth

Today, "stones would cry out" is aptly employed as a warning against secret and unsavory activities conducted by govern-ments or businesses. In Luke the intention was somewhat different. When the disciples hailed Jesus as the Messiah, some of the Pharisees demanded that Jesus rebuke them. He answered, telling the disciples that the story could not be suppressed: "If these [the disciples] should hold their peace, the stones would immediately cry out." The metaphor is that of a wrong great enough to move even inanimate things to speak.

The stones Jesus spoke of were the huge stones of the Temple, mute witnesses to the unfolding events, and the idiom "hold one's peace," well established before the King James Version appeared, means "remain silent."

stone the builders refused
Psalm 118:22
a metaphor for ideas too quickly rejected

As we well know, first impressions can deceive. W. S. Gilbert put it this way in *H.M.S. Pinafore*:

Things are seldom what they seem.
Skim milk masquerades as cream.

Psalm 118, a paean to the strength and mercy of God, says in verse 22, "The stone which the builders refused is become the head stone of the corner." The cornerstone, as the head stone is called in modern English, is taken to be Israel itself or the king of Israel, rejected by other people as insignificant but given deserved recognition by God. This verse was seized upon by the early Christian church as prefiguring Jesus Christ.

straight and narrow
Matthew 7:13–14
in modern usage, the path of virtue

In verse 13 Jesus said, "Wide is the gate, and broad is the way, that leadeth to destruction," meaning that it's easy for people to become self-indulgent. In verse 14 he said, "Strait [narrow] is the gate, and narrow is the way which leadeth into life," meaning that it's not particularly easy to live in a manner that enables one to achieve eternal life. These verses also tell us that far more people follow the path to destruction than the path to eternal life.

Jesus' observation acquires immediacy when we contemplate the disciplined life required of anyone serious about one day becoming a great ballerina, violin virtuoso, or Olympic athlete.

See CAN THE LEOPARD CHANGE HIS SPOTS?

strain at a gnat, swallow a camel
Matthew 23:24
an excellent metaphor for those who spend their time on trivial matters while neglecting what is important

Think of police officers dutifully writing traffic tickets for cars parked minutes too long while crack dealers are going about their evil business unimpeded a short distance away. In this verse from Matthew, Jesus characterized the scribes and Pharisees as "blind guides, which strain at a gnat, and swallow a camel," suggesting that they neglected justice, mercy, and faith while being scrupulous about what Jesus saw as petty affairs, such as collecting Temple tithes of mint, anise, and cumin.

"Strain at" may require some explanation. It is commonly misunderstood to mean "make a violent effort" but was intended to mean "strain out," that is "filter out."

For another ruminant metaphor, *see* CAMEL THROUGH THE EYE OF A NEEDLE.

stranger in a strange land
Exodus 2:22
a metaphor for alienation

In the account of the birth of a child to Zipporah, wife of Moses, we read, "And she bare him a son, and he [Moses] called his name Gershom: for he said, I have been a stranger in a strange land." Moses was expressing the feeling of alienation that troubled him while he was living among the Midianites. In many parts of the Old Testament the Jews are reminded of this feeling, as in Deuteronomy 10:19, for example:

"Love ye therefore the stranger: for ye were strangers in the land of Egypt."

"Stranger in a strange land" was well understood by Robert Heinlein, who used the phrase as the title of a novel.

the **strife of tongues**
Psalm 31:20
contentiousness, or contentious arguments

Seeing the danger presented by those who sowed discord, the psalmist addressed God on behalf of the faithful: "Thou shalt hide them in the secret of thy presence from the pride of man: thou shalt keep them secretly in a pavilion from the strife of tongues."

Chaucer showed he understood the problem in "The Maunciple's Tale" when he wrote, "A wicked tongue is worse than a fiend."

stumbling block
Ezekiel 3:20
an obstacle
See STONE OF STUMBLING.

suffer fools gladly
II Corinthians 11:19
tolerate fools or foolishness without complaint

Paul charged members of the church at Corinth with falling under the sway of false leaders, whose actions were an affront to Christian doctrine. He accused the church members of being duped and tolerating outrages, including slander of Paul himself. In frustration and exhibiting a degree of asperity, he insisted they listen to him even if they thought he spoke foolishly: "For ye suffer fools gladly, seeing ye yourselves are wise."

To this day, anyone who cannot abide stupid behavior in others may say, "I do not suffer fools gladly."

suffer the little children
Mark 10:14
allow them some freedom

Jesus, observing that the disciples were preventing some children from getting near him while he spoke, said, "Suffer the little children to come unto me, and forbid them not; for of such is the kingdom of God."

For an explanation of why Jesus thought thus, *see* KINGDOM OF HEAVEN.

the **sun stood still**
Joshua 10:13
a day miraculously extended, during which many
     wonderful things happened

Joshua and his forces were helped by God to defeat the Amorites, enemies of the Israelites. In this case, God's help took the form of extending the hours of daylight: "And the sun stood still, and the moon stayed, until the people had avenged themselves upon their enemies." Thus, the Israelites were able to finish off their enemies, who might otherwise have been able to regroup or make their getaway in the dark of night.

sweet counsel
Psalm 55:14
an intimate exchange between like-minded persons

Describing an enemy who had once been a friend, the psalmist said of their former relationship, "We took sweet counsel together, and walked unto the house of God in company."

sweeter than honey
Judges 14:18
as sweet as can be

A cliché once widely used to characterize one's beloved but out of favor nowadays—yes, Virginia, there really are clichés that eventually disappear. Perhaps the best-known biblical use of this hyperbole is in the answer to a riddle put by Samson in Judges 14:14. Thinking of the honey he had just eaten from the carcass of a lion, Samson posed this riddle: "Out of the eater came forth meat, and out of the strong came forth sweetness." The correct answer was: "What is sweeter than honey? What is stronger than a lion?"

Among many other Old Testament references to the sweetness of honey, Psalm 19:10 says of the judgments of the Lord that they are "sweeter also than honey and the honeycomb."

For more about Samson's riddle, *see* PLOW WITH MY HEIFER.

sweet influences of Pleiades
Job 38:31
a sign of clear sailing ahead
See LOOSE THE BANDS OF ORION.

swifter than a post
Job 9:25
life passes in an instant

A no-longer-useful metaphor for the brevity of human life. A post in ancient times was a person employed to carry messages. Apparently, postal service was better in those days. Job, seeing himself as rapidly approaching the end of his days and with little chance of improvement in his life, said, "Now my days are swifter than a post: they flee away, they see no good."

swifter than a weaver's shuttle
Job 7:6
another metaphor for the brevity of human life

Anyone who has ever watched the hands of an expert weaver whip a shuttle back and forth across a loom will understand the aptness of Job's despairing words: "My days are swifter than a weaver's shuttle, and are spent without hope." It is worth noting that Job, so sorely afflicted that his days and nights alike were unbearable, nevertheless bemoaned the brevity of life, his dearest remaining possession.

swords into plowshares
Isaiah 2:4
a time of peace

A metaphor for a world in which industrial and agricultural capacity are used to benefit people rather than to wage war—a dream whose time has not yet come. Isaiah gave us a picture of an ideal future when all the nations will come to Zion to be taught by God: "And he shall judge among the nations, and shall rebuke many people: and they shall beat their swords into plowshares, and their spears into pruninghooks: nation shall not lift up sword against nation, neither shall they learn war any more." (Isaiah's words are repeated many times elsewhere in Scripture.)

Meanwhile, let's see if we can't find a few hundred billion dollars more for armies and weapons. Later we'll see to it that people are decently educated, fed, clothed, and housed.

See VALLEY OF DECISION.

take under one's wing
Matthew 23:37
protect or encourage

When we take a person under our wing—perhaps a student,
a young musician, or someone just starting out in the world—
we are extending help. In Matthew 23:37, Jesus spoke of
God's protecting love for the people of Jerusalem: "How
often would I have gathered thy children together, even as a
hen gathereth her chickens under her wings." Foreseeing the
Romans' destruction of the holy city and the Temple, Jesus
lamented Jerusalem's persistent refusal to return to God for
love, freedom, and protection.

a tale that is told
Psalm 90:9
a metaphor for the brevity of life
See THOUSAND YEARS ARE BUT AS YESTERDAY.

tell it not in Gath
II Samuel 1:20
keep the news under your hat

Gath was one of the five city-states of the Philistines, who were
enemies of the Israelites. (It was also the home of Goliath, the
giant David slew.) "Tell it not in Gath" appears in David's
lyric dirge (verses 17–27) mourning the deaths of Saul and
Jonathan: "Tell it not in Gath, publish it not in the streets of
Askelon; lest the daughters of the Philistines rejoice, lest the
daughters of the uncircumcised triumph."
  In short, don't let our enemies find out lest the news give
them cause for celebration.

the **Ten Commandments**
Exodus 20:1–20
the commands God gave his chosen people

These precepts were spoken by God to Moses at Mount Sinai
for transmittal to the Israelites. They were later inscribed in
stone and given to Moses on the "mount of God"(Exodus
24:12).

tender mercies
Psalm 119:77
blessings or gifts from God

Praising God for the gifts bestowed on humanity, the psalmist
said, "Let thy tender mercies come unto me, that I may live:
for thy law is my delight." Rosellen Brown entitled her 1978
novel *Tender Mercies*, produced as a movie in 1982.

tents of wickedness
Psalm 84:10
where sinners dwell
See DOORKEEPER IN THE HOUSE OF GOD.

of **that day and that hour knoweth no man**
Mark 13:32
precisely when God's kingdom will be established on
    earth

Some things we are fated not to know until the moment when
they actually occur. In Mark 13:4 the disciples asked Jesus
when the kingdom of God on earth would come and what the
signs of the coming would be. In verses 5–25 Jesus was explicit about the signs, but as to when the great event would
occur, he said in verse 32, "Of that day and that hour knoweth
no man." Only God knows. In the meantime, added Jesus in
verse 33, "Take ye heed, watch and pray: for ye know not
when the time is." It may come in the next moment.

Looking forward to the thousand years of peace in which

God will reign on earth, millenarians study Mark avidly and from time to time come to believe they have finally ascertained "that date and that hour." Then they gather—usually outdoors and often on high plateaus—to observe, as described in Mark 13:25, the moment when "the stars of heaven shall fall." Soon enough, the moment passes uneventfully—at least it has until now. The millenarians return undaunted to their everyday lives and resume their study of Mark 13.

that thou doest, do quickly
John 13:27
why not get it over with?

These are words that come in handy when someone is walking toward an electric chair or a surgeon's knife, the equivalent of "Why wait? Let's get this show on the road." Jesus was of such mind when he realized the plot against him had gone too far to be stopped. Telling Judas to go about the business of handing him over to the authorities, he said, "That thou doest, do quickly."

their strength is to sit still
Isaiah 30:7
don't count on them to do anything

Isaiah warned the rulers of Judah that they would have to face the encroaching Assyrians without help from any other nation: "The Egyptians shall help in vain, and to no purpose: therefore have I cried concerning this, Their strength is to sit still." What Isaiah wanted the people of Judah to do was put their fate in the hands of God rather than depend on an alliance with Egypt, since the Egyptians would only sit on their hands when push came to shove.

See COVENANT WITH DEATH.

the last Adam
I Corinthians 15:45
Jesus Christ

Paul saw Jesus as the man who perfectly reflected the glory of God: "The first man Adam was made a living soul; the last Adam was made a quickening spirit." The first Adam was a human being who would inevitably encounter corruption; the last, heavenly Adam was an obedient servant of God who would experience grace and life.

James Gould Cozzens, writing of the compromises and moral dilemmas inevitable in the career of a physician, ironically entitled a novel *The Last Adam*.

See OF THE EARTH, EARTHY.

there is death in the pot
II Kings 4:40–41
it's been poisoned, don't eat it

During a time of food shortages, the prophet Elisha instructed that a soup be prepared for his students. The well-intentioned servant who gathered herbs for the soup made the mistake of including poisonous wild gourds along with the herbs. While the students were eating, they cried out, "O thou man of God, there is death in the pot." Unfazed, Elisha had some meal brought to him. "And he cast it into the pot; and he said, Pour out for the people, that they may eat. And there was no harm in the pot."

Just like that.

there is no man that sinneth not
I Kings 8:46
a disturbing, albeit not surprising, observation

In dedicating the Temple, Solomon prayed that God would be forgiving of those who sin and repent, pointing out that "there is no man that sinneth not." We read the same thought in Ecclesiastes 7:20: "For there is not a just man upon earth, that doeth good, and sinneth not." And II Chronicles 6:36 tells us "There is no man which sinneth not."

For further confirmation of Solomon's wisdom, *see* CAST THE FIRST STONE.

there shall be no more death
Revelation 21:2–4
when the kingdom of God is established on earth, that
  is

Happy days may not be here again, but they sure are coming, and Cervantes will be proved dead wrong for having told readers of *Don Quixote* "There is a remedy for everything but death, which will be sure to lay us out flat sometime."

John saw the "new Jerusalem, coming down from God out of heaven, prepared as a bride adorned for her husband." And he said, "God shall wipe away all tears from their [people's] eyes; and there shall be no more death." Incidentally, John showed he knew his Isaiah 25:8, in which it was prophesied of God, "He will swallow up death in victory; and the Lord God will wipe away tears from all faces."

the right hand of fellowship
Galatians 2:9
symbolic acceptance of a person as an equal

In this verse from Galatians, Paul wrote of James, Peter, and John—the leaders of the young Christian church in Jerusalem—that they "perceived the grace that was given unto me, they gave to me and Barnabas the right hands of fellowship." By this act the three leaders accepted Paul and Barnabas into an apostleship equal to their own in authority.

To this day we extend a hand, normally the right hand, in friendship.

the tongue can no man tame
James 3:2–8
will we ever learn to hold our tongues?

In the course of a chapter reading like a primer on ethical behavior, James wrote at length about the need for restraint in speech. And why not? Aren't a great number of our human problems caused by speaking out of turn, speaking without giving some thought to what we will say, speaking with undue harshness, and the like?

In a pair of marvelous metaphors, James likened the human tongue first to a horse's bit, a small device yet capable of turning a great beast's body, and then to a comparably small device, a ship's helm, or tiller: "Behold also the ships, which though they be so great, are driven of fierce winds, yet are they turned about with a very small helm, whithersoever the governor [captain] listeth [causes it to incline]. Even so the tongue is a little member." James went on to describe the kinds of great troubles the tongue can cause and in verse 8 said, "But the tongue can no man tame; it is an unruly evil, full of deadly poison."

Good for James!

they have sown the wind
Hosea 8:7
they have made big trouble

All of us eventually get what is coming to us—particularly those whose actions cause discord. In Galatians 6:7 the apostle Paul wrote, "Be not deceived; God is not mocked: for whatsoever a man soweth, that shall he also reap." So those who sin will be paid in kind. In Hosea 8:7, written at least seven hundred years earlier, the prophet, holding forth against idolators, made the same point: "For they have sown the wind, and they shall reap the whirlwind." The wind may be taken as a metaphor for evil, and the whirlwind for complete disaster. So those who make trouble will be paid back many times over.

In our own century Jerome Lawrence and Robert E. Lee, in entitling their play *Inherit the Wind*, drew on Proverbs 11:29, "He that troubleth his own house shall inherit the wind: and the fool shall be servant to the wise of heart." The playwrights portrayed two advocates locked in courtroom battle over the constitutionality of teaching the concept of evolution, based on Clarence Darrow and William Jennings Bryan in the famous Scopes trial.

they helped every one his neighbor
Isaiah 41:6
a fine compliment

In Isaiah this was written of pagan craftsmen of foreign nations who were makers of idols. Before assuring the Israelites that God would help them against their enemies, Isaiah said of these craftsmen, "They helped everyone his neighbor; and everyone said to his brother, Be of good courage." The efforts of these people could harm Israel, but Isaiah went on in verse 10 to relate God's message to Israel: "Fear thou not; for I am with thee." And then, in verse 29: "Their works are nothing; their molten images are wind and confusion."

they neither sow nor reap
Luke 12:24
the lesser creatures of the earth

Jesus, to allay his followers' anxiety, spoke of God's treatment of the insentient creatures that inhabit the earth along with men and women: "Consider the ravens: for they neither sow nor reap; which neither have storehouse nor barn; and God feedeth them: how much more are ye better than the fowls?"

Since God even looks after these lower creatures, isn't it clear he will do the same for human beings?

they shall run and not be weary
Isaiah 40:31
those who serve God

The power of confidence in God's powers imbues the discouraged with new energy and enthusiasm. The full verse reads: "But they that wait upon the Lord shall renew their strength; they shall mount up with wings as eagles; they shall run and not be weary; and they shall walk, and not faint."

Marathon runners, take notice.

they that are of Caesar's household
Philippians 4:22
the influential, the powerful

In the United States, for example, those who work in and near the Oval Office.

Paul closed his epistle to the Philippians, considered to have been written while he was in Rome or in a Roman provincial capital, by offering them his blessing. He also conveyed greetings from those who accompanied him as well as from those of the imperial establishment: "All the saints salute you, chiefly those that are of Caesar's household."

they toil not, neither do they spin
Matthew 6:28
said of all creatures but human beings
See LILIES OF THE FIELD.

thing not done in a corner
Acts 26:26
anything done openly

A thing not done in a corner is the direct opposite of a covert activity. When Paul was told by Festus that he was off his rocker, Paul responded that he had spoken truthful words in describing his beliefs and activities. What's more, he said, King Agrippa had understood him perfectly: "For the king knoweth of these things, before whom also I speak freely: for I am persuaded that none of these things are hidden from him; for this thing was not done in a corner."

For the next act in this courtroom drama, *see* ALMOST THOU PERSUADEST ME.

things not seen
Hebrews 11:1
intriguing language representing an affirmation of faith

The opening words of Hebrews 11 define faith as "the substance of things hoped for, the evidence of things not seen." In the succeeding verses, we read examples of this faith. Noah, for one, obeyed without question when instructed by God to build the ark, and Abraham, also a man of faith, went to a strange land when so instructed by God. Both heroic men were enabled by their faith to obey and endure.

things which are seen are temporal
II Corinthians 4:18
and unlike spiritual matters, which are eternal

It is easy enough to deal with mundane matters, which change from day to day; it is far from easy to deal with the spiritual, and it is spiritual matters that should occupy our attention, for they are always with us. Paul, addressing the members of his church in Corinth, emphasized love, character, and courage, but most of all spiritual life: "We look not at the things which are seen, but at the things which are not seen: for the things which are seen are temporal; but the things which are not seen are eternal."

thirty pieces of silver
Matthew 26:15
the sum paid for the ultimate betrayal

Moderns equate "thirty pieces of silver" with a bribe or with blood money, money gained at the cost of someone's life. Matthew 26 recounts how Judas Iscariot agreed to accept thirty pieces of silver as his bounty for fingering Jesus to the chief priests of Jerusalem. The deal struck, Judas found his opportunity in the garden of Gethsemane, and the Temple guards seized Jesus there. On the following morning, Judas realized the enormity of what he had done and tried to return the blood money. When the chief priests scorned his offer, Judas committed suicide.

The chief priests judged the silver Judas left behind to be unfit for Temple use. They bought with it a plot of land, "the potter's field," to be used for burial of foreigners and Jerusalem's friendless poor, and it came to be called "the field of blood" (Matthew 27:3–8). "Potter's field" has survived to this day to denote a burial place for unidentified people and the friendless destitute.

See KISS OF DEATH.

this broken reed
Isaiah 36:6
an epithet for Egypt, a weak sister and treacherous

Anyone depending on a broken reed will end up in deep—and hot—water. Isaiah told of how an Assyrian military emissary named Rabshakeh taunted the Israelites, who were trapped inside their own capital under siege by the Assyrian army: "Thou trustest in the staff of this broken reed, on Egypt; whereon if a man lean, it will go into his hand, and pierce it: so is Pharaoh king of Egypt to all that trust in him."

For the events that led up to this incident, *see* THEIR STRENGTH IS TO SIT STILL.

Thomas
John 20:25
one of Jesus' twelve apostles
See DOUBTING THOMAS.

thorn in the flesh
II Corinthians 12:7
a source of continuing annoyance or suffering

In this verse Paul said, "There was given to me a thorn in the flesh, the messenger of Satan to buffet me, lest I should be exalted above measure." Paul's thorn in the flesh is generally thought to have been a physical weakness, and various conjectures have been made about its nature. Among the conditions suggested by medical historians have been epilepsy, malaria, migraine headaches, and recurring eye infections. Obviously, there is insufficient biblical evidence for reliable diagnosis.

Thorns, which abound in the Near East, are symbols of vexation in Numbers 33:53 and elsewhere in the Bible, and of a pestiferous nuisance in Matthew 7:16. Whatever the original intent of Paul, his metaphor—more often given now as "thorn in one's side"—enjoys widespread use among parents of obstreperous children and among those of us who must work alongside an annoying or destructive colleague.

thou art the man
II Samuel 12:6–7
the classic accusation made against a person believed
     guilty of a crime

The court prophet Nathan used these words to rebuke David
for conniving to have Uriah killed. It happened this way: Nathan set David up by telling him a story about an anonymous
man who had taken unfair advantage of another. Angered by
the story, David made his decision: "The man that hath done
this thing shall surely die." Nathan then let David have it right
between the eyes: "Thou art the man." Sure enough, from
then on David's life went downhill into frustration, contentiousness, and disappointment.

For David's role in Uriah's death, *see* FOREFRONT OF THE
BATTLE.

though he slay me
Job 13:15
my faith is unshakable

There were gremlins abroad even during the days of King
James I. Errors somehow manage to creep into the best-ed-
ited of texts, so why should Scripture be different? One such
error, dubbed "a sublime mistranslation," is ascribed to the
great team of translators who converted the Hebrew of the
Old Testament and the Greek of the New Testament into the
English of the poetic King James Version. The gremlin stood
ready when it came time to render the opening words of Job
13:15. The King James Version gives the passage as "Though
he slay me, yet will I trust in him," conveying the idea that
Job's faith was supremely unshakable. In the Revised Stan-
dard Version, the passage comes a lot closer to the meaning
of the Hebrew and is more in line with what one might expect
from a frustrated, angry Job: "Behold, he will slay me; I have
no hope."

Quite a different meaning, yet King James wins out in quo-
tability, don't you agree?

thou hast made me as the clay
Job 10:9
I am entirely in your hands

Clay is a biblical metaphor for the human body, as distinguished from the life-spirit. In biblical times clay was essential in making pottery, and God is often characterized in Scripture as the master potter, who can shape humanity into any form. Job, desperately seeking an explanation for his sufferings, said to God, "Remember, I beseech thee, that thou hast made me as the clay; and wilt thou bring me into dust again?"

See DUST THOU ART.

a thousand years are but as yesterday
Psalm 90:4
infinite time

Psalm 90:4 speaks of the eternity of God: "A thousand years in thy sight are but as yesterday when it is past, and as a watch in the night." "Watch in the night" merits explanation. In biblical times, the night watch was divided into three parts of a few hours each. Thus, God's tenure is so long that, for him, a thousand years pass very quickly.

A well-known hymn written by the English theologian Isaac Watts (1674–1748) gives verse 4 this way:

A thousand ages in Thy sight
Are like an evening gone;
Short as the watch that ends the night
Before the rising sun.

See WATCHMAN, WHAT OF THE NIGHT?

a threefold cord is not quickly broken
Ecclesiastes 4:9–12
a metaphor for teamwork

In these verses the author of Ecclesiastes begins by telling us "two are better than one" and goes on to explain why: "For if they fall, the one will lift up his fellow: but woe to him that is alone when he falleth; for he hath not another to help him up." The passage concludes by citing the advantage of co-operation when facing an attack by an assailant: "And if one prevail against him, two shall withstand him; and a threefold cord is not quickly broken." So, while two are better than one, three are even better.

As every alert resident of any modern city knows.

threescore and ten
Psalm 90:10
the human life span

This biblical reckoning is surely showing signs of superannuation. Recognizing that every one of us eventually must die, the psalmist said, "The days of our years are threescore and ten; and if by reason of strength they be fourscore years, yet is their strength labor and sorrow; for it is soon cut off, and we fly away." Much of Psalm 90 deals with the fleeting nature of human existence. Verses 5 and 6 liken a person's life to a night's sleep, which is of short duration, and to grass, which withers and is cut down—Walt Whitman used the psalmist's metaphor in entitling *Leaves of Grass*. Verse 9 of the psalm says life is "a tale that is told"—once past, it is done with. Shakespeare went much further in *Macbeth*:

Life's but a walking shadow, a poor player
That struts and frets his hour upon the stage,
And then is heard no more; it is a tale
Told by an idiot, full of sound and fury,
Signifying nothing.

See ALL THINGS COME ALIKE TO ALL.

through a glass darkly
I Corinthians 13:12
vaguely, ambiguously, mysteriously
See SEE THROUGH A GLASS DARKLY.

thy love is better than wine
Song of Solomon 1:2
thy love for me, that is

The extended tribute to love between woman and man that is the Song of Solomon opens with "Let him kiss me with the kisses of his mouth: for thy love is better than wine" and continues in the same vein for eight chapters.

Many centuries after this verse was written, a popular song extolled a lover's kisses as "sweeter than wine," proving the durability of the metaphor.

thy love to me was wonderful
II Samuel 1:26
I loved you greatly
See PASSING THE LOVE OF WOMEN.

thy people shall be my people
Ruth 1:16
I will follow you to your homeland and remain with you there
See WHITHER THOU GOEST, I WILL GO.

tidings of great joy
Luke 2:10
good news

What better words than "tidings of great joy" can be employed to preface a message of good news, particularly one given to people awaiting the birth of a child? In Luke 2 the shepherds keeping watch over their flock by night were anxious. They had seen a strange light in the skies and did not know they were seeing "the glory of the Lord." Then an angel appeared to them, with the words "I bring you good tidings of great joy, which shall be to all people. For unto you is born this day in the city of David a Savior, which is Christ the Lord."

Christmas carolers each year recall these "tidings of comfort and of joy."

till death do us part
Ruth 1:16
as long as I shall live
See WHITHER THOU GOEST, I WILL GO.

a **time to keep silence, and a time to speak**
Ecclesiastes 3:7
a wonderfully wise observation

A lot of marriages would be saved if the wisdom of this insight were more widely recognized.
See TO EVERY THING THERE IS A SEASON.

tithe
Leviticus 27:30
a tenth of one's annual income, set aside for support of sacred rites and observances

Tithing, which is mentioned in many places in Scripture, has a long history. In early times it appears to have been a means of supporting the priests and the Temple, but it was also used as a form of tax collection for secular purposes. Leviticus 27 established formulas to be used in computing one's obligations to the Lord. For example, verse 30 tells farmers, "And all the tithe of the land, whether of the seed of the land, or of the fruit of the tree, is the Lord's; it is holy unto the Lord."
See RENDER TO CAESAR.

to every thing there is a season
Ecclesiastes 3:1–8
everything in its proper time

This is the beginning of one of the most famous and most often quoted sequences of biblical verses: "To every thing there is a season, and a time to every purpose under the heaven: A time to be born, and a time to die...." The extended passage continues in this vein, ending with "A time to love, and a time to hate; a time of war, and a time of peace." In simple words of haunting beauty, these verses counterpose life's happy experiences and its inevitable sorrows. Preachers, poets, and writers—these last have found many book titles in Ecclesiastes 3—are usually inclined to find moral uplift and consolation in the passage. It was in this spirit that a eulogist at the funeral of President John F. Kennedy read aloud the eight verses in their entirety, as have many eulogists before and after him.

Edith Wharton, alluding wryly to "a time to plant, and a time to pluck up that which is planted" in verse 2, wrote in her novel *The Age of Innocence*: "In the rotation of crops there was a recognized season for wild oats; but they were not sown more than once."

See ALL THINGS COME ALIKE TO ALL *and* THREESCORE AND TEN.

tower of Babel
Genesis 11:9
the edifice intended by its presumptuous builders to
   reach all the way to heaven
See BABEL.

tower of ivory
Song of Solomon 7:4
a metaphor for womanly beauty

Since love is blind, "Thy neck is as a tower of ivory" finds use in describing a lady love as well as a lovely lady. The use of ivory to describe a woman's neck must not be taken to mean that the Song of Solomon responds only to beauty in women. In 6:14 it says of a man, "His hands are as gold rings set with the beryl: his belly is as bright ivory overlaid with sapphires."

And these metaphors are only a few of many ready and waiting in the Song of Solomon.

See SONG OF SONGS.

travel the second mile
Matthew 5:41
don't be vindictive

In current usage, "travel the second mile" means to do more than is required or expected, accommodate, bend over backward. The halls of the U.S. Congress abound in legislators versed in biblical metaphor, so there—even after long and acrimonious debate—our elected representatives often speak of their willingness to travel the second mile. Then there is that kind person inside and outside Congress who can always be counted on to travel the second mile in giving financial or emotional support to a sister or brother ever in need and asking repeatedly for help.

Matthew 5:41 is interpreted somewhat differently. When Jesus said to his disciples, "Whosoever shall compel thee to go a mile, go with him twain," he was counseling against vindictiveness and urging the disciples to turn the other cheek rather than bend over backward to be subservient. The verse is thought to allude to a practice of Roman soldiers and civil authorities, who took advantage of subjugated people by forcing them to carry the baggage of their conquerors.

See TURN THE OTHER CHEEK.

a tree is known by its fruit
Matthew 12:33
good results arise from honorable intentions, bad results
    from evil intentions

In Matthew 12 Jesus used this metaphor in defending his ministry of healing and restoration against charges that he was possessed of demonic powers. He countercharged that his critics were unable to judge his work correctly because their hearts were evil: "Either make the tree good, and his fruit good; or else make the tree corrupt, and his fruit corrupt: for the tree is known by his fruit." Bad sources do not yield good works.

the **truth shall make you free**
John 8:32
the truth Jesus was teaching, that is

Today, these words from John are often treated as a philosophic statement about truth and liberty and used to adorn newspaper mastheads, university halls, and libraries. In their biblical context, the intention is rather different. When Jesus said, "And ye shall know the truth, and the truth shall make ye free," he was capping a brief discourse to his disciples about the truth and efficacy of what he was revealing through his life and teaching.

turn the other cheek
Matthew 5:39
don't indulge in retaliation

This is perhaps the most frequently heard and most widely ignored of all biblical metaphors. Whereas the law of Moses and Roman law called for giving as good as one got, Jesus opposed vindictiveness and revenge. Teaching that strife only begets more strife, Jesus said in Matthew 5:39, "Whosoever shall smite thee on thy right cheek turn to him the other also."

Such thinking forms the core of the policy of nonviolence counseled by Mahatma Gandhi, Martin Luther King, Jr., and others, but thus far neither the nations of the world nor most ordinary people appear eager to adopt it.

See TRAVEL THE SECOND MILE.

in the **twinkling of an eye**
I Corinthians 15:52
in an instant

This metaphor is of special interest because of its antiquity—its first citation in the *Oxford English Dictionary* is dated 1303. This venerable history is mentioned here, as comparable histories might well have been mentioned in many other entries of this volume, to call attention to the fact that while the King James translators created many metaphors and were true to many others in the original Hebrew and Greek, they did not ignore colloquial English in doing their work.

Believing the day of resurrection was imminent, Paul said, "In a moment, in the twinkling of an eye, at the last trump: for the trumpet shall sound, and the dead shall be raised incorruptible, and we shall be changed." So in an instant the people who have put their trust in God will be resurrected into a new order of being.

two are better than one
Ecclesiastes 4:9
See THREEFOLD CORD IS NOT QUICKLY BROKEN.

two-edged sword
Hebrews 4:12
any thing or idea that cuts both ways
See DOUBLE-EDGED SWORD.

Tyre, whose merchants are princes
Isaiah 23:8
an epithet for a seat of power and for those who wield power and will inevitably fall from power

The great Phoenician trading center that was Tyre had been defeated by the forces of Sennacherib, and Isaiah spoke of the reasons for the city's collapse: "Who hath taken this counsel against Tyre, the crowning city, whose merchants are princes, whose traffickers are the honorable of the earth? The Lord of hosts hath purposed it, to stain the pride of all glory, and to bring into contempt all the honorable of the earth." So God was evening things out. The expression "merchant princes," denoting merchants of great wealth, may or may not owe its existence to this passage from Isaiah, but one is sorely tempted to give Scripture the credit. One may certainly credit Scripture for its widespread use.

U

---

an **uncertain sound**
I Corinthians 14:6–8
an ambiguous message

Paul remarked in I Corinthians 12 that a divine gift enabled some people to speak in tongues and some listeners to interpret this speech accurately. Yet he was aware that all people did not have the gift of tongues, nor did all listeners understand what they were hearing when someone spoke in tongues. In the course of a discussion of this subject in chapter 14, Paul said, "If I come unto you speaking with tongues, what shall I profit you, except I shall speak to you either by revelation, or by knowledge, or by prophesying, or by doctrine....If the trumpet give an uncertain sound, who shall prepare himself to the battle?" For "trumpet" read "I"; for "give an uncertain sound" read "speak in tongues." In other words Paul was suggesting that much ecstatic speech is meaningless. In using the trumpet metaphor, he was saying that he wanted his message to come through loud and clear.

General Maxwell Taylor used the apt and modest title *Uncertain Trumpet* for his 1960 book on U.S. defense policy and strategy, particularly under the Eisenhower administration.

See UNKNOWN TONGUE.

an **unclean spirit**
Mark 1:21–23
demonic possession

In the biblical world—and for far too long thereafter—it was thought that mental disorders were caused by evil supernatural beings. Because the mentally ill were uncared for, they were seen as dirty, hence the expression "unclean spirit." Jesus went to preach in Capernaum and had an encounter there with a person possessed by a supernatural being:

"There was in their synagogue a man with an unclean spirit and he cried out, Saying, Let us alone; what have we to do with thee, thou Jesus of Nazareth? art thou come to destroy us?" Immediately, Jesus exorcised the unclean spirit.

underneath are the everlasting arms
Deuteronomy 33:27
the arms of God, that is
See EVERLASTING ARMS.

an **understanding heart**
I Kings 3:9
common sense and the ability to recognize and respond
    to people's needs

Solomon, whose name still epitomizes wisdom—I Kings 4:30 says, "Solomon's wisdom excelled the wisdom of all the children of the east country, and all the wisdom of Egypt"—was told by God he would be granted anything he asked for. Solomon replied, "Give therefore thy servant an understanding heart to judge thy people, that I may discern between good and bad."

A high IQ doesn't mean much without an understanding heart.

the **unknown god**
Acts 17:23
an agnostic's epithet for God

This phrase is taken as suggesting that God is unknown but not unknowable by those who have the necessary faith. Paul perceived the Athenians as idolators. In the course of a sermon to them, he said, "For as I passed by, and beheld your devotions, I found an altar with this inscription, TO THE UNKNOWN GOD." He went on to explain that the unknown god was the Christian God. Archaeologists have looked in vain for an altar bearing the inscription Paul described. Inscriptions to "unknown gods" (plural) have been found on ancient Greek altars, but it is thought that the ancient Greeks dedicated altars in this way to avoid unintentional slights to any of their gods.

John Steinbeck used "To the Unknown God" as the working title for one of his early novels, which eventually appeared as *To a God Unknown*. The protagonist, a farmer obsessed by his pagan religion, commits suicide at the outdoor altar where he customarily worshiped.

an **unknown tongue**
Acts 2:2–4
ambiguous language

These verses from the Acts of the Apostles tell how, during a church service at the time of the Pentecost, "There came a sound from heaven as of a rushing mighty wind." All present were "filled with the Holy Ghost, and began to speak with other tongues." The passage states that the "other tongues" were actual foreign languages. Although the people present were of many different nations, all heard the words spoken and understood them. It was like a great meeting at the United Nations, where the electronic marvel of simultaneous translation enables all in attendance to hear the speeches in their own languages. (Today, "tongues" is generally understood to be ecstatic speech.)

Paul, much concerned with the practice of speaking in tongues that was prevalent in some Christian communities of his time, said, "In the church I had rather speak five words with my understanding, that by my voice I might teach others also, than ten thousand words in an unknown tongue." In short, though Paul recognized that speaking with tongues was a spiritual gift, he wanted to speak and be understood unambiguously when he was preaching.

See UNCERTAIN SOUND.

unstable as water
Genesis 49:3–4
a characterization of a person of dubious morality

"Unstable as water" is not a particularly striking simile, but it is worthy of mention for the circumstance in which it was used. Jacob, aware he had not long to live, called his sons together and to Reuben, his eldest, said, "Thou art my first-born, my might, and the beginning of my strength, the excellency of dignity, and the excellency of power: unstable as water, thou shalt not excel; because thou wentest up to thy father's bed; then defiledst thou it." Translation: Reuben was to be denied the share of his father's estate normally due a firstborn son. And why? Genesis 35:22 provides the explanation: "Reuben went and lay with Bilhah his father's concubine."

unto whom much is given
Luke 12:48
in modern usage, akin to *noblesse oblige*

The passage from Luke contains an admonition by Jesus to those privileged to know of the coming of the Lord: "For unto whomsoever much is given, of him shall be much required: and to whom men have committed much, of him they will ask the more." When the Lord suddenly appears, said Jesus, those who have not known of the coming—and therefore have not prepared themselves—will be punished less severely than those who have known and have not prepared themselves.

In the modern world, anyone who starts out in life with a mental, spiritual, or physical—need we add financial?—advantage must take care not to coast, but strive to achieve to the fullest.

See FIVE WERE WISE, FIVE FOOLISH.

upon this rock
Matthew 16:18
a metaphor suggesting solidity and permanence

A structure or institution built on rock—especially this rock—will withstand a destructive force many orders of magnitude greater than anything measurable on the Richter scale. In Matthew 16:18 Jesus suggested the durability of the church he was founding. He addressed Peter, whose name until then had been Simon: "Thou art Peter, and upon this rock I will build my church; and the gates of hell shall not prevail against it." (This saying of Jesus to Peter is considered to be the grounds for the institution of the papacy and the primacy of the Roman Catholic Church.) Simon's new name was derived from the Greek word *petros*, meaning "rock," and so Jesus in renaming Simon signaled the great and enduring role Peter would play in the future of the church.
See ROCK SOLID.

the **upright man**
Ecclesiastes 7:29
a straight arrow
See MAN UPRIGHT.

use a little wine for thy stomach's sake
I Timothy 5:23
drink in moderation to help your digestion

This is advice akin to "an apple a day keeps the doctor away," yet it also evokes the image of a toper in need of a reasonable excuse to commence the day's drinking. The writer of I Timothy, by way of offering advice on clean living, gave us, "Drink no longer water, but use a little wine for thy stomach's sake and thine often infirmities." Come to think of it, he may have known something about the purity of water in biblical times.

Today, the economically privileged are likely to be heard ordering Perrier or Evian water—before going on to a glass or bottle of the white or red.

valley of decision

Joel 3:12–16

a place real or imaginary where an event of lasting
  importance, long feared or eagerly anticipated, is
  brought to realization

These verses from Joel depict the day of judgment, when "the
heavens and the earth shall shake." After telling the people,
in verse 10—and against all advice from Isaiah 2:4—to "beat
your plowshares into swords, and your pruninghooks into
spears," Joel went on to tell them that the Lord would sum-
mon the nations harassing Jerusalem to the valley of Jehosha-
phat to be judged: "Multitudes, multitudes in the valley of
decision: for the fear of the Lord is near in the valley of
decision." There God would deliver his verdict upon the assembled nations and condemn them to final destruction.

And Marcia Davenport had the title for her best-selling
novel of 1942, *The Valley of Decision*.

See SWORDS INTO PLOWSHARES.

vanity of vanities

Ecclesiastes 1:2–5

all of life is emptiness and futility

Humanity's pursuits and activities lead inevitably to dead
ends, according to the unknown writer of Ecclesiastes: "Vanity of vanities, saith the Preacher, vanity of vanities; all is
vanity. What profit hath a man of all his labor which he taketh
under the sun? One generation passeth away, and another
generation cometh: but the earth abideth for ever." Striving
to view life realistically, the writer could find no escape from
his judgment that life was ultimately futile.

Thackeray rang down the curtain on his great novel *Vanity
Fair* with "Ah! Vanitas Vanitatum! Which of us is happy in this

265

world? Which of us has his desire? or having it, is satisfied?—Come, children, let us shut up the box and the puppets, for our play is played out."

Ernest Hemingway found verse 5 especially arresting: "The sun also ariseth, and the sun goeth down, and hasteth to his place where he arose." His novel *The Sun Also Rises* closes with its main characters unchanged in outlook. Disillusioned at the beginning of the book, they remain disillusioned at the end. All is vanity.

We are left with a question: How could a book as apparently heretical as Ecclesiastes have made its way into Scripture?

vengeance is mine; I will repay
Romans 12:19
leave the avenging to me

Paul told his followers not to worry about getting even with anybody: "Dearly beloved, avenge not yourselves, but rather give place unto wrath: for it is written, Vengeance is mine; and I will repay, saith the Lord." So don't distract yourself with thoughts of retribution. Leave all that to God—who is much better at that sort of thing.

a **vexation only to understand the report**
Isaiah 28:19
how could they have done such a thing!

Isaiah was not discussing the rhetoric of government spokespersons and others paid to obfuscate. Rather he was detailing the undesirable outcome to be visited upon Judah for making alliances with the nation's enemies: "Morning by morning shall it pass over, by day and by night: and it shall be a vexation only to understand the report." That is, merely to hear news of the devastation sure to come would be more than a body could bear.

virgins, five wise and five foolish
Matthew 25:2
the unmarried women in the parable of the wise and
  foolish virgins
See FIVE WERE WISE, FIVE FOOLISH.

a virtuous woman is a crown to her husband
Proverbs 12:4
a minority view of what a wife should be

This ancient view of the role of a wife still infuses too much
of American political and economic life and infuriates those
who believe a wife should be something more than a mere
adjunct to her husband. The full verse reads, "A virtuous
woman is a crown to her husband: but she that maketh [him]
ashamed is as rottenness in his bones."

And what of a husband who maketh a wife ashamed? Not
dealt with in Proverbs 12.

See PRICE FAR ABOVE RUBIES.

a voice crying in the wilderness
Isaiah 40:3
today, any impassioned protester acting alone or
  virtually alone to whom little or no attention is paid

In Isaiah the verse is much narrower in intention: "The voice
of him that crieth in the wilderness, Prepare ye the way of the
Lord, make straight in the desert a highway for our God."
Attention everyone, big things are about to happen. In an
almost identical translation, both Matthew 3:3 and Luke 3:4
picked up Isaiah's thought: "The voice of one crying in the
wilderness, Prepare ye the way of the Lord, make his paths
straight." The New Testament passages reflect the beliefs of
early Christians who regarded John the Baptist, preaching in
the wilderness of Judea, as fulfilling the prophecy of Isaiah.

But the discussion is not yet complete. This beautiful passage from Isaiah represents yet another inspired mistranslation by the King James scholars. The Hebrew original is better rendered in this way: "A voice crying, In the wilderness

prepare ye the way of the Lord...." So the voice was not crying in the wilderness; that tiny comma after "crying" rather than after "wilderness" tells us the voice was commanding that the way of the Lord be prepared in the wilderness.

See ALL FLESH IS GRASS.

the **voice is Jacob's voice**
Genesis 27:22
I smell a rat

Or, to continue with the coinage of metaphor, something's rotten in the state of Denmark. And it all stemmed from the importance of a father's blessing. To the ancient Hebrews a father's blessing imparted a mystical power and once uttered could not be revoked.

The full verse reads, "Jacob went near unto Isaac his father; and he [Isaac] felt him, and said, The voice is Jacob's voice, but the hands are the hands of Esau." What was all this about? Esau, born before his twin brother, Jacob, was entitled to the larger share of their blind father's estate. When Esau returned from hunting one day, he found himself famished, and his crafty younger brother persuaded him to sell his birthright for a bowl of the pottage Jacob was cooking. Esau must have been pretty simpleminded to go along with this. At any rate, Jacob was then encouraged by his mother, Rebekah, to impersonate Esau and gain Isaac's blessing. So Jacob put on Esau's clothes and covered his hands with goatskin to simulate the hairiness of Esau. It was then that Isaac said the voice was Jacob's but the hands were those of Esau.

Did the scam work? You bet it did. Isaac gave his blessing to Jacob.

See MESS OF POTTAGE.

the **voice of the turtle**
Song of Solomon 2:11–12
a sign of a pleasant season on the way

Spring is bustin' out all over, and now it's time for love: "Lo, the winter is past, the rain is over and gone; the flowers appear on the earth; the time of the singing of birds is come, and the voice of the turtle is heard in our land." The turtle, of course, is the turtle dove, and who has not enjoyed the cooing of a dove? Turtles presumably make some sort of sound, but who has ever had the good fortune to hear it?

For literary uses of "voice of the turtle" and other memorable phrases, *see* LITTLE FOXES.

the **wages of sin is death**
Romans 6:16–23
woe to them who sin

"Wages" here is construed as singular, as it often was centuries ago, but of particular interest is its meaning. Paul used the word not in the sense of "payment for service rendered," but as something close to "retaliation." Sinners are not paid in any way. Rather, they can anticipate that their less-than-wholesome activities will be observed and will meet with suitable punishment.

In Romans 6 Paul was discussing law and sin, making it clear which side he was on in the ongoing battle between good and evil. In verse 16, for example, he asked, "Know ye not, that to whom ye yield yourselves servants to obey, his servants ye are to whom ye obey; whether of sin unto death, or of obedience unto righteousness?" And in verse 16, at the end of the chapter, Paul laid it on the line: "For the wages of sin is death; but the gift of God is eternal life through Jesus Christ our Lord."

walk by faith
II Corinthians 5:6–7
true believers don't ask for proof of God's existence

Skilled pilots fly blind when they have to, relying only on their cockpit instruments. The very brave start from scratch and build great and worthy enterprises against mighty odds—and without any instruments. Both pilots and entrepreneurs, as well as missionaries and humanitarians, have the impelling confidence available only to those who "walk by faith." Acknowledging humanity's inability to understand completely the meaning of Christ's love, Paul said that nevertheless "we are always confident, knowing that, whilst we are at home in the body, we are absent from the Lord: (For we walk by faith, not by sight)." In the absence of a clear vision of what lay ahead, Paul relied on faith in God, and the dimly seen goal of that faith was a glorious eternal life.

It is such faith or something resembling religious faith that enables visionaries—unfunded by governments, foundations, or wealthy benefactors—to initiate programs on a shoestring that one day may do much to advance humanity.

walk on water
perform the impossible

Extraordinary people—astrophysicists, industrial tycoons, football coaches—who accomplish feats thought to be impossible can be said to walk on water. In Mark 6 Jesus saw that contrary winds were making it impossible for his disciples to make headway in their voyage across the Sea of Galilee. So (in Mark 6:48), "walking upon the sea," he went out to their ship, and the wind abruptly ceased.

walk with God
Genesis 5:22
a metaphor for practicing one's faith fully, that is, for living in intimate association with God

In the Old Testament, "walk with God" is repeated many times. In Deuteronomy 10:12, for example, we read, "What doth the Lord thy God require of thee, but to fear the Lord thy God, to walk in all his ways, and to love him, and to serve the Lord thy God with all thy heart and with all thy soul." A eulogist wishing to pay a great compliment to a deceased person of outstanding character, integrity, and serenity may say, "He walked with God." In Genesis 5:22, the person of whom this was written was Enoch, the sixth descendant of Adam.

the **walls of Jericho**
Joshua 6:20
a metaphor for a seemingly impregnable defense—a
  Maginot Line—that suddenly collapses

After successfully crossing the Jordan River under the command of Joshua, the invading Israelites prepared to attack
Jericho. With their priests leading the way, they carried the
holy ark around the wall of the city once a day for six days.
On the seventh day, at a blast from all the priests' trumpets,
"It came to pass, when the people heard the sound of the
trumpet, and the people shouted with a great shout, that the
wall fell down flat. . .and they took the city."
  The power of faith.

wars and rumors of wars
Mark 13:7
signs of the beginning of the end

Jesus in this verse counseled, "When ye shall hear of wars and
rumors of wars, be ye not troubled: for such things must
needs be; but the end shall not be yet." Even so, warfare and
the clamor—an archaic meaning of "rumor"—of warfare
would be among the terrible events culminating in the end of
the age and the coming of the Messiah.
  Philip Caputo, evoking the words of Mark 13, used the title
A Rumor of War for his recollections of Marine combat in
Vietnam.
  See MANY SHALL COME IN MY NAME.

wash one's hands of an affair
Matthew 27:24
a metaphor useful when a scheme dips toward
  impracticality or unreasonable risk

To avoid blame, clever people in the loop wash their hands
of a failing affair. In Matthew 27:24 Pontius Pilate decided it
was time to absolve himself of complicity in the plot against
Jesus, whereupon he "took water, and washed his hands

before the multitude, saying, I am innocent of the blood of this just person: see ye to it." In other words, he was avoiding responsibility by establishing an alibi before a large number of witnesses.

Modern bureaucratic language being what it is, "official deniability" is now one of the phrases of choice among those who act deviously or illegally. They cut off the paper trail short of a high official to be shielded, and when the plan goes awry, that person is off the hook. "Wash one's hands," "official deniability," "out of the loop," "paper trail," "off the hook"—Pilate launched a cottage industry that shows no sign of obsolescence.

wasted the country
I Chronicles 20:1
devastated it

In modern times, particularly in the parlance of the Vietnam War, "waste" has been used to mean "kill," more broadly "devastate." And it is the latter meaning we encounter in this verse from Chronicles: "Joab led forth the power of the army, and wasted the country of the children of Ammon."

Does anything ever change?

See VANITY OF VANITIES.

watch in the night
Psalm 90:4
nighttime guard duty
See THOUSAND YEARS ARE BUT AS YESTERDAY.

watchman, what of the night?
Isaiah 21:11–12
has anything happened during the night?

In one of Isaiah's visions, the prophet saw himself keeping watch atop a tower, and he was asked, "Watchman, what of the night? Watchman, what of the night? The watchman said, The morning cometh, and also the night: if ye will inquire,

inquire ye: return, come." The entire exchange is wondrously ambiguous and obscure, but "watchman, what of the night?" lives on as a literary way of asking for news if there be any. And the watchman's response, verse 12, "The morning cometh, and also the night," appears to suggest that nothing worth reporting occurred during the watch of Isaiah's vision.

See BABYLON IS FALLEN, IS FALLEN.

waters cannot quench love
Song of Solomon 8:7
hyperbole on the phenomenon known as true love

If we can credit the Song of Solomon, the condition known as love is a natural for harmless exaggeration: "Many waters cannot quench love, neither can the floods drown it."

the **way of all the earth**
Joshua 23:14
a euphemism for death

Joshua, with a premonition of imminent death, said in a farewell to his people, "Behold, this day I am going the way of all the earth." David, employing the same metaphor in giving his deathbed instructions to Solomon, said in I Kings 2:2, "I go the way of all the earth: be thou strong therefore, and show thyself a man."

the **weaker vessel**
I Peter 3:1–7
woman
See GIVE HONOR UNTO YOUR WIFE.

we carry nothing out
I Timothy 6:7
cemeteries house classless societies
See BROUGHT NOTHING INTO THIS WORLD.

weeping and gnashing of teeth
Matthew 8:12
an overt manifestation of extreme pain or rage

For a present-day example of weeping and gnashing of teeth, observe people at O'Hare Airport who have just been told they have missed the last flight home. When Jesus said, "There shall be weeping and gnashing of teeth," he was speaking of those of little faith, saying that at the time of judgment, they would be "cast out into outer darkness."

weeping may endure for a night
Psalm 30:5
don't give way to despair

Even problems that seem insurmountable will prove transitory. Psalm 30, a hymn of praise to God, counsels against despair: "Weeping may endure for a night, but joy cometh in the morning." So peace of mind, according to the psalmist, will eventually be restored even to those experiencing the worst of troubles.

we like sheep have gone astray
Isaiah 53:6
we have failed to follow the path of the Lord
See LOST SHEEP.

well done, good and faithful servant
Matthew 25:21
a compliment paid for diligence

With these words in the parable of the entrusted talents, two hardworking servants were complimented for making good use of money their master had provided to support them during his long absence. A wicked and slothful servant, who had also been given money, had done nothing but bury his single talent in the ground and was therefore scolded.

The word "talent" is worthy of comment. In biblical times it was a unit of currency worth several hundred dollars. But the parable gave "talent" an additional sense that persists to this day: a power of body or mind given naturally to someone for use and improvement.

we will not serve your gods
Daniel 3:18
we will not abandon our religion

The cry of uncommonly brave people who are willing to face martyrdom rather than submit to forced conversion. In modern times we have as yet found no comparable rallying cry to encourage whistle-blowers to endure hardship rather than remain safely and anonymously in the ranks of the vast majority who get along by going along. In Daniel it was with the words "We will not serve your gods, nor worship the golden image which thou hast set up" that Shadrach, Meshach, and Abednego defied Nebuchadnezzar. They preferred martyrdom, even in a fiery furnace, to apostasy, as did many other Jews in the successful Maccabean revolt of the second century B.C.

See HEAR, O ISRAEL *and* SHADRACH, MESHACH, AND ABEDNEGO.

what God hath joined together
Mark 10:9
a married couple

Even in the Golden Age of Divorce, now in its most shining hour, who is there who does not listen intently as a minister performing a marriage ceremony says, "What therefore God hath joined together, let not man put asunder"? The allusion is to Adam and Eve in the account of the Creation.

See BILL OF DIVORCEMENT.

what is a man profited?
Matthew 16:26
no important or lasting good comes from
   moneygrubbing

Jesus counseled eloquently against chasing mindlessly after power and wealth: "For what is a man profited, if he should gain the whole world and lose his own soul?"

what is man?
Psalm 8:4
we are an insignificant part of the universe

An often posed and much debated question. The psalmist addressed God with these words: "What is man, that thou art mindful of him?" When read in conjunction with verse 3, this questioning of man's significance in the face of the grandeur of the heavens expresses the paradox beautifully: "When I consider thy heavens, the work of thy fingers, the moon and the stars, which thou hast ordained; What is man, that thou art mindful of him?"

whatsoever a man soweth, that shall he also reap
Hosea 8:7
we get what's coming to us
See THEY HAVE SOWN THE WIND.

wheels within wheels
Ezekiel 1:15–21
today, hidden motives and circumstances at work

In Scripture the meaning of this phrase is far less clear. The Book of Ezekiel opens with a dazzling description of the cherubim Ezekiel saw in a vision. He described these guardians of God's throne as winged, human-headed lions with different animal faces on front, back, and sides. Beside each cherub were wheels, described in verse 16: "The appearance of the wheels and their work was like unto the color of a beryl:

and they four had one likeness: and their appearance and their work was as it were a wheel in the middle of a wheel." To visualize a wheel within a wheel, think of two wheels cutting each other transversely so the assembly can move off in any of four directions. Got the picture?

Our modern application of "wheels within wheels" suggests secret or conflicting agencies at work to thwart or help us so that nothing can be taken at face value.

when all men speak well of you
Luke 6:26
time to watch your step

The last of Jesus' four woes—"Woe unto you, when all men shall speak well of you! for so did their fathers to the false prophets"—warns that general acclaim lulls the recipient into perilous self-satisfaction. So, when everything's coming up roses, it's time to begin looking carefully for the thorns.

when deep sleep falleth upon men
Job 4:13–14
a time of dread for the troubled

Macbeth found out that, for conspirators at least, night does not always bring "innocent sleep, sleep that knits up the raveled sleave of care." The night may be a time of fear or a time for spirits to roam and visions to be experienced, as it was for a friend of Job's. He insisted on regaling Job with advice that had come to him during a trancelike revelation. The account begins with these words: "In thoughts from the visions of the night, when deep sleep falleth on men, Fear came upon me, and trembling, which made all my bones shake. Then a spirit passed before my face; the hair of my flesh stood up."

Good night, moon.

See also SLEEP OF A LABORING MAN IS SWEET

when I became a man, I put away childish things
I Corinthians 13:11
once I had grown up, I spent my time on adult matters

Today, any adult less than competent at sports may invoke this saying of Paul's to get out of the loathsome duty of playing baseball or the like with a pack of sturdy children. Paul, of course, had an entirely different thought in mind. He contrasted childhood and maturity to make the point that growth in understanding is properly part of the life process. Certain activities and attitudes must be left behind in order to make time for growth in secular knowledge, maturing judgment, and spiritual development. Jesus praised childlike qualities, but Paul belittled childish attitudes and interests: "When I was a child, I spake as a child, I understood as a child, I thought as a child: but when I became a man, I put away childish things."

In short, I know better now.

where shall wisdom be found?
Job 28:12
a vexing question unanswerable by human beings

In times of national stress, this question is often raised. The answer? Only God knows. The famous twenty-eighth chapter of Job is the Bible's most penetrating probe of the question "Where shall wisdom be found? and where is the place of understanding?" Verse 13 says, "Man knoweth not the price thereof; neither is it found in the land of the living." Verse 23 says, "God understandeth the way thereof, and he knoweth the place thereof." So wisdom, according to Job, is hidden in a secret place to which God alone knows the way.

Pro-life, pro-choice; pro-choice, pro-life: Where does wisdom lie?

See EYES TO THE BLIND.

where the carcass, there the eagles
Matthew 24:28
weakness invites oppression

When a defenseless target turns up, plenty of predators and scavengers will be close by, ready to do their ugly work. In Matthew 24 Jesus spoke of the coming of the Son of man, in verse 28 saying, "Wheresoever the carcase [carcass] is, there will the eagles be gathered together." Job 39:28–30 used a similar figure, speaking of hawks as well as eagles, leading one to believe that bird-of-prey metaphors were well established by biblical times.

whited sepulcher
Matthew 23:27
a savage epithet for a hypocrite

In Matthew, Jesus said, "Woe unto you, scribes and Pharisees, hypocrites! For ye are like unto whited sepulchers, which indeed appear beautiful outward, but are within full of dead men's bones, and of all uncleanness." Jewish custom in biblical times called for whitewashing the exterior of burial tombs, or sepulchers, to warn passersby of the uncleanness within. A Jew who touched a tomb would become ceremonially unclean and thus barred from the Temple area and shunned until ritual purification could be completed.

Whitewash may have improved the appearance of tombs, but it did not change the inner decay. This is what gives "whited sepulcher" its durable potency: Hypocrites may look splendid to people about them, but inwardly they are rotten.

"Whited sepulcher" appears also in Eugene O'Neill's play *Ah, Wilderness!* used by a father, during one of those it's-time-you-and-I-had-a-talk-son talks with his son, to characterize a prostitute.

See SCRIBES AND PHARISEES.

whiter than snow
Psalm 51:7
a metaphor for moral virtue

While those who live in northern climates may not find this figure at all striking, we must recall that snow was anything but common in the land of the Bible. Laboring under a strong feeling of personal guilt, the psalmist prayed for moral renewal, asking God to blot out his iniquities so that he might start over: "Wash me, and I shall be whiter than snow."

Shakespeare, more intimately acquainted with snow and knowledgeable about slander, also used "snow" metaphorically in *Henry IV, Part II*: "Be thou as chaste as ice, as pure as snow, thou shalt not escape calumny."

See LET US REASON TOGETHER.

whither thou goest, I will go
Ruth 1:16
the ultimate expression of devotion to a beloved person

Ruth, a Moabite, spoke these words to Naomi, her Jewish mother-in-law. In Moab Naomi had lost her husband and two sons, the husbands of Ruth and Orpha. Naomi declared that she would return to her family in her native land, and Orpha kissed her farewell. But Ruth opted for the love and trust of Naomi: "Intreat me not to leave thee, or return from following after thee: for whither thou goest, I will go; and where thou lodgest, I will lodge: thy people shall be my people, and thy God my God: Where thou diest, will I die, and there will I be buried."

These words evoke the spirit of the marriage vow from *The*

Book of Common Prayer: "To have and to hold from this day forward, for better for worse, for richer for poorer, in sickness and in health, to love and to cherish, till death do us part." But isn't it doubly wonderful that when Ruth said her piece she was addressing her mother-in-law?

whom the lord loveth he chasteneth
Hebrews 12:6
God just doesn't bother with those he doesn't love

Written to offset perceived faintheartedness at a time when there was no major oppression of Christians, "whom the Lord loveth he chasteneth" is used now to take the edge off the pain of punishment imminent and punishment just received. In its biblical intention, the statement makes a different point: As a loving father applies discipline to make certain a child will behave properly in the future, so God disciplines those he loves: "For whom the Lord loveth he chasteneth, and scourgeth every son whom he receiveth." Or, as given in Proverbs 3:12, "For whom the Lord loveth he correcteth; even as a father the son in whom he delighteth."
  See SPARE THE ROD AND SPOIL THE CHILD.

whosoever shall exalt himself
Matthew 23:12
every prideful person is looking for a comeuppance

A centuries-old English proverb, in multifarious formulations, tells us pride goes before a fall. An early citation for this proverb in the *Oxford English Dictionary* is a 1382 work by the theologian John Wycliffe: "Pride goth befor contricioun; an befor falling the spirit shal ben enhauncid." In Matthew 23:12, at the conclusion of a condemnation of the hypocrisy and ostentation of the scribes and Pharisees, Jesus said, "Whosoever shall exalt himself shall be abased; and he that shall humble himself shall be exalted."
  See PRIDE GOES BEFORE A FALL.

whosoever will save his life shall lose it
Matthew 16:25
the wise focus on their religious responsibilities, not on security and comfort

The statement from Matthew is a paradox that is resolved only when the thought is expressed completely. Jesus adjured his disciples to renounce their worldly lives: "Whosoever will save his life shall lose it; and whosoever will lose his life for my sake shall find it." Now we understand what Jesus meant: Anyone who struggles to retain this mundane life rather than fulfill obligations to God will fail to gain eternal life. Jesus taught consistently that self-sacrifice was the true way to serve God and gain life eternal, a principle especially meaningful to first-century Christians facing martyrdom at the hands of the Romans.

why hast thou forsaken me?
Psalm 22:1
the painful cry of believers who feel they have been abandoned by God

Psalm 22, lamenting the psalmist's profound troubles and appealing for divine help, begins with despairing words, "My God, my God, why has thou forsaken me?"

In Mark 15:34, the psalmist's words are used by Jesus, then "at the ninth hour" on the cross. In this account, "Jesus cried with a loud voice, saying 'Eloi, Eloi, lama sabachthani?' which is, being interpreted, My God, my God, why hast thou forsaken me?" (The word *sabachthani* is Aramaic, the remaining words Hebrew, and a more common transliteration of this cry currently is "Eli, Eli, lema sabachthani.") As verse 37 relates, Jesus soon "gave up the ghost," giving us an enduring metaphor first for the act of dying and later on for resignation, for ceasing to struggle. The metaphor, in the sense of dying, appears many times in Scripture. Job 11:20, for example, speaks of "the giving up of the ghost."

why tarry the wheels of his chariot?
Judges 5:28
what's keeping him?

It seems that since long before the modern era, mothers have worried when their children stayed out late. The mother of Sisera, commander of the Canaanite armies, expected that he would return victorious and check in with her after doing battle with the Israelites: "The mother of Sisera looked out at a window, and cried through the lattice, Why is his chariot so long in coming? why tarry the wheels of his chariot?" Alas, Sisera lay dead far from home, murdered by a woman who had taken him into her home after his defeat by the Israelites.

All of this suggests that a mother's worries are not always baseless.

See STARS IN THEIR COURSES.

wickedness sweet in the mouth
Job 20:12
a warning to avoid sin

Brief pleasures gained through sinful behavior turn bitter rapidly once retribution catches up with the sinner, as it inevitably does—we are told. This phrase is an example of the so-called help given by one of Job's friends, who found himself shocked by the defense Job offered for his behavior. What the friend said was, "Though wickedness be sweet in his mouth, though he hide it under his tongue. . .Yet his meat in his bowels is turned, it is the gall of asps within him." Not only was the food Job ate becoming rotten within him, but like snake venom, it was poisoning him.

Ugh.

See MISERABLE COMFORTERS *and* WORMWOOD AND GALL.

widow's mite
Mark 12:41–43
a modest offering that represents self-sacrifice by the
  giver

This well-established English locution denotes a small contribution given cheerfully by someone who can ill afford it.
Although a widow's mite may have little financial value, it
acquires great significance in light of the situation of the
giver. Mark makes clear just how small a widow's mite is. Jesus
observed people contributing money for support of the Temple: "Many that were rich cast in much. And there came a
certain poor widow, and she threw in two mites, which make
a farthing." When we consider that a farthing was formerly a
British coin equal to one-fourth of a penny, we have a good
idea of how little the widow was able to donate. Notwithstanding, the widow's mite came from the heart and so was of great
significance. Jesus said it all for us: "This poor widow hath
cast more in, than all they which have cast into the treasury."
   Do we often find the same spirit of giving among those of
our contemporaries who make remarkably grand and ostenta-
tious—and tax-deductible—contributions to charity?
   See LET NOT YOUR LEFT HAND KNOW WHAT YOUR RIGHT HAND
DOES.

wife of thy bosom
Deuteronomy 13:6
a warm way of referring to the one dearest to a good
  husband

In a stern, extended warning against those who may try to
entice us into idolatry, Deuteronomy tried to touch all bases.
Imbedded within one lengthy conditional clause, Deuteronomy included all the following among the potential tempters:
"Thy brother, the son of thy mother, or thy son, or thy daughter, or the wife of thy bosom, or thy friend, which is as thine
own soul." We surely must shut our ears to sweet talk, no
matter where it comes from.
   See DREAMER OF DREAMS.

wine that maketh glad the heart of man
Psalm 104:15
a tribute to the bounty of God, still appropriate on the
  occasion of opening a special bottle

In full the verse reads, "And wine that maketh glad the heart
of man, and oil to make his face to shine, and bread which
strengtheneth man's heart." Wine, one of the chief products
of ancient Israel's agriculture, was in those times fermented
mostly from the juice of grapes, with pomegranates and dates
accounting for small percentages. Consumption of wine was
almost universal, and only overindulgence was condemned.
See USE A LITTLE WINE FOR THY STOMACH'S SAKE.

wings of the dove
Psalm 55:6
a metaphor for peace

People in love, who often and understandably are concerned
only with their own lives, are inclined to think of the dove
exclusively as a romantic symbol. Thus, when they say, "Oh
that I had wings like a dove!" they are expressing their longing for a beloved to whose side they would fly if they could.
But the gentle bird is also associated with the idea of peace.
The latter image is closer to what the psalmist had in mind in
this verse: "Oh that I had wings like a dove! for then would
I fly away, and be at rest." The psalmist was giving voice to
an impulse to exchange an evil environment for a place that
offered peace. And this may be what led Henry James, preoc-

cupied with the problem of the artist in an alien environment, to use *The Wings of the Dove* as the title of one of his best novels. *See* DOVE.

wings of the wind
Psalm 18:10
a metaphor for God's power

It was long the custom for painters to represent the wind as bearing wings, a convention traceable to the Old Testament, in which the psalmist said of God, "Yea, he did fly upon the wings of the wind." And soon in this Psalm, we find that God "thundered in the heavens" and "shot out lightnings." All this by way of manifesting God's majesty and power.

wisdom above rubies
Proverbs 31:10
priceless wisdom
See PRICE FAR ABOVE RUBIES.

wisdom shall die with you
Job 12:2–3
a putdown for an insufferable know-it-all

Job had had it up to here with a friend's lengthy explanation of why God was treating Job so shabbily. Finally, Job responded, "No doubt but ye are the people, and wisdom shall die with you. But I have understanding as well as you; I am not inferior to you: yea, who knoweth not such things as these?"
Way to go, Job!

wise as serpents, harmless as doves
Matthew 10:16
street-smart but well-intentioned

It's a jungle out there. To succeed in any line of work you had better keep your wits about you. Jesus sensed that his disciples would meet opposition of all kinds when they went out on their ministries. So in this verse from Matthew he said, "I send you forth as sheep in the midst of wolves: be ye therefore wise as serpents and harmless as doves."

wise men from the east
Matthew 2:1
the first to pay homage to the infant Jesus

According to Matthew 2:1, "When Jesus was born in Bethlehem of Judaea in the days of Herod the king, behold, there came wise men from the east to Jerusalem." Since people in Matthew's day most likely thought of the men bearing gifts as astrologers or magicians, "magi" (from a Greek root meaning "magic") may be a more apt translation than "wise men."

Today, most people think of the wise men as kings and three in number, carrying the names Caspar, Melchior, and Balthasar, even though there is no New Testament evidence for any of this. Notwithstanding, the wise men brought three gifts to the infant, and with those gifts earned the everlasting gratitude of children in most parts of the world.

See GOLD, AND FRANKINCENSE, AND MYRRH *and* TIDINGS OF GREAT JOY.

without are dogs
Revelation 22:13–15
bad people will be kept out

With the apocalyptic vision of Revelation nearing its climax, John reported Jesus' enigmatic message "I am the Alpha and the Omega, the beginning and the end, the first and the last." Then John went on more straightforwardly, speaking of the stainless city of God, where those who follow God's commandments "have the right to the tree of life, and may enter in through the gates into the city." But who are they who will be excluded from the city of God? John wrote, "Without are dogs, and sorcerers, and whoremongers, and murderers, and idolaters, and whosoever loveth and maketh a lie." So man's best friend, classified with those who are evil and foul, does not fare too well in this passage, perhaps because dogs were known to feed on dead flesh.

This view of Lassie should come as no surprise. We cherish our pet dogs beyond reason but in our speech reveal ourselves to hold dogs in low regard. Witness some of our expressions in regular use: "dirty dog," "dog it," "go to the dogs," "lie down with dogs, get up with fleas," and "bitch" in its less than literal sense. From time to time in Scripture, in Exodus 22:31, for instance, dogs are mentioned in a favorable light as watchdogs, but more often they are looked upon with less than high regard. Since dogs lead John's list of those that will be excluded from the city of God, one wonders whether John thought of them as the worst of the lot. But that reasoning would make adulterers, last mentioned, the least of sinners, wouldn't it?

See ALPHA AND OMEGA *and* DOG IS TURNED TO HIS OWN VOMIT.

wives, submit yourselves unto your husbands
Ephesians 5.22
subordinate yourselves completely

Little did Paul know how long people would take his advice literally: "Wives, submit yourselves unto your own husbands, as unto the Lord." Paul was writing in the first century A.D., of course, and knew only the patriarchal domination in the home that was almost universal in his time. Although changing times have been accompanied by changing social attitudes, even in modern Western societies many marriages still appear to reflect the spirit of this verse from Ephesians.

Stay tuned for further developments.

See GIVE HONOR UNTO YOUR WIFE.

woe unto them that call evil good, and good evil
Isaiah 5:20

those who speak with forked tongues will come to a bad end

Shame on those whose moral sense is totally perverted, especially the wretches paid to speak of "incursions" rather than "invasions," "economic dislocations" rather than "unemployment," "negative economic growth" rather than "depression," "acceptable environmental hazards" rather than "life-threatening pollution." In the midst of a succession of stinging judgments on the manifestations of a decadent society, Isaiah 5 declares, "Woe unto them that call evil good, and good evil; that put darkness for light, and light for darkness; that put bitter for sweet, and sweet for bitter."

We moderns may say with Isaiah, Woe unto speechwriters and politicians that subvert truth. Single-mindedly pursuing their own programs and skillfully exploiting the lexicon of public relations, such people say they are merely putting their own spin on events. Disinterested observers say they are telling lies.

woe unto you, when all men shall speak well of you
Luke 6:26

watch out for sweet-talkers

See WHEN ALL MEN SPEAK WELL OF YOU.

the **wolf shall dwell with the lamb**
Isaiah 11:6
when peace and brotherhood come to the world

Isaiah prophesied that one day everything would be hunky-dory. The golden age would come with the ascendancy of David, Israel's ideal king and the Lord's vice-regent: "The wolf also shall dwell with the lamb, and the leopard shall lie down with the kid; and the calf and the young lion and the fatling together; and a little child shall lead them."

Oh well, so it hasn't turned out that way yet.

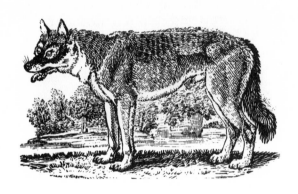

the **words of the wise are as goads**
Ecclesiastes 12:11
listen to those who know what they are talking about

When the writer of Ecclesiastes said, "The words of the wise are as goads, and as nails fastened by the masters of assemblies," his intent was to remind us to heed sage advice given by teachers, editors, and other wise mentors. Today, we may more often cite Benjamin Franklin's version of a similar proverb, "A word to the wise is enough," meaning that intelligent people need only the merest hint of advice in order to take appropriate action.

By every measure possible, we have an ample supply of wise listeners, but where have the wise speakers gone?

words without knowledge
Job 35:16
words, words, empty words—the dubious art of talking
without saying anything

Job's young accuser attacked him for making plaintive, self-righteous, rebellious claims on God's attention: "Therefore, doth Job open his mouth in vain; he multiplieth words without knowledge." Later, in Job 38:2, we have a chance to read again of words without knowledge. This time it is God who speaks to Job in a voice that comes out of the whirlwind: "Who is this that darkeneth counsel by his words without knowledge?" God will soon overawe Job, who had spoken of God in human terms and shown ignorance of the mysteries that underlie God's creation.

work out your own salvation
Philippians 2:12
but in full awareness of the presence of God

Parents telling adolescent sons or daughters they will have to look after themselves may use this often-quoted line from Philippians. But they should first make certain they understand the context in which it appears. At the time Paul was writing, big troubles—feuds and petty jealousies—were besetting the church he had established in the Macedonian city of Philippi, and Paul was not on the scene. In writing to the Philippians, Paul first reminded them of the example set by Jesus, making it clear that anyone acting in the tradition of Jesus would not put up with such shenanigans. Then, in verse 12, Paul wrote, "Wherefore, my beloved, as ye have always obeyed, not as in my presence only, but now much more in my absence, work out your own salvation with fear and trembling." So Paul was not walking away from the problem. Having reminded the Philippians of Jesus' example, Paul could leave the solution to them, confident that they would act correctly and that they would have God's support if they worked "with fear and trembling," that is, with proper humility toward God.

And parents who decide one day to let their offspring work out their own salvations will first do everything they can to make their sons and daughters capable of doing so.

wormwood and gall
Jeremiah 9:15
a deadly metaphor for bitterness and sorrow as
   retribution for evil

According to Jeremiah, among the punishments God would inflict upon his people—at least the disobedient among them—were two of special note: "Behold, I will feed them, even this people, with wormwood, and give them water of gall to drink." Since wormwood was a plant proverbial for its bitter taste, and gall was an herb both bitter and poisonous, God apparently intended a double dose for the morally deficient.

See WICKEDNESS SWEET IN THE MOUTH.

Y

yea, yea; nay, nay
Matthew 5:37
speak the whole truth and nothing but the truth

The cryptic message "yea, yea; nay, nay" serves to remind us of how common the crime of perjury is in our time, bringing into question the utility of administering oaths intended to ensure that witnesses tell the truth. Oaths had been so badly abused by the time of Jesus that no person's vow was certain to be truthful. Some oaths were frivolously given, some were blasphemous, and many were intended to deceive. Jesus, wanting his followers to speak directly and honestly, forbade them to use oaths of any kind lest they fall into the old discredited practices. In Matthew 5:37 he said, "Let your communication be, Yea, yea; Nay, nay: for whatsoever is more than these cometh of evil."

Could Jesus possibly have foreseen the duplicity so common today among people occupying high office?

ye cannot serve two masters
Matthew 6:24
you can't have it both ways
See GOD AND MAMMON.

ye that labor and are heavy laden
Matthew 11:28–30
those burdened by toil, suffering, or fear

Verse 28, "Come unto me, all ye that labor and are heavy laden, and I will give you rest," is an invitation to all who are troubled to join with Jesus. Observing his fellow Jews struggling to comply with complex religious law, Jesus urged them in verses 29–30 to follow his own, simpler precepts: fellow-ship and worship of God. "Take my yoke upon you and learn of me; for I am meek and lowly in heart: and ye shall find rest unto your souls. For my yoke is easy, and my burden is light."

ye that ride on white asses

Judges 5:10

all of you who ride around in stretch limos

The prophetess Deborah, after the death of Sisera (Judges 4), addressed the rulers and leaders of Canaan scornfully: "Ye that ride on white asses, ye that sit in judgment."

She may have spoken for all of us.

See STARS IN THEIR COURSES.

your goodness is as a morning cloud

Hosea 6:4

quick to vanish, that is

God, finding both Ephraim and Judah (the Northern King-dom and the Southern Kingdom) disloyal to their covenant with him, spoke as a father might to errant children: "O Ephraim, what shall I do unto thee? O Judah, what shall I do unto thee? for your goodness is as a morning cloud, and as the early dew it goeth away."

your old men shall dream dreams, your young men shall see visions

Joel 2:28

when people again obey God

Joel is speaking of that time when evil will be no more, when God's people return to the paths of righteousness: "I will pour out my spirit upon all flesh; and your sons and daughters shall prophesy, your old men shall dream dreams, your young men shall see visions." Make no mistake—Joel was not derogating those who dream dreams and see visions, as some action-oriented moderns are inclined to do. Some of the most important events and principles described in the Bible were revealed in dreams and visions. So turn to God in thought and deed, and he will restore to you full participation in all the good things he promised.

Z

zealot

Acts

in modern usage, a person zealous, even fanatical, in
support of a cause

In the time of Jesus, the Zealots were a nationalistic party of
rebels against Roman rule. They played a major role in the
rebellion of A.D. 66–70, which ended in the destruction of the
Temple. Zealous in their observance of God's law, they were
fanatical in their opposition to foreign domination, and some
refused to pay Roman taxes and lived as brigands.

INDEX TO
SCRIPTURAL PASSAGES

The Old Testament

The New Testament